TO JAY

How We Play the GAME

How We Play the GAME

A History of High School Hoops in Mason County

Danny Weddle

Eagle Creek Press
Solon, Ohio

Printed in the United States of America.

Eagle Creek Press
32513 Seneca Drive
Solon, OH 44139

ISBN: 978-0-9839725-3-2

Printed by Total Printing Systems, Newton, Illinois.

Cover Illustration by Stephanie Stewart

For Glenda, my best friend
and wife of 33 years.

For Danielle, Erica and Faith.
I am blessed to be your father.

Acknowledgments

There were many days when I asked myself why in the world I thought I could write a book. Some days I was very frustrated, but most of the time I was excited about the project, which I started in March 2011.

I have many people to thank for helping me pull this off. My wife, Glenda, and my daughters, Danielle, Erica and Faith, were very patient and supportive. Erica helped me with Microsoft Word and was my first reader and proofreader.

Bill Smoot, the son of former Maysville girls' basketball coach, Helen Smoot, took the time to read the first few chapters.

I spent many hours pouring over the microfilm at the Kentucky Gateway Museum Center (KMGC) in Maysville. Staff members Myra Harding, Cay Chamness, Sue Ellen Grannis, Mary V. Clarke, Paula Ruble and Dr. Jim Shires provided extraordinary service to me for this book. The KGMC is a researcher's dream. I wish more local residents would take advantage of the resources at the facility. This book would not have been possible without the archive of newspaper microfilm available at the KGMC.

The city of Maysville has been blessed to have outstanding newspaper coverage throughout the years. Many of the stories and facts in this book came from the local newspapers including the Evening Bulletin, the Daily Bulletin, the Public Ledger, the Daily Independent and The Ledger Independent.

Carol Bennett provided me with photos and directed me to her mother-in-law, Stella Bennett, a member of the Fee girls' state championship teams.

John Clark and Randy Harrison, fellow researchers at the KGMC, pointed out stories and facts needed for this book.

Tony Sapp and Rick Swartz compiled record books for the Maysville, St. Patrick and Mason County teams. The books were a tremendous help in writing this book, and I called Tony and Rick numerous times over the past year. If they didn't have what I needed when I called, they tracked it down for me.

Paris scorekeeper Eugene "Puck" Puckett answered my questions about the Maysville vs. Paris games.

Mike Fields of the Herald-Leader and Jody Demling and Jason Frakes of the Courier-Journal gave me the lists of their newspapers' Coach of the Year Award winners.

Daniel Weddington helped with the Kentucky High School Athletics Association archives at the Eastern Kentucky University Library.

Eldon May, the KHSAA Sports Information Director, tracked down several bits of information for me including the all-tournament teams from the girls' state tournaments.

J.T. Teegarden provided me with information about the Brooksville and Bracken County teams.

Gerald Orme gave me a photo of the 1981 Mason County state runner-up team.

Steve Appelman gave me the photo of the last Maysville team.

Bob Hendrickson, publisher of the Ledger Independent, gave me permission to use photos from the newspapers.

The Ledger Independent has had a long line of talented photographers who shot the basketball photos including Virgil Hunt, Bob Warner, Terry Prather, Leo McKay and Brian Hitch.

Jason Butler took the photo of Mason County's 2008 state championship team.

Ron Bailey, who has become a local historian, sent me several photos.

The McKay family gave me permission to use the photo of the 1948 St. Patrick team taken by Pat McKay, and passed along to me by Chris O'Hearn.

Jackie Thomas, Anita Curtis and Sparky McDowell provided me with school yearbooks. Sparky also let me borrow his copy of MAYSVILLE HIGH SCHOOL GIRLS' BASKETBALL written by Debbie Day.

I spent about two hours interviewing former Ledger-Independent sports editor Laurnie Caproni. His insights added much to this book.

My boss, Robert Roe, the General Manager of WFTM radio,

scanned photos and provided encouragement. At times he was more excited about the book than I was.

A big thanks to Rachel Foley for coming up with the title of the book.

I am indebted to my editor, Marsha Franklin. I was intimidated by sending the manuscript to the longtime English teacher at Mason County High School, but she was the perfect person to edit the book.

It was an honor to have Stephanie Stewart design the book cover.

I am confident this book would not have been published without the assistance of Fran Stewart of Eagle Creek Press. I was busy writing the book without any idea of how to complete the task until Fran offered to put it together.

Thanks to Total Printing Systems for printing the book.

– DW

Contents

Introduction

I had several reasons for writing a book about local high school basketball. Number one was my love for the game.

While in the fourth grade at Forest Avenue School, I became a fan of the Maysville Bulldogs when I attended my first game at the Maysville Gymnasium. I was hooked.

Later in the season I saw my first Maysville vs. Mason County game in the spacious Mason County Fieldhouse.

Little did I know, a few months later, I would be moving to Washington in the Mason County School District.

I quickly became a Mason County Royals fan.

I also have a fond memory of shooting hoops outdoors with my friends while listening to WFTM's Don Stahl call the play-by-play of Maysville's upset of Louisville Central in the 1972 state tournament.

In 1979 I broadcast my first basketball game on WFTM. I have called more than 1,000 games in my career.

An interview I recorded in 1987 with legendary Maysville coach Earle D. Jones also was an impetus for writing this book. I did the interview with Jones as the 40th anniversary of the Bulldogs' state championship was approaching. I realized that interview was just scratching the surface of local basketball history. There was surely enough information for a book.

I also knew it was a history worth preserving and there were many stories that had not been documented.

This community has an intense love for the game. Here is what I wrote in the Maysville-Mason County Tourism Visitors Guide a few years ago:

"Basketball has been important in Maysville and Mason County for more than 80 years. The community has produced great players and championship teams guided by legendary coaches. Fans are passionate about their teams. As soon as one season ends, talk of the next season begins."

There were days when I thought I was crazy for trying to write a book, but on most days I was excited about the project.

This book is not an almanac. I could not mention every player or every game, but I have tried to highlight many of the outstanding players and memorable games—including championship victories and heartbreaking losses.

I have covered more than 100 years in this book. Many players, coaches and games are mentioned. I have done my best to check the facts, but in works like this, mistakes of commission or omission are inevitable. I apologize in advance for any such errors.

I hope you enjoy the book.

Chapter 1 A New Game in Town

Dr. James Naismith invented the game of Basket Ball at the Y.M.C.A in Springfield, Mass. in 1891, and the game spread across the country.[1]

The first documented reference to basket ball in Maysville was in the September 30, 1896 edition of the *Public Ledger*:

"The baseball season being over, it is now in order for several of our enthusiasts to organize a basket ball team. But wait until the Y.M.C. A. gets quartered for the winter, and there'll be lots of fun in that line."[2]

Baseball was big in Maysville and would remain so for many years. Maysville's baseball team beat the Cincinnati Reds in back-to-back years. With 1,500 people on hand, Maysville won 4-2 on June 28, 1895,[3] and a crowd of 2,500 watched the Maysville team edge the Reds 3-2 on August 10, 1896.[4]

Basket ball was a new feature at the Y.M.C.A in the winter of 1897.[5] Teams were formed at the Y.M.C.A. and the games began. Basket ball was becoming more popular with the Y.M.C.A. members who used the gymnasium.[6]

The *Public Ledger* wrote "This is indeed a game that has gotten a hold in this city."[7]

The Reds beat the Blues 19-13 on March 25, 1897[8] in the first game reported. The *Evening Bulletin* gave this account of the contest: "The best game of basket ball thus far played in the local association gymnasium was witnessed last evening by a number of interested spectators."[9]

Less than two weeks later, the Reds were winners over the Blues again, this time by the score of 30-24.[10]

There were also games between the Young Men's and Business Men's Classes at the Y.M.C.A. in 1897.[11]

There was very little mention of basket ball in the newspapers in 1898. The *Public Ledger* did report that a game on December 16, 1898 was the first game played in Maysville with five men on a side."[12]

Basket ball games were played at the Y.M.C.A. on Tuesday and Friday evenings during the winter of 1899. The Y.M.C.A. report in the *Public Ledger* on Feb. 27 noted the boys "should be congratulated, too, upon the fact that they were learning to play a clean, gentlemanly game."[13]

The Maysville Y.M.C.A. traveled to Cincinnati on March 23, 1899 to play the Cincinnati Y.M.C.A. Frank Wormald started at center for Maysville. Ed. Swartz was the right forward. Simon Childs was the left forward. H.E. Gabby was the right back and J.J. Easton was the left back. Leon Squires, Samuel Egnew and Arthur Helmer were the substitutes.[14]

Cincinnati beat Maysville 27-9. The *Evening Bulletin* reported that the local team "played at some disadvantage because the boys had been accustomed to work on a small floor.[15] It was the first time the local boys had played against a team from another city.[16] Wormald made a goal from a distance of over 35 feet near the close of the game.[17]

The sport continued to grow in the fall of 1899. The Y.M.C.A report in the *Evening Bulletin* on Dec. 9 said "Basket ball plays a prominent part in our work and more time is given over to it than at any previous time. Several good teams are being developed."[18]

The Maysville Y.M.C.A. team was trounced by the Cincinnati Y.M.C.A squad 72-7 in Cincinnati on January 11, 1900.[19]

League play continued that winter. A large crowd watched the Regulars edge the Germans 22-20. Sam Egnew, Ed. Swartz, Chas. Slack, Leon Squires and G.A. Helmer were on the Regulars team. The Germans included Simon Childs, Wm. Oldham, Chas. Helmer, Austin Rosenham and J.W. Rasp.[20]

Even though the game had been played in Maysville for more than four years, newspaper reports in February 1901 outlined some of the rules. This report was in the February 14, 1901 edition of the *Public Ledger*:

The rules to govern these games are the Official Basket Ball Rules, edited by Luther Gulick, M.D., and published by the American Sports Publishing Company of New York. The latest edition can be seen at the Y.M.C.A office at any time. With an understanding of the rules the games can be much more enjoyed. The interpretation put upon the rules by our local Secretary is according to that [practiced] by all the best Physical Directors and Basket Ball players of the United States. Section 3 of Rule XII. Says: "Officials are expected to be as strict as possible, both with players and spectators. In all cases not covered in these rules officials are to use their own [judgement] in accord with the general spirit of the rules." Section 31 of Rule X.: "There shall be no protests against the decision of the officials, except in regard to

Interpretation of rules." Section 35 of Rule X.: "Any remarks on the part of a player during progress of the game derogatory in any way to the officials shall be called a foul by the referee."[21]

Two weeks later, another article in the *Public Ledger* detailed how the game was being played at the Y.M.C.A.:

That basketball has a firm hold upon the young members of the Y.M.C.A no person would doubt who goes there. Even the middle aged and a few old "vets" are held with delight when witnessing a game and the two latter classes never miss a night when there is a game. Basket ball is not rough, in that players are not allowed to kick, strike nor tussle for the ball. That most dangerous mixup which is fatal to life and limb is avoided. The principal features are: Five numbers are chosen to each side. The positions are right and left guards, two goal men and a center man. Each having his opposite, take positions, which are arranged across the field properly marked and bounded. The ball is tossed from center by the umpire at the blowing of the whistle. The game has begun and continues for fifteen minutes, when time is called to allow a rest for ten minutes; then the second half starts. And at its end the side having the largest number of points is declared the winner. A player caught taking the ball from a man, for roughness, speaking to the officers, for advancing or running is declared fouling, and the points are not only counted against him but for the opposite side. Field goals are made from the field while the game is in progress. A goal throw is made when a foul is declared. The former counts two points, the latter one for the side making them. Two referees, one umpire and a time-keeper are appointed and these officers are sole arbiters of the game. No appeal lies and no right to question their decision is allowed, though the Captains can argue a point and contend for a due observance of the rules. The game is well calculated to drill the players along the line of physical development, self-control and evenness of temper. Thus briefly is outlined the game, and when fully comprehended is most fascinating and decent. The public is cordially invited to see the games now being played, and once witnessing the interest and good accomplished a practical demonstration of the working of one phase of the four-sided ideas of the Y.M.C.A. is exhibited.[22]

A big crowd packed the Y.M.C.A. on March 7, 1901 to watch the Heavyweights beat the Heinies 21-11. The management of the physical department expressed regret that the gym was not larger.[23]

The Y.M.C.A.'s statistical report for the year ending June 1, 1901 showed that over 20 games were played in the basket ball league.[24]

Basket ball was not limited to the winter months in 1901. The *Evening Bulletin* gave this report on the popularity of the game in June 1901:

Basket ball grows more popular with every season of its age. Surely in Maysville it has never enjoyed more than the past season, and now with the fine court at the ball park the boys propose giving the people entertainment throughout the summer.[25]

Maysville's first game that summer was scheduled to be at home against its old nemesis, the Cincinnati Y.M.C.A., but it was rained out.[26]

In December 1901, four teams were chosen, a basket ball league was organized, and plans called for a team to be chosen to represent the Y.M.C.A. in all match games.[27]

The Covington Y.M.C.A. defeated the Maysville Y.M.C.A. 39-27 on February 14, 1902 in the first game of basket ball ever played in Maysville against a visiting team. The game was played in the Convent Hall. Covington led 30-9 at the end of the first half.[28]

Bruce Crawford was the Maysville center. Charles Slack was the right forward. Austin Rosenham played the left forward position. Conrad Rasp was the right guard, Lee Dinger was the left guard.[29]

Admission to the game was 25 cents for gentlemen, 15 cents for ladies and children.[30]

The Glendale, Ohio, team came to town on March 7, 1902 and edged Maysville 36-33 in what the *Evening Bulletin* called "The fastest game of basket ball ever played by the Maysville team."[31]

The game was not without controversy and attendance was low. The *Evening Bulletin* had this report:

Several points during the game were in dispute, and the referee's decision was tested. Maysville made a goal and while the ball was in the air a foul was called on the home team, and the officials said that goal did not count, but it opened the way for a contested game.

The game did not have the patronage of the people it deserves. The majority of those present were ladies, and their loyalty is appreciated very much. The show at the Opera House took many away, and even some who should give loyal support to the game and to the association.[32]

Glendale beat Maysville again the next day. Crawford missed the game for some unknown reason, and Glendale played rough.[33]

Maysville lost to Latonia 19-14 on April 11, 1904. The *Public Ledger* wrote "The occasion was graced by the presence of many ladies, and the game was a spirited one from start to finish."[34]

A rematch between the two teams scheduled to be played in Latonia on April 23 was called off.[35]

Fans attending a game between Captain Slack's and Captain Rasp's teams on January 18, 1905 were invited to stay for a German lunch and listen to a solo by Captain Charles Slack, who was described by the *Public Ledger* as "the handsome tonsorial artist."[36]

By 1906, basket ball had been around long enough to form an "Old Timers" team at the Y.M.C.A. The "Old Timers" – Captain C. Slack, W. Weis, C. Helmer, R. Rasp and C. Wright lost to the 1906 squad 16-13.[37]

Y.M.C.A. basket ball news no longer appeared in the local newspaper after 1906, and the game spread to the schools. Who could have imagined how big the game would become in Maysville and throughout the state of Kentucky?

Chapter 2 Early High School Hoops

There is nothing in the local newspapers that specifies a game as the first ever played on the high school level. Thc first rcports of games didn't appear in the newspapers until 1909, however, when the Maysville High School Athletic Association held its annual election in 1907, Charles B. Gibson was elected as the Basket Ball Captain.[38]

Once the game reports started appearing in the newspapers, the early focus was on girls' basket ball. 1909-10 was the first season for girls' basket ball at Maysville High School.[39]

The Maysville basket ball teams had a new facility to play their home games in. The new Maysville High School building was dedicated on June 17, 1909. The $75,000 structure included an auditorium on the third floor.[40] The auditorium would serve as Maysville's home court until the Maysville Gymnasium opened in 1930.

Two girls' teams from Maysville High School squared off in a game at Beechwood Park on October 30, 1909. The Blues beat the Whites 28-15. The *Public Ledger* wrote: "Because of the splendid guarding of Miss Natalie Wood the Whites were able to score only once in the first half, while Miss Zweigart's goal throwing was a conspicuous feature of the game." Zweigart had nine field goals in the first half.[41] Zweigart's first name was Jennie and she was a forward.[42]

The Maysville girls traveled to Paris and lost 25-9. "The Maysville girls play the cleanest game of basket ball I have ever seen," said Mr. Johnson, the Paris coach.[43]

The *Public Ledger's* story on the game said the Maysville girls had only played six weeks.[44]

The Maysville girls picked up a 20-8 road win over an Ashland squad, which according to the *Public Ledger* "became slightly confused because of the unfamiliarity with the line rules, while they were unable to use their goal throwers because of the strength and quickness of the Maysville guards."[45]

Maysville routed Ashland 19-3 when the two teams met later in the season in Maysville.[46]

The Maysville girls traveled to Lexington On February 22 and lost to the State University team 38-3. The *Lexington Herald* report, reprinted in the *Public Ledger*, said "although the visitors were at a disadvantage on account of age and training, they played fairly good ball and won the admiration of the audience by their tenacity and pluck."[47]

This uncredited photo shows the third-floor auditorium that served as Maysville's home court until the Maysville Gymnasium opened in 1930.

High school basket ball in Mason County was not limited to Maysville. May's Lick High School also had team. Despite having two experienced college players, the May's Lick girls only had two field goals and lost to Maysville on February 26, 1910.[48] The final score was 18-4.[49]

The Maysville girls took a road trip to central Kentucky and suffered losses to Caldwell High School of Richmond (14-8) and Kentucky Wesleyan in Winchester (21-9) on back-to-back nights. The gym in Richmond had a low ceiling and bad goals. The girls had to spend the night in a Winchester boarding house because the train for the trip home was delayed four hours in Winchester making it impossible to make the connection in Paris.[50]

Maysville challenged May's Lick to a rematch under the following conditions:

1. That the game be played either indoors or outdoors on a field free from obstructions not more than five feet shorter than the regulation field as called for in Spalding's Guide Book.

2. That the referee be a person from outside Mason County, well known in basketball circles.

3. That the umpire be a person who is accustomed to officer games and one satisfactory to both teams.

4. That the game be played as formerly— open field and five girl teams— otherwise strictly in accordance with Spalding's Guide for Women.

5. That the game be played within three weeks.

6. That each team send two representatives to some convenient place to meet and arrange details.[51]

This was the last challenge Maysville was going to give or accept from May's Lick. The Maysville team found out there was ill feelings toward Maysville from the May's Lick community following the first game.[52]

There is no report of the rematch ever being played in the 1909-10 season.

The Maysville girls decided to close out the 1909-10 season after a game between the two school teams in April because it was getting too warm to practice.[53]

In boys' action in the 1909-10 season, May's Lick High School and the Lewisburg Athletic Club played a series of games. May's Lick, with two professors in the lineup, won the first game.[54]

The Minerva High School Athletic Association was organized in October 1910. Eugene Boyd was elected captain of the boys' basketball team, and Katie Dwyer was elected captain of the girls' basketball team.[55]

The Minerva girls were scheduled to host Brooksville on November 25,[56] but there was no report after the game.

The only game score published in the 1910-11 season was a 35-17 victory for May's Lick over Flemingsburg in Flemingsburg.[57] The one-sentence report did not say if it was a boys' or a girls' game.

The May's Lick girls had games scheduled that season against Flemingsburg,[58] the Bourbon College team,[59] and Paris.[60] The May's Lick boys had a game scheduled at Augusta.[61]

The Maysville girls defeated Bellevue 11-5 in 1912.[62]

The two scores reported in the 1911-12 season were the May's Lick boys' 51-5 loss to Paris,[63] and the May's Lick girls' 18-15 victory over Maysville.[64]

Two Maysville High School first and second boys' teams played against each other on April 18. The game was billed as the only chance to see the boys play on the newly equipped floor. The *Public Ledger* wrote that the boys' game was "slightly different" from the girls'.[65]

The lineups for the teams, chosen by Dr. Quigley, were:

First Team

Center - Ben Allen
Right Forward - Jerome Zeigler (Captain)
Left Forward - Frances Hopper
Right Guard - Tom Barbour
Left Guard - Vincent Ellis
Substitute - Hugh Power

Second Team

Center - George Fitzgerald (Captain)
Right Forward - Ernest Zeigler
Left Forward - Clay Smith
Right Guard - Lisle Threlkeld
Left Guard - Abe Galanty
Substitute - Clarence Pollitt[66]

There was no report on how the game turned out.

The First District School beat the Maysville High School boys' team 6-4 in the fall of 1912.[67]

The Maysville boys beat the MHS Alumni 18-10. The *Public Ledger* wrote "The disconcerting part of the game for the Alumni was the basketball rules have been somewhat changed in the last few years and some members of the team were very much confused at the provisions of the present rules."[68]

The boys' team ended up with a record of 14-1 in 1913.[69]

The Maysville High School girls' team didn't start the season until late January when two teams from the high school played against each other.[70]

A couple of weeks later, the Maysville girls lost to Paris 37-2. Both points were on foul goals. The line-up for Maysville was Miss Lykins, center; Miss Stevenson and Miss Smith, forwards and Miss Young and Miss Calvert, guards.[71]

That game was probably fresh in the Maysville girls' minds as they got ready to host Paris in February 1914. The *Public Ledger* wrote "the Maysville girls have been practicing very strenuously and are playing in better form than at any time during the season."[72] There was no report on how the game turned out.

The Maysville boys' team got off to a fast start in the 1913-14 season and finally received some press coverage. The boys were 4-0 against other schools heading into a much anticipated home game against Portsmouth. The wins were over Germantown (28-18), Flemingsburg (28-8), Minerva (18-9) and Brooksville (23-14).[73]

A capacity crowd was on hand to see Maysville beat Portsmouth 23-13. McNamara, the Maysville center had six goals and one point from a foul goal. The rest of the Maysville line-up included Hunt, Stevens, Coryell and Zeigler.[74]

The Maysville boys opened the 1914-15 season with an 8-5 road loss to Germantown. Several Maysville fans made the trip to Germantown in automobiles.[75]

A week before Christmas, the Maysville boys hosted Paris and suffered a 20-14 loss in a game The *Bourbon News* described as "snappy from start to finish."[76]

After being called basket ball since its inception, the sport's spelling was changed to basketball in early 1915.[77]

The Maysville boys' and girls' teams swept a doubleheader against Germantown on January 8. The boys avenged their season-opening loss with a 29-12 victory, while the girls won a defensive battle by the score of 6-5.[78]

The next few games were a struggle for the boys' team. Maysville was outscored 21-1 in the second half of a 37-12 loss to Ashland in the

MHS auditorium on January 22. Roy Hampton, who scored all but one of the goals, and E. Parker were the Maysville forwards. Marsh played center. The guards were Mathews and S. Parker. Shea was the lone substitute.[79] Marsh was known as Big "Granny" Marsh and was one of the stars of the team.[80]

Maysville lost to Augusta 27-15 in a game played in Augusta.[81]

Two hundred fifty people attended the Maysville at Portsmouth game, with Portsmouth winning 40-12.[82]

In what the *Public Ledger* called "The most exciting basketball game that has been witnessed in Maysville for a long time," the Maysville girls and Newport played to a 17-17 tie. The Maysville line-up had Flossie Jones at center, Georgia Clark at left guard, Carroll Matthews at right guard, Elizabeth Peed (with a team-high seven points) at left forward and Francis Dixon Ball at right forward.[83] [84]

The Maysville girls traveled to Newport for the rematch and were defeated by the score of 27-13. Flossie Jones had all the goals for Maysville.[85]

The May's Lick boys' team was undefeated in the 1914-15 season.[86]

Roy Hampton was elected captain of the 1915-16 Maysville boys' team.[87] Hampton might have been the first outstanding athlete at MHS. The *Public Ledger* wrote that Hampton "has been one of the most consistent players Maysville High School has ever had.[88] The school yearbook, *Advocate,* described Hampton as "a bear, throwing goals from any angle." He was also the captain of the 1916 baseball team. Hampton was a splendid fielder, a .375 hitter and the mainstay of the pitching staff.[89]

G.C. Mance was listed as the Maysville coach in a preseason news story,[90] but Professor C.S. Dale was the coach when the season opened. Dale also served as the coach for the Maysville Night High School team.[91] Mance, who served as faculty manager[92] of the school, was the referee for many of Maysville's games.[93] Later in the season, Mance took over as the coach.[94]

The season opener — a home game against May's Lick— was for bragging rights in the county. Neither team had lost to a team from Mason County the previous season.[95] Maysville won 10-7.[96] Hampton was held scoreless.

In a home game against Brooksville, Maysville fell behind early, but rallied to lead 17-7 at the end of the first half and went on to win 26-16.[97]

Players on Maysville's first and second teams, in addition to Hampton, were Ed Parker, student manager; Stanley Parker, Gordon Smoot, Clarence Wood, Jr., Cecil Dickson, Charles Kerr, Henry Shea, Charles G. Downing, Giles Rice, John C. Everett, John Glascock, William Geisel, Donnell McNamara, Charles Hancock and John

Robert Currey. The May's Lick squads included J. Pogue, Spencer Manion, W. Rees Wood, Collopy, H. Rees, T. Pogue, Gaither and Collins. Professor E.L. Dix was the May's Lick coach.[98] Ellsworth Cablish was listed as a member of the Maysville team in a newspaper story the next week.[99]

Maysville's early season success was creating even more interest in the sport. The *Public Ledger* wrote "The classy playing of the locals during the last two weeks has attracted the attention of lovers of the net game in this vicinity and each performance is drawing larger crowds. In view of this fact the management has made special arrangements for a large crowd Friday evening." [100]

That game drew the largest crowd of the season, and Maysville, despite being without two starters, defeated Dayton 37-26, thanks in part to a splendid game by Hampton.[101]

After leading 12-9 at halftime, Maysville picked up a 23-15 victory over Germantown in the MHS auditorium. Smoot played rough in the first half and was replaced by Wood in the second half.[102]

Hampton scored 17 points to lead Maysville past Carlisle 29-18. Parker played well on defense.[103]

Maysville continued to roll with home victories over Ft. Thomas (29-13), the MHS Alumni (13-11) and Carlisle (30-3).[104]

Maysville hit the road and defeated Manchester 24-9. The Maysville team was pictured in the Sunday edition of the *Cincinnati Enquirer*. The newspaper touted the Maysville squad as the leaders of this section of the state.[105]

Next up was a train trip to northern Kentucky to play three different schools.[106] The *Public Ledger* wrote "A large following of fans will make the trip with the boys and these adherents think the chances of the M.H.S. boys are so good that they are wagering their last cent on them."[107]

If that was the case, the fans came home broke because Maysville lost all three games— 25-20 to Dayton, 25-12 to Bellevue and 41-18 to Ft. Thomas. The season recap in the school yearbook, *Advocate*, said all three floors were not large enough to play upon, and the Dayton floor had a number of posts in the center.[108]

February 4, 1916 was the date of the first-ever game between the Maysville and Paris boys' teams.[109] Maysville outscored Paris 31-6 in the second half to win 42-8. The attendance was listed at 300— the largest of the season. Maysville center Clarence Wood made a basket with Paris' heavy center, Humpty Adair, hanging on his shoulders. The *Public Ledger* wrote "The feat was one of the prettiest pieces of basketball ever seen in this city and much applause greeted the stunt."[110]

The home court advantage must have been huge that season

because Maysville traveled to Paris for the rematch and lost 25-24. Then, Maysville avenged its 13-point road loss to Bellevue by beating that team 39-17 in the MHS auditorium in the final game of the season.[111]

Maysville finished the season with a 12-4 record and was undefeated at home. The team went to see the movie "The Cheat" at the Opera House before attending a banquet at Traxel's. Letter winners, based on attendance at practice instead of playing in a number of games, included Gordon Smoot, Clarence Wood, Charles Downing, Roy Hampton, Chenoweth Everett, John Glascock, J.E. Parker Jr., Henry Shea, Cecil Dickson and Ellsworth Cablish. [112]

The 1915-16 Maysville girls' team was coach by Rosine Dickman, a Latin teacher at the high school.[113]

The girls opened the season with a 15-6 road victory over Carlisle.[114]

Maysville picked up another win over Carlisle, and beat the alumnae team. The girls suffered two losses to Highlands and two losses to Bellevue for a season record of 3-4.[115]

Letter winners included Margaret Smith, Ailene Berry, Flossie Jones, Irene Gilcher, Carroll Matthews and Eleanor Wood.[116]

The 1916-17 Maysville girls' team, coached by Elsie Heller, a four-year member of the Kentucky State team, went 6-3. Eleanor Wood was the captain.[117]

The girls opened the season with a 54-1 victory over Augusta in the MHS auditorium.[118]

When the two teams met again in Augusta, Maysville won 26-0.[119]

A January game between Maysville and Paris was marked by a phenomenal performance by Lena Rose of Paris. The *Public Ledger* reported that Rose scored 34 points in Paris' 54-9 win.[120] The game report in *The Daily Bulletin* credited Rose with 46 points, and had the final score 50-9. The *Daily Bulletin* wrote: "Miss Rose's performance was nothing short of spectacular and she was warmly applauded for her excellent work. Being of much larger build than any of her opponents, Miss Rose would often hold off her opponents with one hand and with the other toss the ball into the basket. Her work was by far the most phenomenal ever witnessed in M.H.S. auditorium and established an individual record for High School basketball in this city."[121]

The school annual, *The Calx*, wrote that the game at Ft. Thomas "seemed unfair, for the girls were compelled by Ft. Thomas to play boys' rules, contrary to the agreement."[122] The train was late and the team did not arrive until a few minutes before game time. Ft. Thomas edged Maysville 10-9.[123]

The girls posted a 32-9 victory over Flemingsburg[124] before being routed by Paris 52-8 in Paris. Rose had another big game for Paris. Her point total was not listed, but the *Public Ledger* reported that she did a great deal of the scoring.[125]

The 1916-17 team members were Eleanor Wood (captain), Ailene Berry, Frances Dixon Ball, Corina Slye, Margaret Smith, Edna Stevens, Elizabeth Calvert, Lillian Middleman, Margaret Lingenfelser, Louise Adair, Fannie Thomas, Violet Muse, Esculene Traxel and Helen Nauman.[126]

Professor Lewis Duke coached the Maysville boys in 1916-17.[127]

The Maysville boys opened the season with a 50-20 win over Germantown. After reaching the 50-point mark, Maysville allowed Germantown to score the last 11 points of the game. Maysville forward Gordon Smoot was put out of the game in the second half for using improper language. Maysville's second team posted a 26-10 victory over Germantown.[128]

New eligibility rules went into effect in November 1916. Every member of the team playing in a game against another school was required to have a passing grade in all but one subject.[129]

Maysville's 36-10 win over Manchester was marred by a couple of fights. Maysville center Clarence Wood Jr. and a Manchester player by the name of Coleman were tossed out of the game in the first half after fighting. Wood was allowed to return to action in the second half. The big skirmish happened in the second half when Manchester's Cole and Maysville's Browning started to fight. The *Public Ledger* wrote: "the larger part of the audience rushed to the floor and had it not been for the fact that the faculty were present the Manchester boy might have suffered severe injury."[130]

Maysville lost to Lexington 32-22 in what the *Public Ledger* called "one of the best games ever played on the local floor."[131] The school annual said it was the first home defeat in three years.[132]

The alumni team, which included Roy Hampton, the star of the 1915-16 squad, beat Maysville 31-12. It was the first time the alumni had defeated the high school team.[133]

Maysville bounced back with a 55-6 home court rout of Augusta.[134]

Maysville lost to Paris 39-18 in Paris,[135] but avenged that loss with a 29-16 victory at home.[136]

Ft. Thomas edged Maysville 26-24 in Ft. Thomas. That was the same night the Maysville girls lost to Ft. Thomas 10-9. The *Public Ledger* wrote: "The students claim that the referee of the game did not give them a fair deal by calling fouls on the least thing. They also claim that on account of the small floor they were greatly handicapped.[137] The school annual called the Ft. Thomas gymnasium a "cigar box."[138]

The 1916-17 team members were Frank Browning, Clarence Wood, Markham Hicks, John Everett Jr., Gordon Smoot (captain),

Charles Downing, Stanley Parker and Norman Bowman.[139]

The first games of the 1917-18 season played at the MHS auditorium were between May's Lick and Germantown. The games were scheduled to be played outdoors in May's Lick, but they were moved indoors in Maysville because of inclement weather. May's Lick won the games by the scores of 18-14 and 26-10.[140]

Expectations for the Maysville boys' team were not too high because many of the top players had graduated the previous spring.[141]

With "Uncle" George J. Noel as the new coach, Maysville opened the season with four straight wins (two over Flemingsburg and one each against Manchester and Augusta).[142]

The winning streak was snapped by a 51-13 loss to Paris in Paris. That was followed by a 41-30 road loss to Richmond.[143]

The school annual listed the Maysville at Manchester game as a 35-28 victory for Maysville.[144] The *Public Ledger* reported the game as a 35-28 loss for Maysville, but did not provide any details.[145]

Maysville closed out the season with a 24-21 loss to Paris in the MHS auditorium.[146]

The 1917-18 squad included Raymond Dawson (captain), Collis Dickson, Goebel Baugh, William Tully, Robert Owens, Clifford Purdon, John Walker and Clifford Thomas. The school annual described Dawson as "one of the quickest little forwards that ever played on our floor," and listed his point total for the season at 120.[147]

In a 28-18 win over Flemingsburg, the *Public Ledger* wrote that Dawson "performed some quick work in dribbling and dodge work."

The 1917-18 Maysville girls team routed Augusta 50-3,[148] but ran into Lena Rose again and lost to her Paris team 38-14 at Paris.[149] The school annual wrote of the loss to Paris "The girls could be excused for this defeat, since they simply couldn't hold down a lady three times their size, and it was such a one who made comparatively all the points."

Maysville edged Paris 31-30 at home in the final game of the season. The *Public Ledger* wrote that the girls "displayed some of the neatest goal shots and clever guarding that has been seen for several seasons."[150] The school annual wrote "even the 'Invincible Rosie' was here, but she couldn't escape our girls."[151]

The start of the 1918-19 season was delayed because of an influenza epidemic. Schools, churches and theaters were ordered closed on October 7.[152] Maysville city schools reopened on December 2. In the middle of February only nine of the 38 schools in the county were open. None of the closed schools would reopen the rest of the year. Dover was the only high school that was open.[153] At least 80 flu-related deaths were reported in Mason County.[154]

Many teams had started to play before the Maysville boys had started to practice. C.S. Dale returned as Maysville's coach.[155]

Maysville lost to the alumni team 40-8. The alumni team included former MHS players who were playing for various college teams.[156]

Maysville beat Manchester 39-17 at home, but lost 33-20 in the rematch at Manchester. All of the team could not get to Manchester. The school annual, *The Calx*, said Maysville lost at Manchester in back-to-back seasons because of "poor transportation facilities."[157]

About 20 boys and Coach Dale made the trip to Augusta in a truck and Maysville defeated Augusta 42-2.[158]

Maysville recorded its first win over Ashland, but it was not without controversy. When the final whistle blew, Maysville was leading 21-19. Ashland contested the score by claiming not enough time had been played. Ashland, after being given an additional five minutes, admitted defeat with Maysville up 23-21.[159] It was the first game played in Ashland's new gymnasium.[160] Ashland got revenge by beating Maysville 25-20 in Maysville.[161]

The school annual claimed Paris beat Maysville 25-15 because Paris played some of their former "stars" who had just returned from military service.[162]

Collis Dickson was the captain of the 1918-19 team. The other members of the team were Raymond Dawson, John McDonough, William Smith, Glenn Collins and Gus Cooper.[163]

The 1918-19 Maysville girls team beat Paris and lost to the alumni, Winchester Wesleyan and Paris.[164]

In a game billed as the county championship in October 1919, Minerva doubled up May's Lick 22-11.[165]

George Noel took over for C.S. Dale as the Maysville boys coach for the 1919-20 season.[166] Maysville made its first appearance in the state tournament in 1920, losing to Pikeville College 23-16 in the first round.[167] The state tournament must not have been a big deal back then because there was no mention of the game in the school annual. Team members included Charles Kennan (captain), William Tully, William Rice, Glenn Collins, John McDonough, Reed Crawford, Thomas Pickett and William Smith.[168]

Miss Scottie Stevenson, a graduate of MHS and Miami University, coached the Maysville girls to a 1-4 record. The win was over Portsmouth in the only home game of the season. Abbie Shea was the captain. The girls' roster also included Lyde Chenault, Frieda Nauman, Clarice Day, Margaret Stevenson, Dolly Ford, Martha Day and Jessie Figgins.[169]

The 1920-21 Maysville boys team, coached by Noel, opened the season with six straight wins and finished with an 11-5 record. William Rice was the captain. He was joined on the team by William Tully, T.J. Pickett, Reuben Dickson, Milton Russell, Church Matthews,

John Stevenson and Ernest Brodt.

The 1920-21 Maysville girls team went 3-2 under Coach Stevenson. The team included Lyde Chenault (captain), Clarice Day, Frieda Nauman, Martha Day, Susie Pickett, Dolly Ford, Margaret Stevenson and Elizabeth Brady.

The big story of the 1921-22 season was the state runner-up finish by the Sardis girls. The girls played all of their home games on an outdoor court. They practiced in a barn on the W.A. Simons farm or on a frozen outdoor court. Once a week they traveled to Maysville to practice in the gymnasium at the Christian Church. Dave Hopkins was the coach. Sardis defeated Flemingsburg in the district tournament and beat Paducah and Glendale in the state tournament before losing to Ashland 26-13 in the state championship game to finish the season with a 20-1 record.[170]

Ada Fowler was named an all-state player. Other team members were Susan Cracraft, Ruby Crockett, Elizabeth Fowler, Mabel Dye, Clara Bierly, Dora White, Clarine Mullikin and Aldora Cracraft.[171]

"We were tough," Ada Fowler Cracraft recalled in 1980. "The boys wouldn't play us when we practiced.[172]

"We went to Bracken County for a game, and they didn't want to play us. They thought they were going to play Mt. Olivet."[173]

The 1921-22 season was forgettable for the Maysville teams. The girls, with a new coach - Emily Lindsley - lost to Sardis, Flemingsburg and Carlisle.[174]

The Maysville boys, coached again by George Noel, and with Church Matthews as the captain, also struggled. The school annual, *The Calx,* wrote:

"M.H.S. did not have a very successful season in basketball this year for several reasons. We had games scheduled with strong teams in the first of the season, when we had had but little practice. And, furthermore, we started out with practically a new team, having only one old man on it. However, after much hard practice and with the aid of the coaching ability of Mr. Noel, the team braced up and we were able, in the last of the season, to defeat some of our strongest rivals."[175]

For the 1922-23 season, Coach Noel moved over to the girls team and George Schneider took over as the boys' coach. The girls were the district runners-up and had a 4-4 record. Three of the losses were to Flemingsburg and the other one to Sardis. Team members were Gertrude McNamara, Susie Pickett, Louise Calvert, Martha Purdon, Dorothy Caplinger, Margaret Helpenstein and Virginia Goodwin.[176]

The school annual, *The Calx,* called the boys' team "one of the most formidable quintets that M.H.S. has ever produced."[177]

John Chenault, the team captain, was voted best athlete in the school and won two medals at the state tournament as best all-round player and all-star captain.[178]

Former Maysville player Flossie Jones was the new coach of the Maysville girls in the 1923-1924 season. The team edged Flemingsburg 9-7 in the district championship game and was the first MHS girls' team to play in the state tournament.[179] Maysville trailed Ashland 12-2 at the end of the first half in the opening round game at the state tournament. Dorothy Caplinger, who scored Maysville's two points in the first half, fouled out early in the second half. Louise Calvert scored the other two points before suffering a broken collar bone when she collided with an Ashland player at the beginning of the fourth quarter. The final score was Ashland 21, Maysville 4.[180] Maysville's season record was 10-3.[181]

The Maysville boys had a new coach for the 1923-24 season, Frank Scott. The team won seven games and lost six. Two of their losses were to Minerva by the lopsided scores of 40-19 and 32-14. Maysville lost to Carlisle 25-24 in the district tournament.[182] John Stevenson was the Maysville captain.[183]

The Daily Independent referring to the Maysville football team as the Bulldogs in 1924.[184] The Bulldogs nickname did not start showing up in newspaper accounts of the basketball games on a regular basis until the 1926-27 season. Prior to then, the most of the newspaper reports called the teams the Gold and White. The girls' basketball team was sometimes referred to as the Gold and White lassies.

The Minerva boys' team was an interesting story in the 1923-24 season. After the 40-9 victory over Maysville, Minerva had outscored its opponents 475-189 in 16 games. Only one other team in the state had scored as many points in the same number of games.[185]

Minerva did not get to display its scoring talents in post season play. The team was barred from the district tournament at Flemingsburg because it was not a member of the state athletic association. The Minerva team manager claimed the Flemingsburg district tournament managers notified every school but Minerva about the deadline to become a member of the association.[186]

Chapter 3 Maysville's First State Title

There were high hopes for the Maysville girls' team at the start of the 1925-26 season. Maysville was coming off a 12-3 season and only lost one regular player—Hilda Welte—to graduation.[187] *The Daily Independent* wrote "Miss Flossie Jones, coach of the girls has an abundance of material and should have easy sailing with every team in this district."[188] The *Public Ledger* was in even bolder in its preseason report "The girls' team is expected to be developed into one of the best female outfits in the state."[189]

The season opener was no contest. Maysville routed Tollesboro 40-3 in the MHS auditorium. The *Public Ledger* wrote "The game was hardly a good practice game for the local lassies, who won the contest in a walk."[190] Gladys Keith led the way with 17 points. Catherine Fee, the team captain, added 13 points.

The team was brought down to earth with a 38-10 road loss to Portsmouth. A large crowd, including about 25 people from Maysville witnessed the game. The *Public Ledger* wrote "The Maysville girls were handicapped by being stage-frightened, particularly in the first half."[191]

After not playing in nearly a month, and despite being without two starters-Jane Moses and Katherine Simpson - Maysville cruised past Augusta 43-4 at home.[192] The next night, Fee scored 10 points to lead Maysville to a 23-10 home court win over Brooksville.

Maysville went to Augusta and posted a 28-4 victory. Fee tossed in 18 points.

Maysville had easy wins over Brooksville (24-8 at Brooksville) and Germantown (22-8 at home).

The Georgetown Buffalettes, the defending state champions and winners of 30 consecutive games, came to town on January 30. The Georgetown girls were known as the "wonder team" and had attracted nationwide attention.[193] Five hundred fans attended the game crowding the recently installed new seats in the auditorium. The *Public Ledger* wrote the fans "were far beyond being comfortable and giving ample proof of the dire need of a new gymnasium in Maysville." The Maysville girls had a 5-2 lead at the end of the first quarter. Georgetown rallied to lead 10-7 at the half and 18-9 at the end of the third quarter. The Buffalettes had an 18-12 lead early in the fourth quarter when their star player, Miss Sharpe, left the game with an injury. Maysville made three straight field goals to pull within one at 19-18.[194] *The Daily Independent* wrote "The crowd was in an uproar, clamoring and praying for the needed field goal which would give Maysville victory. But the strain was too much. With three seconds to go and the ball in Maysville territory, Georgetown call time out, and on resuming play held fast until the gong."[195]

Elizabeth Sharpe scored 15 of Georgetown's 19 points. Fee had 12 of Maysville's 18 points. *The Daily Independent* called Sharpe "one of the greatest girl players ever seen on this court."[196]

Maysville won its next three games against school teams by a combined score of 109-16. Fee scored in double figures in all three games- 13 in a 31-1 home rout of Carlisle, 16 in a 39-4 home win over Paris and 19 in 39-11 victory over Paris in the return game at Paris.

The week separating the games against Paris featured a game against the alumni. The former players were no match for the Maysville girls. With her team leading 20-1 at the end of the first quarter, Coach Jones made many substitutions and the Maysville girls won 56-9.[197]

Fee was held to five points in a 29-14 road loss to Georgetown. The *Public Ledger* wrote "The Maysville girls seemed rattled throughout their contest, and at no time did they hit their stride. Moses, at guard, and Keith, at forward, played fine games, but the other members of the team were unable to get going."[198] Sharpe scored 19 points for Georgetown.

Maysville traveled to Flemingsburg to close out the regular season. The capacity crowd included about 250 fans from Maysville. After leading 8-3 at the half, Maysville pulled away for a 31-7 victory.[199] Fee scored 19 points.

The 11th District Tournament was held at Brooksville.[200]

Fee scored 19 points and Keith added 10 as Maysville shutout Augusta 37-0.

Maysville beat Carlisle 28-9 in the semifinal round.[201] It was 14-point game for Fee.

Fee scored 16 points to lead Maysville to a 26-8 win over Germantown in the championship game.[202] The Maysville girls were headed back to the state tournament.

Maysville was rated the second best team in the state.[203] Georgetown was the favorite to win the state tournament, but the Buffalettes would be shorthanded. Their second best player,"Red" Lemmons, had the mumps and would not play in the tournament.[204]

Maysville played the 10 a.m. first round game in the state tournament at the University of Kentucky on March 11. Maysville doubled up Reidland, the First District champion, by the score of

24-12.[205] Fee was the leading scorer with 14 points, but *The Daily Independent* called Elizabeth Broshears the "star of the game," and added that "the fleet guard being every place on the floor, breaking up plays, displaying good guarding and scoring six points."[206]

Maysville never trailed in a 25-18 win over Shepherdsville in the quarterfinal round on Friday morning. Fee led all scorers with 15 points. The *Public Ledger* received first hand information on the game thanks to the efforts of Clarence Lynch, manager of the local office of the Postal Telegraph Company.[207]

The semifinals of the girls' tournament were played Friday night and both games resulted in upsets. Maysville defeated West Louisville 17-10 in the first semifinal, and Henderson shocked Georgetown 17-14 in the second game. Fee with nine points and Broshears with eight were the only Maysville players to score.[208]

The championship game between Maysville and Henderson was played at 2:30 on Saturday afternoon in front of approximately 1,500 fans. Maysville, which had become a crowd favorite, led 3-2 at the end of the first quarter, 10-4 at the half and 16-6 after three quarters. Despite being outscored 10-7 in the fourth quarter, Maysville maintained a comfortable lead and won 23-16. The headline in the March 15, 1926 *Public Ledger* screamed STATE BASKETBALL CHAMPIONS. Fee scored 12 points in the championship game and was named to the all-state team. Broshears scored 9 points. Keith tossed in two points. The state championship trophy was a silver basketball, regulation size, mounted on an ebony base. Each member of the team and Coach Jones received a small gold basketball. The state championship trophy and the 11th District championship trophy were displayed in one of the show windows of the P.J. Murphy Jewelry Store.[209]

People started lining the streets in downtown Maysville a long time before the team arrived home by bus shortly after noon on Sunday. Several cars met the bus and accompanied the team to town. Other cars joined the procession when the bus reached the city. The bus and cars proceeded west on Second Street to the C. and O. depot and then back to the Union Bus Station where a celebration took place. The team was taken to the Elite Confectionary and presented with a box of candy by the Bellas brothers.[210]

The *Public Ledger* wrote "It also is thought to be a surety that the winning of the state championship by the local girls will furnish the incentive for the erection of a gymnasium in Maysville, which would mean the further promotion of athletics in Maysville High School and would be the best step the city has taken in years."[211]

A reception was held in the high school auditorium Monday morning. Each faculty member expressed admiration for the team. Several alumni and members of the student body gave speeches. The

The 1926 Maysville girls' state championship team.

entire high school paraded the streets Monday afternoon.[212]

The Maysville Rotary Club hosted a banquet for the state champions. J. Barbour Russell presented the team with two large boxes of Babe Ruth and Red Grange candies. The following verse was tucked into each box:

"Here's to 'Our Maysville Girls' who won the prize,
And made all folk of Maysville open their eyes,
Babe Ruth, the 'Home-runner', the man of this age,
'Red' Grange, the foot-ball kicker, all the rage,
Have nothing on the Maysville gold and white,
That won the Championship of Kentucky alright,
So while Ruth and Grange candy is sweet as can be,
Maysville Girls have the good will from me."

Russell also presented each member of the team and Coach Jones with a complimentary ticket to the movie, "Irene," to be shown at the Opera Theatre.[213]

Mr. and Mrs. Eugene Merz composed a song and dedicated it to the state champions. The song, "The Champion Team of Kentucky," was sung by the Rotarians to the tune of "Marching Through Georgia." Here are the words to the song:

I.

Sing a song of Triumph, boys
A song of Basketball!
Sing a song of valiant deeds,
That made the mighty fall,
Every team a winner there,
But Maysville best of all,
The Champion Team of Kentucky!

CHORUS

Hurrah, Hurrah, we'll sing the jubilee,
Hurrah, Hurrah, we'll shout and cheer with glee;
We've got the finest bunch of girls,
That you may ever see,
The Champion Team of Kentucky!

II.

Maysville is a proud old town
They're boasting here today,
Our school and our girls,
Is all you hear them say,
They are so good to look upon,
And Gee! How they can play!
The Champion Team of Kentucky!

Chorus. (As above.)

III.

Let us do them honor then,
They're winners you'll agree,
Simpson, Moses, Newell, Broshears.
Keith and Captain Fee;
Tolle and Decker, all are sports
And fine as they can be,
The Champion Team of Kentucky!

Chorus. (As above.)

The Commercial Club entertained the team with a dinner in the high school auditorium.[214]

The Maysville girls never made it back to the state tournament. The region tournament was added to the postseason playoffs beginning in the 1926-27 season. Maysville won the 1927 district tournament, but lost to Ashland 34-9 in the region tournament. Ashland also eliminated the Maysville girls in 1928, 1930 and 1931.

The Maysville girls' state championship surely played a huge part in the construction of the Maysville gymnasium. The facility was dedicated on January 3, 1930. The *Public Ledger* wrote "Lovers of basketball in Maysville saw the realization Friday evening of their fondest hope, which they long cherished, when they witnessed the formal opening of the splendid new gymnasium on East Third Street." The largest crowd ever to witness a basketball game at Maysville at the time was estimated at 1,200 for the Maysville vs. Paris girl-boy doubleheader that night.[215]

Virginia Atkinson of Maysville scored the first official goal in the gymnasium. The Maysville girls won 12-8. The Maysville boys completed a sweep of the doubleheader with a 20-13 victory. A dedication ceremony was held between the games.[216]

Chapter 4 Minerva Boys, May's Lick Girls Go to State

One year after the Maysville girls brought home a state championship, the Minerva boys team, coached by E.A. Allison, made a run at a state title.

Minerva opened the 1927 district tournament with a victory over Ewing. The *Public Ledger* listed the score as 29-12.[217] *The Daily Independent* reported it as 30-12.[218] There was no debate about the second round score- Minerva routed Germantown 32-2. That was followed by a 28-9 win over Orangeburg. French Smoot scored eight points to lead Minerva past Brooksville 20-17 in the championship game. Smoot was named Most Valuable Player and was on the All-District Team.[219]

The Region 6 tournament was played at Ashland. Minerva defeated Owingsville 38-12 in the first round and Rowan County 24-10 in the semi-final round.[220]

Despite losing to Ashland in the championship game by a score of 29-18, Minerva earned a berth in the state tournament as the Class B champion. Albert Bean scored 13 points in the championship game[221] and was named First Team All-Region.[222]

Minerva was named Best Sportsman Team in the tournament and was given a silver loving cup by the state Y.M.C.A.[223]

In the first draw for the state tournament, Minerva was pitted against Wickliffe.[224] But Ashland Coach Jimmy Anderson protested the first draw claiming it was conducted contrary to the Kentucky High School Athletic Association rules. Those rules stipulated that each team must play a first round game. The draw conducted by the University of Kentucky had allowed two teams to receive a first round bye. The KHSAA agreed with Anderson and a second draw was conducted.[225]

Minerva drew Memorial High School of Hardyville and came away with a 28-21 victory. Smoot led the way with 12 points. Minerva drew a bye in the second round[226] and advanced to the Class B finals to play the Millersburg Military Institute Cadets (teams were divided into Class A and Class B based on the size of the school).

Minerva led 5-3 at the end of the first quarter and 13-8 at the half. Neither team scored in the third quarter. M.M.I. rallied in the fourth quarter. The Cadets scored their 15th point with two minutes to play and then pulled away. *The Daily Independent* wrote "A minute and twenty seconds remained when the cadets came to life, Christian made two foul shots and then the next three tip-offs were converted into field goals by some fast passing and snappy shooting."[227] M.M.I. won 23-16. Smoot scored 10 points for Minerva.[228] M.M.I. defeated London 34-25 in the state championship game. The other members of the 1927 Minerva team in addition to Smoot and Bean were James Jennings, Vernon Watson, D.F. Weaver, Garrett Stewart, Johnny B. Stewart and John L. Mains.[229]

The Minerva boys opened the 1928 District tournament by routing Rectorville 55-3. *The Daily Independent* wrote "It was too one-sided to be interesting."[230] The second game wasn't much better- Minerva 41, Orangeburg 8. Smoot scored 13 points in Minerva's 32-17 semifinal win over Germantown. Tournament favorite Maysville was upset by Brooksville in the first round. Then, Augusta knocked off Brooksville in the semifinal round, pitting Augusta against Minerva in the championship game. The score was tied at 3-3 at the end of the first. Minerva led 11-5 at the half and 21-12 after three quarters. Minerva went on to win 30-20. Smoot had another 17-point game and Jennings added 10 points.[231]

Smoot scored 14 points to lead Minerva past Mt. Sterling 25-16 in the first round of the 8th Region Tournament. The *Public Ledger* called Smoot "one of the classiest forwards turned out in Mason County."[232]

The Class B title game between Minerva and Jenkins was no contest. Minerva led 10-6 at the end of the first quarter, 25-8 at the half 37-10 after three quarters and won 43-14. Three Minerva players scored in double figures. Griffith with 14 points, Jenkins with 12 and Smoot had 10.[233]

Minerva lost to Ashland 34-23 in the championship game. Smoot scored 14 points. Minerva was named the Most Sportsman-Like Team and was headed back to the state tournament.[234]

Vernon Watson, a running guard for Minerva, had been playing for two months with from a badly infected right leg. Watson became seriously ill at the state tournament banquet and was taken to the University of Kentucky Hospital. He was transferred to Hayswood Hospital in Maysville.[235]

Even without Watson, Minerva continued its trend of first round blowout wins with a 34-14 victory Corydon.[236]

There was a rumor in Maysville that the Minerva team had been ordered to leave Lexington because of an epidemic of scarlet fever in Minerva. While two cases of the disease were confirmed in Minerva, and two Minerva school girls had become ill and were sent home from school, the team was allowed to stay in Lexington and continue to play in the state tournament.[237]

Minerva's season came to end with a 21-11 second round loss to Carr Creek.[238]

The May's Lick girls made their first trip to the state tournament in 1930. May's Lick had a starting lineup of Frances Slattery and Mary Cracraft as the forwards, Minnie Beckett at center and Mary Laytham and Helen Slattery as the guards. Paynter and Ruth Lowe were the substitutes.

Beckett scored 17 points to lead May's Lick to a 27-3 victory over Sardis its opening game in the 29th District Tournament played in the new Maysville gymnasium. Sardis did not have a field goal.[239]

In the second round, Tollesboro led May's Lick 7-2 at the end of the first quarter. May's Lick rallied to lead 9-7 at the half and won 28-14. Beckett led the way with 17 points.[240]

Beckett scored 10 points in May's Lick's 22-9 semifinal win over Orangeburg. Beckett was held to one point as Maysville beat May's Lick 18-15 in the championship game. Beckett was named First Team All-District. Laytham and Frances Slattery were named Second Team All-District.[241]

May's Lick opened 8th Region Tournament play with a 29-5 victory over Raceland. Cracraft scored 12 points and Beckett added 11.[242]

Haldeman was May's Lick's opponent in the Class B finals. Neither team led by more than three points. The game was tied 8-8 at the end of the first half. May's Lick 16-15 won. Beckett scored 11 points.[243]

Ashland defeated May's Lick 35-14 in the championship game. Beckett was named to the all-tournament team.[244]

May's Lick posted easy wins in its first two games in the state tournament-33-11 over New Castle in the opening round[245] and 39-5 over Whitehall in the second round. Beckett scored 19 points in the win over Whitehall.[246]

In the Class B finals against Woodburn, May's Lick was up 6-2 at the end of the first quarter, but Woodburn led 12-7 at the half and 20-8 after three quarters. Beckett was held to seven points, and Woodburn went on to win. *The Daily Independent* had the score as 22-14.[247] The *Public Ledger* listed the score as 22-12.[248]

Powered by a fast break offense which resulted in many shots from under the basket, May's Lick, coached by Claude Jones, opened the 1931 district tournament with a 45-10 win over Tollesboro. Frances Slattery, playing forward, scored 13 points. May's Lick center Dorothy Hitt added 12 points. The other starters were Margaret O'Rourke and Francis Hitt as forwards and Ruth Lowe as the lone guard. Elizabeth Slattery and Tilly Worthington were the subs.[249] Anna Cooper was also a member of the team.[250]

May's Lick met Ewing in the Class B finals. After trailing 9-4 in the first quarter, May's Lick came back to lead 12-9 at the end of the first half and 17-9 after three quarters on the way to a 20-11 victory. Frances Slattery was the leading scorer with 8 points. Manion was a substitute for May's Lick.[251]

With a 21-7 win over Maysville in the championship game May's Lick was the first Class B team to win the girls' 29th District title. Frances Slattery was named the Most Outstanding Girl Player in the tournament. Slattery and Dorothy Hitt made the All-District Team. Lowe was named to the Second Team All-District.[252]

There was controversy at the draw for the regional tournament. Maytown school representatives claimed that the May's Lick girls should be a Class A team based on enrollment figures in the yearbook that listed May's Lick as having 90 pupils. Maytown had 76 students. Two drawings were conducted. The first with May's Lick in Class B and the second with May's Lick in Class A. The Kentucky High School Athletic Association ruled that since May's Lick played in the district tournament as a Class B team with a correct enrollment of 70, it would be a Class B team in the regional tournament. The first draw was adopted. The decision had major ramifications for the local teams. In the second draw, May's Lick was paired against Ashland, while Maysville would have played Paintsville. When the first draw was adopted, Maysville had to face Ashland.[253] Maysville lost 22-8, while May's Lick defeated Frenchburg 18-7.[254]

May's Lick beat Haldeman 17-12 in the Class B finals and advanced to play Ashland in championship game.[255]

Ashland led 9-2 at the end of the first quarter, 20-4 at the half and 22-4 after three quarters. The final score was Ashland 24, May's Lick 6. Frances Slattery was named to the All-Region Team. Dorothy Hitt was named Honorable Mention All-Region.[256]

May's Lick lost to Woodburn 35-11 in the opening round of the state tournament. Frances Slattery scored nine points.[257]

Chapter 5 Coaching Changes, Washington Girls Go to State & the End of Girls' Hoops

While the Maysville girls' basketball program had stability once Flossie Jones took over as coach in 1924, the boys' program had five coaches in seven seasons from 1925 to 1931.

After a two-year stint by F.B. Richardson as the coach in the 1924-25 and 1925-26 seasons, the school brought in experienced coaches who had had success elsewhere.

The broad search for coaches actually started with the football program. The football team played the 1923 and 1924 seasons without a coach, and no coach was in place at the start of the 1925 season.

The alumni, school board, faculty and members of the community held a meeting on September 28, 1925 to secure a coach. *The Daily Independent* wrote "It is high time that this city was placed on par with many of the cities and smaller towns, as well, in central Kentucky. Each of these schools have special coaches and in additional to them receive special training from some members of the big Universities of the State."[258]

No coach was secured at that meeting. The next week the school board set aside $200 for a coach. The alumni planned to provide the rest of the money.[259]

Maysville, still without a coach, opened the season by shutting out Falmouth 27-0.[260]

The following Monday, former University of Cincinnati star football, basketball and baseball player, Joe Linneman arrived on the C&O No. 2 train. Linneman was the new football coach at Maysville High School. He guided the team to a 9-1 record[261] in his only season at Maysville.

W. Robert "Bob" Long took over as the football and basketball coach in 1926. Long was the first in a string of five men to coach both football and basketball at Maysville. Long, a graduate of Georgetown College, was an assistant coach in Mason City, Iowa, the previous season.[262]

Maysville lost 14-12 to Brooksville in the second round of the 1927 district tournament and finished the season with an 8-12 record. Long stayed just one season and was succeeded by Hobart Walker who had coached football and basketball at Frankfort the previous two seasons.

Walker, like Long, was a graduate of Georgetown College. Walker had taken two special courses at Notre Dame under the supervision of Knute Rockne and was completing a course under Rockne at the time he was hired by Maysville.[263]

Walker's one season at Maysville ended with a 19-17 first round loss to Brooksville in the district tournament.

Walker resigned to take the football and basketball coaching positions at Carlisle.[264]

Maysville then turned to former University of Kentucky quarterback Turner Gregg who had coached at Greenville the previous three years.[265] Gregg guided the Bulldogs to back-to-back district titles. His 1929-30 team had a 20-4 record, but lost to Mt. Sterling 19-18 in the first round of the regional tournament. The *Public Ledger* reported that Gregg "apparently confident of victory, had his athletes change their style of play, instructing them to use a fast-breaking offense system instead of slow, well organized system of attack which carried them through a successful season and to the district championship, the purpose being to conceal their merit with a view to defeating the winner of the Ashland-Paintsville game." The newspaper added "Considering the style of play they were using, the Maysville boys gave a very good performance."[266] Turner left after that season.

Maysville hired former University of Alabama football player Walter Hovater as its new coach in 1930. Hovater was the head football coach at Georgetown College for three seasons. He took the Maysville football team to Blue Licks State Park for its first-ever preseason training camp.[267]

Eleven games into the 1930-31 season, Flossie Jones resigned as the Maysville girl's coach due to her increasing duties as a teacher. Hovater, took over the girls' team.[268]

On his first night as the coach of both the boys and girls teams, Hovater guided the boys' team to a 38-14 win over Lawrenceburg and the girls to a 34-19 victory over Sardis in front of a rowdy crowd at the MHS gym. *The Daily Independent* wrote: "The fans displayed poor sportsmanship in razzing Referee Mohney on his decisions".[269]

When the boys' and girls' teams played at different locations on February 13, Amy Goodwin was in charge of the girls' team.[270] The girls routed Morehead 29-5.[271]

Hovater guided the basketball team to a 19-7 record. The Bulldogs won the district tournament but lost to Ashland 15-13 in overtime in the semifinals of the regional tournament.

The girls' team was the district runner-up and lost to Ashland in the regional tournament to finish with a 17-5 record.

That was Hovater's only season at Maysville. He resigned to accept a position on the football coaching staff at the University of

Alabama.[272]

In August of 1931 the Maysville Board of Education hired a coach that would change the course of basketball for Maysville High School and the area.

Earle D. Jones, who had compiled a 71-11 record in three season at Kavanaugh,[273] beat out 63 other applicants for the job.[274]

Jones, a graduate of the University of Kentucky, guided Kavanaugh to three district titles and two regional championships. The 1929-30 team won the Class A championship at the state tournament[275] before losing to Corinth in the state championship game. The Tigers went 1-1 in the 1930 national tournament in Chicago.[276]

Jones brought his Kavanaugh team to Maysville in 1931 and routed the Bulldogs 41-15. Kavanaugh outscored Maysville 25-6 in the second half.[277]

Kavanaugh returned to the state tournament in 1931. The Tigers lost in the quarterfinal round. Jones resigned from Kavanaugh in the spring of 1931.[278]

Harry Gammage, the head coach of athletics at the University of Kentucky, sent a telegram to the Maysville Board of Education stating that he considered Jones the "best young coach in Kentucky."[279]

In its story about Jones being hired at Maysville, *The Courier-Journal* wrote "A report that Jones had signed with Versailles High apparently was incorrect."[280]

Jones was Maysville's sixth coach in eight seasons.

In a little over a month after being hired at Maysville, Jones guided the football team to a 19-7 season-opening victory over Falmouth.[281]

The 1931 Maysville football team ended up with a record of 5-3-1.

Jones coached both the boys' and girls' basketball teams. Twenty boys turned for the first basketball practice.[282]

One of the Bulldogs' top returning players-Donnie Root- missed the first nine games of the season due to a neck injury suffered during the football season.

After compiling a 10-7 record in the regular season, the Bulldogs beat Augusta, Brooksville and May's Lick win the district tournament.

The Maysville girls had a 6-4 regular season record. The girls lost to Ashland 44-1 at Ashland. Anne Rozan scored Maysville's lone point and was nicknamed "One Point Rozan."[283]

The Maysville girls had a formidable opponent in the district tournament-Washington. In their first game in the 1932 district tournament, the Washington girls, coached by Vigil Fryman, nearly shutout Orangeburg, winning by the score of 13-1. Four players scored for Washington - Minnie Davis with 4 points, Marie Fields scored 3 points, Grace Woodward followed with two points and Mary Alice Gifford added one point. Three points are unaccounted for. Other players seeing action for Washington included Winifred Frodge, Louise Cracraft and N. Davis.

Washington and May's Lick met in the Class B finals. The game was tied 3-3 at the half.[284] Washington outscored May's Lick 9-5 in the second half for a 12-7 victory to advance to the championship game to play Maysville- an 11-9 winner over Mt. Olivet in the Class A finals.[285]

Washington and Maysville split their two regular season games with the home team winning each time. It was 13-10 at Washington and 18-10 at Maysville. The championship game was a defensive struggle. *The Daily Independent* wrote "The two teams put forth a brilliant zone defense and neither was able to work in for many short shots and what were attempted were rushed."[286]

Maysville led 1-0 at the end of the first half. The game was tied 2-2 at the end of third quarter and 3-3 at the end of the fourth quarter. All six points were on free throws. Neither team scored in the two overtime periods, and according to the rules, girls' games were declared a tie after two overtimes. The officials suggested that each team shoot five free throws to break the tie. But both coaches favored another overtime period. Washington outscored Maysville 4-0 in the third overtime on a field goal by Fields and two free throws by Cracraft for a 7-3 victory.[287]

1932 was the first year the regional tournaments were held in the Maysville Gymnasium. A committee was formed to make arrangements to take care of the players. Another committee displayed the colors of the participating teams in the gymnasium. A third committee was in charge of a tournament dance. Roy Knight was the tournament manager.[288]

The Maysville Bulldogs beat Flemingsburg 39-20 in the first round. Root missed the game with a knee injury.[289] He played against Paris in the Class A final but did not score. The Bulldogs lost to the Greyhounds 18-15 to end their first season under Coach Jones with a 14-8 record.

The Washington girls continued to play stingy defense in their first game in the regional tournament against Center Hill. Washington led 2-1 at the end of the first quarter and 10-1 at halftime. Center Hill outscored Washington 5-0 in the third quarter to cut the lead to four at 10-6. Washington outscored Center Hill 8-0 in the fourth quarter to win 18-6.[290]

In what *The Daily Independent* called "the greatest deluge of field goals ever witnessed on the Maysville court"[291] Washington scored 75 points in a rout over Clintonville in the Class B finals. *The Daily Independent* listed the final score as 75-4.[292] The *Daily Bulletin* had it as 75-3.[293] Four Washington players scored in double figures- Woodward with 14 points. Cracraft and Fields each scored 13. Davis was credited with 11 by *The Daily Independent*,[294] while The *Daily Bulletin* had her with 10 points.[295]

Maysville edged Vanceburg 18-17 in the Class A finals setting up a rematch of the district championship game. A trip to the state tournament was on the line because only the region champion would advance to state in 1932.

The region championship game was another defensive struggle. Margaret January gave Maysville a 2-0 lead with a crip shot in the opening minute of the game. Field goals by Davis and Cracraft gave Washington a 4-2 lead at the half. January hit a free throw to make it 4-3. Woodward's field goal gave Washington a 6-3 lead. Carolyn Quigley hit a free throw for Maysville. Washington was up 6-4 heading into the fourth quarter. Quigley tied the game with a field goal from the side. In the last half minute, Fields made a field goal to give Washington an 8-6 win.[296] Washington was headed to the state tournament.

Quigley was named Most Valuable Player. Quigley, January, Cracraft and Fields were named to the All Region Team.[297]

Washington, with 45 students, was the smallest school in the girls' state tournament.[298]

Clay City was Washington's opening round opponent. The game was played in the Transylvania College gym.[299] Clay City led 5-2 at the end of each of the first two quarters and defeated Washington 11-8. Minnie Davis scored four points. Cracraft and Fields each scored two points.[300]

The Kentucky High School Athletic Association voted in 1932 to discontinue the girls' state tournament. It would be 43 years before the KHSAA held another state tournament for girls.

Chapter 6 A Major Flood & a State Runner-up

The closest Coach Earle D. Jones came to having a losing season was in 1932-33 when the Maysville Bulldogs went 8-7 and lost to Augusta in the district tournament.

The 1933-34 squad won 17 games, edged Brooksville 26-25 in the district championship game, beat Carlisle 17-15 in the first round of the regional tournament, lost to Cynthiana 24-21 in the semifinals.

Maysville opened the 1934-35 season with 15 consecutive victories. The winning streak was snapped with a 35-31 loss to Augusta in February. The Bulldogs bounced back with an 11-game winning streak which included a 17-7 victory over Paris in the championship game of the regional tournament. In their first appearance in the state tournament under Jones, the Bulldogs beat Dixon 15-12. Maysville's season ended with a 28-13 loss to Newport in the quarterfinal round.

Maysville lost to Minerva 28-27 in the second round of the 1936 district tournament. Harry Denham, the leading scorer for the Bulldogs that season, went on to play basketball and football at the University of Kentucky.

The 1936-37 season was interrupted by the record-setting Ohio River flood in January. The river was already above flood stage[301] when Maysville ran its season-opening winning streak to 11 games with a 24-13 victory over Carlisle on January 19.

The rain continued to fall and the river continued to rise rapidly. The Maysville schools were closed on January 22 when the river level hit 66 feet,[302] 16 feet above flood stage.

Three days later the river had reached 74.6 feet, about six feet higher than the 1913 crest.[303] The city of Maysville was placed under Martial Law on January 26.[304] Another order went to out to prevent a spread of typhoid fever.

"Everybody was supposed to have a Typhoid shot," Jones recalled in a 1987 interview. "It wasn't pleasant, but everybody had to have one."

The river crested at 75.425 feet on January 27,[305] and fell below flood stage on February 4.[306] Martial Law was lifted on February 10.[307]

The Bulldogs returned to action on February 10 with a 32-17 road win over Versailles. Clarence "Red" Cracraft, who had patrolled the city during the flood as a member of the local National Guard, scored a game-high 16 points. Another local guardsman, Carl Staker, scored five points.[308]

Maysville ran its record to 13-0 with a 32-5 romp over Brooksville. The winning streak was broken with a 32-27 loss to M.M.I. The Bulldogs put together a 12-game winning streak which included district and regional championships and a 27-23 victory over Shady Grove in the first round of the state tournament. Maysville trailed St. Xavier 16-6 at halftime of the quarterfinal round game[309] and lost 25-22, ending the season with a 25-2 record.

Staker played at the University of Kentucky and was the captain of the 1941-42 team.

The 1937-38 season had all of the makings of a rebuilding year for the Maysville Bulldogs. Four starters from the 1937 state tournament team had graduated. Two other players were ineligible because they had played the quota of semesters,[310] and team captain Gene Wood had suffered a broken neck in an automobile accident.[311]

The Bulldogs ended the regular season with back-to-back losses and drew Brooksville in the first round of the district tournament. Brooksville entered postseason play with a 22-1 record.[312] Brooksville had beaten Maysville 25-19 in December.

In the district tournament game, Maysville led 5-4 at the end of the quarter. The game was tied 7-7 at the half. Brooksville was up 16-14 at the end of the third quarter. Maysville opened the fourth quarter on a 8-1 run en route to a 22-19 victory. The *Public Ledger* called it "one of the biggest upsets ever recorded in tournament play in the Thirty-seventh District."[313]

The Bulldogs defeated Augusta 20-13 in the semifinals, but were upset by Mt. Olivet 18-16 in the district championship game.

Maysville, playing without All-District forward "Tex" McDonald and substitute George Burke who had both suffered badly sprained ankles in practice,[314] beat Flemingsburg 33-27 in its opening game of the regional tournament.

McDonald was back in the starting lineup as the Bulldogs routed Paris 31-15 in semifinals.[315]

Maysville met Cynthiana in the championship game. Maysville led 9-7 at the end of the first quarter. Cynthiana took a 14-13 lead into the locker room at the half. Maysville was on top 20-19 at the end of the third quarter. With two minutes left in the game, Cynthiana led 25-23. Joe Fitch hit a free throw to cut Maysville's deficit to one. A field goal by Joe Knight put Maysville in the lead at 26-25. Cynthiana had a chance to regain the lead but missed a shot,[316] and Maysville won its third regional title in four years.

Maysville drew Russell in the first round of the state tournament.

Public Ledger

Front row (L-R): D. Fitch, Knight, Maley, White, McDonald, G. Burke, Antle, Walker, Ritchie, Wallingford. Back Row (L-R): Coach Jones, Toncray, Calvert, Green, R. Burke, Grace, Orme, Rubinacher, Farris, J. Fitch, Case, Holland, mgr.

The game was tied at 15-15 at the half. Maysville led 30-20 after three quarters and won 44-31.[317]

The Bulldogs jumped out to a 5-1 lead in the quarterfinal round game against Highlands. Maysville was up 9-7 at the end of the first quarter, but Highlands outscored Maysville 6-2 in the second quarter to lead 13-11 at the half. Highlands had a 16-13 lead after three quarters. Maysville opened the fourth quarter on a 6-1 run to regain the lead at 19-17. There were three ties down the stretch including 23-23 at the end of regulation. McDonald's crip shot after Knight missed a free throw gave Maysville a 25-23 win in overtime. The Bulldogs had finally advanced to the state semifinals.[318]

Maysville met Frenchburg in the semifinals. The Bulldogs led 7-5 at the end of the first quarter and 16-6 at the half, and went on to win 26-20.[319]

Sharpe advanced to the championship game by beating St. Xavier 26-23 in the other semifinal game to run its record to 29-1.

Gene Wood was on the minds of Maysville's fans, players and coach during the championship game. Earl Ruby of *The Courier-Journal* wrote: "Maysville rooters roared Wood's name as the Bulldogs battled and in every huddle the players whispered 'let's make a basket for Wood,' and in the dressing room Coach Jones told them 'go in and win for Wood.'"[320]

Sharpe led 12-8 at the end of the first quarter and 18-12 at the half. Maysville cut the deficit to three at 22-19 after three quarters. Sharpe took a five-point lead at 24-19 early in the fourth quarter.

McDonald and Knight made back-to-back baskets to get Maysville to within one at 24-23. Sharpe answered with six straight points and went on to win 36-27.[321]

McDonald and Fitch were named to the all-tournament team.[322]

Coach Jones and the team returned to Maysville on Sunday afternoon. The *Public Ledger* called the Bulldogs "the wonder team" and Jones "The Miracle Man." The state runner-up trophy was displayed in the window of the Owl drug store on Sunday and was moved to the high school on Monday.[323]

The 1938-39 team won the district championship but lost to Paris 24-21 in the semifinals of the regional tournament to finish with a 16-9 record.

Two days after completing the 1939-40 regular season with a six-game winning streak and a 17-4 record, it was discovered that leading scorer Billy Ritchie had turned 20 the previous summer making him too old to play that season.

An unnamed school had filed a complaint about Ritchie with the Kentucky High School Athletic Association. After receiving a letter from KHSAA President W.F. O'Donnell, Maysville High School Principal Roy Knight contacted Ritchie who admitted to being 20 years old. Ritchie's birthday was on July 23. Ritchie told the *Public Ledger* he misrepresented his age because he wanted to participate in athletics throughout his high school career. Maysville had to forfeit all of the football and basketball games Ritchie had played in.[324]

Maysville was suspended from the KHSAA until July 1, 1940 and was thus barred from playing in the postseason tournaments.[325]

Jones received an encouraging letter from University of Kentucky Coach Adolph Rupp:

Dear Earl (sic),

Sorry to see in the paper this morning that you had a little trouble. These things will come up. However, everyone knows that You, Knight and Shaw wouldn't have had it happened for anything in the world. In my books you still won the games. The world may look pretty dark this morning but old Adolph is still your pal. You still have a good team without him. See you at the Tournament.[326]

It was a tough time for Maysville basketball but the program would rebound the very next season.

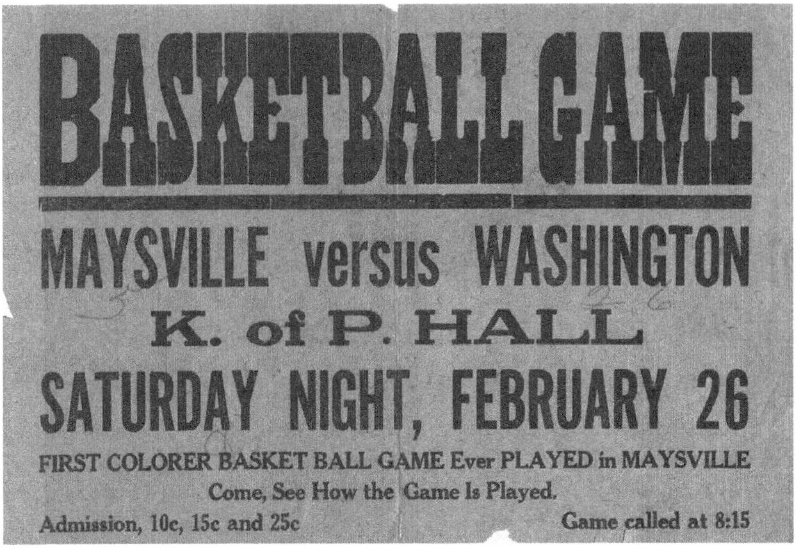
BASKETBALL GAME
MAYSVILLE versus WASHINGTON
K. of P. HALL
SATURDAY NIGHT, FEBRUARY 26
FIRST COLORER BASKET BALL GAME Ever PLAYED in MAYSVILLE
Come, See How the Game Is Played.
Admission, 10c, 15c and 25c
Game called at 8:15

Carol Bennett provided this 1927 advertisement for the first basketball game played between African-American teams in Maysville.

Chapter 7 State Titles for Fee Girls; Fee Boys Are Runners-up

While the 1931-32 season marked the end of girls' basketball and the beginning of the Coach Earle D. Jones era at Maysville High School, the girls' and boys' basketball teams at Maysville's African-American school - John G. Fee Industrial High School - were state powers. Fee had had winning teams for years, but the combined success of the Kittens and the Wildcats that season was unprecedented.

The John G. Fee High Industrial High School opened on September 2, 1930.[327] The African-American teams finally had a home court at their school. The previous high school building, (known as the Maysville Colored High School), on Fifth Street did not have a gymnasium. The teams played their "home" games at the Knights of Pythians Hall or on the outdoor court at Beechwood Park.

The first basketball game played between African-American teams in Maysville took place on February 26, 1927 at the Knights of Pythians Hall.[328] The Maysville boys lost to Washington 19-6. "Mac" Johnson led Washington in scoring with 10 points.[329] It was Washington's second win over Maysville that season. The opposing centers, Ross of Maysville, and "Lanky" Lee of Washington, each scored eight points in Washington's 11-7 victory before a packed house at the Washington Gymnasium. Lee won the individual prize for making the first field goal in the new gym.[330]

Washington was undefeated heading into a game against Portsmouth. Washington lost to the fast pro team of Portsmouth 14-10 but touted its undefeated record in Kentucky. The story in *The Daily Independent* said "If there is any refutation, We are still booking games."[331]

In 1928, the Maysville boys and girls teams swept a doubleheader against Versailles at Beechwood Park. The boys won 25-23 and the girls shutout the visitors from Woodford County 20-0.[332]

In 1929, the Maysville girls edged Millersburg 10-7.[333]

Both the girls' and boys' teams at Fee played in the 1931 state tournament for African-American schools. Fee sent 10 girls and 10 boys to the tournament in Lexington. The Fee girls were favored to win the championship.[334]

In the opening round, the girls lost to Lexington 8-7, and the boys beat Danville 17-15.[335]

The boys beat Louisville 22-14 in the second round before losing to Frankfort 26-11 in the third round.[336]

Robert Hall was the captain of the 1932 Fee team.[337] G.D. Clarke was the coach.[338]

The Wildcats defeated Paris 34-11[339] before suffering losses to Frankfort (30-15) and Portsmouth (36-20).[340]

The Fee girls didn't open the 1932 season until January 30. Players returning from the 1931 team were Florine Ewing, Thelma Corde, Catherine Foster, Elizabeth Clemmens, Margaret Corde, Margaret Ryan and Petronella Jackson.[341]

There was very little newspaper coverage of the rest of the regular season. One game that did get mentioned was the Wildcats' 28-15 victory over the Lexington Bearcats in February.[342]

Fee's regular center Lank Rowley returned to action in late February after missing some games. A report in *The Daily Independent* said "Preacher" Smith played in Rowley's absence and "he held down that position with the grim determination of a regular and has proven himself an asset to the team in general."[343]

The 1932 state tournament was played in Frankfort. Fee defeated Paris 29-25 and Frankfort 22-16 to advance to the championship game against Louisville Central.[344] Fee had to settle for a runner-up finish after losing to Louisville Central 34-25. Eugene Rowley led the Wildcats in scoring with nine points. John Fields followed with eight points. Hall added 4 points, and Lank Rowley and Turner scored two points apiece.[345] The story in *The Daily Bulletin* reported the final score of the championship game as 34-27 and listed a Fee win over Winchester in the state tournament without the score.[346]

The Fee Wildcats had a new coach for the 1932-33 season, James Jackson, a former coach of the Washington Wildcats. Jackson had studied at the University of Wisconsin under Dr. Walter Meanwell, the dean of basketball coaches in America at that time.[347] Jackson had introduced the game of basketball in the African-American schools in this area several years before becoming Fee's coach.[348]

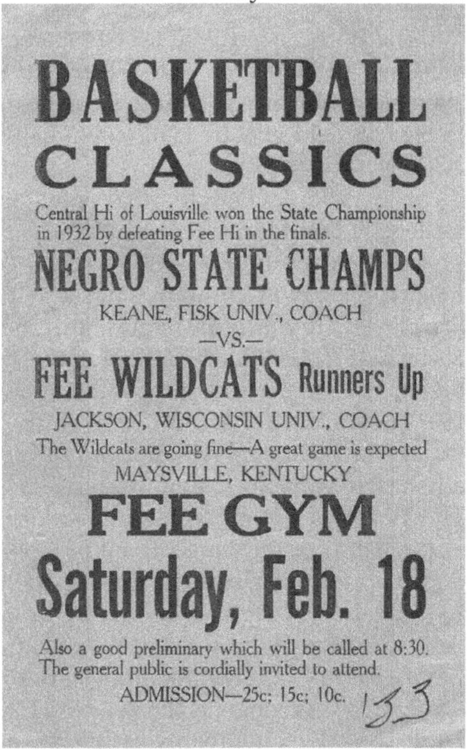
BASKETBALL
CLASSICS
Central Hi of Louisville won the State Championship in 1932 by defeating Fee Hi in the finals.
NEGRO STATE CHAMPS
KEANE, FISK UNIV., COACH
—VS.—
FEE WILDCATS Runners Up
JACKSON, WISCONSIN UNIV., COACH
The Wildcats are going fine—A great game is expected
MAYSVILLE, KENTUCKY
FEE GYM
Saturday, Feb. 18
Also a good preliminary which will be called at 8:30.
The general public is cordially invited to attend.
ADMISSION—25c; 15c; 10c.
1933
Carol Bennett also provided this 1933 flier advertising a rematch between the state tournament finalists played in Maysville.

Fee won and won big in its first season with Coach Jackson. In a home game against Lexington Dunbar, the Wildcats led 12-0 at the end of the first quarter and 18-4 at the half and won 34-13. Dunbar edged Fee 35-33 in Lexington.[349]

The Wildcats jumped out to a 16-5 lead at the half and routed Mt. Sterling 37-10. James Beatty led the way with 15 points.[350] When Fee and Mt. Sterling met again a couple of weeks later, Robert Hall scored 20 points to lead the Wildcats to a 55-13 victory.[351]

Olympic track and field star Dehart Hubbard had a team of former college and high school stars nicknamed the Lion Tamers. Fee, shorthanded due to injuries sustained in a game at Richmond, had a 12-10 lead at the half, but lost to the Lion Tamers 48-40.[352]

Fee was looking to avenge a two-point road loss to Richmond when the two teams met in Maysville. The Wildcats led 31-12 at the half en route to a 52-30 win. Beatty scored 16 points, Hall tossed in 14 points and Captain Eugene Rowley added 10 points.[353]

Despite a 10-point game by Eugene Rowley, Fee suffered a 35-24 road loss to Danville.[354]

In the rematch with Danville, Fee was held scoreless in the first five minutes of the game, but rallied to win 24-20.[355]

Defending state champion Louisville Central came to Maysville in February and edged Fee 33-32.[356]

Fee led Paris Western 33-14 at the half and won 47-25. Hall scored 19 points and Eugene Rowley added 14 points.[357]

The Wildcats enjoyed a 21-14 lead over Alabama State College at halftime. But Alabama State rallied and led 32-30. "Jug" Green, an all-state guard, hit a long shot to tie the game at 32-32 with two minutes to play. A field goal by Hall with a half minute remaining gave Fee a 34-32 victory.[358]

The Wildcats left for the state tournament at Kentucky State College in Frankfort on March 8.[359]

1932 champion Louisville Central and 1932 runner-up Fee were the favorites, but Central was upset by Winchester in the third round. Fee played Hopkinsville in the quarterfinals and trailed by nine points at the half. The Wildcats rallied in the second half and the game was tied at 32-32 at the end of regulation play. Fee outscored Hopkinsville 10-2 in overtime for a 42-34 victory.[360]

Fee edged Jackson Senior of Louisville 28-27 in the semifinals to advance to the state championship game for the second straight year. The Wildcats got off to a slow against Frankfort and trailed 20-11 at the half. Fee outscored Frankfort 14-10 in the second half but the deficit was too big to overcome and the Wildcats lost 30-25.[361]

Members of the state runner-up team were Eugene Rowley, James Beatty, Robert Hall, Andrew Whaley, Lank Rowley, Houston Green, Emory Gentry, John Smith and Charles Hicks.[362]

Emma Clement was the new coach of the Fee Kittens for the 1932-33 season. Wilson Green was the assistant coach.[363] The Kittens ran their record to 4-0 with a 5-4 win over Lexington Dunbar. The Kittens also defeated Dunbar 20-7 in Lexington. [364]

In another low scoring game Fee beat Mt. Sterling 8-4 at Mt. Sterling.[365] When the two teams met again a couple of weeks later in Maysville Captain Florine Ewing scored 18 points and the Kittens won 26-6.[366] Ewing scored 16 points in a 31-1 home court victory over Richmond.[367]

The Kittens continued to play stingy defense in the state tournament and upset Danville 20-13. Fee cruised past Lawrenceburg by the score of 21 to 2. The Kittens met Bowling Green in the quarterfinals and won 20-5. Fee trailed Lexington, the 1932 state champion, by two points with five minutes left in the semifinal game. All but three Fee players had fouled out. Despite playing three against five, the Kittens rallied to win 15-12. Fee guard Carrie Rice had to be carried off the court.[368]

Fee routed Richmond 34-12 in the championship game. The Kittens were state champions with a 16-0 record. No team scored more than 13 points against Fee. Ewing was named all-state center for the third time. The *Public Ledger* wrote, "Her brilliant shooting electrified the fans."[369] The Daily Independent wrote that Ewing's "sensational shooting and dribbling gave the fans a never to be forgotten thrill."[370] Rice was named all-state guard, and Margaret Corde received an

Kentucky Gateway Museum Center, Maysville, Kentucky

Front row (L-R): Thelma Corde, Margaret Corde, Florence Ewing, Carrie Rice, Viola Berry. Back Row (L-R): Coach Emma Clement, Petronella Jackson, Alline Commodore, Margaret Ryan, Elizabeth Clement, Stella Jackson, Nannie Mae Morgan.

overnight bag for being the most brilliant student on the winning team.[371]

Other members of the 1933 state championship team were Thelma Corde, Viola Berry, Petronella Jackson, Alline Commodore, Margaret Rice, Elizabeth Clement, Stella Bennett, Nannie Morgan and Pauline Foster.[372]

The Kittens returned to the state tournament in 1934. Players making the trip with Coach Clement were Captain Margaret Corde, Thelma Corde, Frances Johnson, Carrie Rice, Alline Commodore, Stella Jackson, Myrtle Foster, Petronella Jackson, Nannie Morgan and Gladys Thomas. Fee boys basketball coach James Jackson also accompanied the team to Lexington.[373]

The Kittens routed Bowling Green 21-2 in the quarterfinals.[374]

Fee trailed Lexington Dunbar 5-0 at the half in the semifinal game, but rallied to win 11-9.[375]

The Kittens' opponent in the championship game was Danville. Fee had lost to Danville by one point in the regional tournament. The Kittens jumped out to a 13-1 lead at the half on their way to a 24-10 victory. In her first two seasons at Fee, Coach Clement had guided the Kittens to two state championships. Rice, Johnson and Petronella Jackson were named to the all-state team. Margaret Corde received a set of Shakespeare's works for being the best scholar on the team.[376]

Reflecting back on her playing days at Fee nearly 80 years later, Stella Jackson Bennett said Clement was a "good coach." Bennett remembered the girls' team practicing against the boys' team, and big crowds attending the games.[377]

The Fee Wildcats won the 1939 district championship with victories over Paris (42-22), Winchester (42-27) and Richmond (45-35). W.H. Humphrey and Gene Commodore were named to the all-district team.[378]

Fee lost to Richmond 38-19 in the first round of the regional tournament. In consolation play, Fee beat Danville 40-32, but lost to Lincoln Ridge 40-35.[379]

Despite the early exit from the regional tournament, the Wildcats went to the National Tournament for African Americans for the first time in 1939. The tournament was held in Tuskegee, Alabama.[380]

Fee returned to the National Tournament in 1940. The team's itinerary included stops at My Old Kentucky Home in Bardstown, Abraham Lincoln's birthplace in Hodgenville, three African-American schools in Nashville - Fisk University, Tennessee State College and Meharry Medical College - and Alabama State Teachers College in Montgomery, Alabama. The tournament was played at Tuskegee Institute. The trip home, on a different route, included visits to Atlanta College and Lookout Mountain in Chattanooga, Tennessee. White people in Maysville donated oil, gas and money for the trips.[381]

Fee defeated Cynthiana 26-18 in the first round of the 1941 district tournament[382] and won the regional tournament at Richmond with a victory over 1940 state champion Richmond. Principal W.H. Humphrey was still the coach. He was assisted by Robert A. Hall, Langston Rowley, Eugene Greene, James Beatty, John Fields and others. Players making the trip to Frankfort were Eugene Commodore, Richard Jones, Addison Fields, William Thompson, James Samuels, Charles Hord, Gerald King, Frank Owens, Eugene Morton and James Breckenridge. The team was once again invited to the national tournament.[383]

John Fields was the head coach at Fee in 1946. The 1946 Eastern Mountain Regional tournament was played in Middlesboro. Fee drew a first round bye. Charles Commodore scored 18 points to lead the Wildcats to a 42-32 win over Lynch in the quarterfinal round. Fee defeated Harlan 43-38 in the semifinals. James Hopkins led the Wildcats in scoring with 15 points and Charles Routt added 12 points. Fee beat Benham 37-31 in the championship game.[384]

One of Fee's starting guards, Hughes, became ill, was put to bed and missed the Wildcats' opening round game against Henderson in the state tournament. Henderson led 10-4 at the end of the first quarter, 17-7 at halftime and 27-17 at the end of the third quarter. The final score was Henderson 33, Fee 21. The game story in the *Public Ledger* said Fee had appeared in the state tournament in three successive years.[385]

The Wildcats defeated Murray 47-35 in the consolation game.[386]

Fee hosted the Eastern Mountain Regional Tournament for the first time in 1947. Games were played in the Fee gym and the Maysville High School gym. Seats were reserved for white patrons.[387]

Expectations were not very high for the Wildcats. A story in the *Public Ledger* said "Fee High has experienced one of its worst seasons in years and will have to show improvement in every department of play if it expects to be a contender."[388]

Fee drew a first round bye and met Hazard in the quarterfinals. The game was tied at 26-all at the end of regulation and tied 28-28 at the end of the first overtime. The second overtime period was sudden-death. Charles Routt hit a long shot to give the Wildcats a 30-28 win.[389]

Fee faced Middlesboro in the semifinals. The Wildcats were without their regular center, Charles Commodore, who was attending his father's funeral. The game was played on Saturday afternoon before a full house at Fee. The Wildcats were clinging to a 57-56 lead as time was running out. Middlesboro made a field goal but the officials ruled the game had already ended. The *Public Ledger* wrote "Pandemonium then reigned." Slater led Fee with 25 points.[390]

Fee played the Ashland Hornets, the tournament favorite, in the championship game on Saturday night. The crowd at the Maysville High School gym was estimated at 1,500 and included many white people. Commodore was back in the lineup for the Wildcats. Ashland led 7-4 at the end of the first quarter. The score was 13-13 at the end of the first half. Ashland was up 23-20 after three quarters and the Hornets won 32-27. Slater was Fee's leading scorer with 10 points.[391]

Fee was scheduled to play in the postseason tournament in Lynch in 1948 but there were no reports on the game. The Wildcats closed out the season at home against the Walnut Hills Y.M.C.A.[392]

The 1949 Eastern District Basketball Tournament was held in Middlesboro. Fee defeated Jenkins 41-34 in the first round and beat Wheelwright 40-26 in the quarterfinals.[393]

The Wildcats downed Middlesboro 41-32 in the semifinals. Joe Cunningham scored 18 points and Warner came off the bench to add 16 to lead Fee to 51-44 victory over Ashland in the championship game. Cunningham was named one of the top 10 performers in the tournament.[394]

Fee lost to Harrodsburg 39-37 in the opening round of the Eastern Region Tournament at Dunbar High School in Lexington. Cunningham scored 13 points and G. Warner added 10.[395]

Chapter 8 MHS 1941-1946

After missing the postseason in 1940 due to being suspended by the KHSAA, the Maysville Bulldogs compiled a 13-9 record in the 1940-41 regular season. Maysville posted wins over May's Lick (34-28), Orangeburg (38-20) and Minerva (40-34) in the district tournament. The Bulldogs cruised to wins over Carlisle (37-22) and Renaker (54-24) in the first two rounds of the 10th Region tournament. Maysville pulled out a 30-26 victory over Morgan in the championship game. The Bulldogs were headed back to the state tournament. A 51-27 win over Catlettsburg in the first round ran the Bulldogs' winning streak to nine games and their record to 20-9. Maysville's opponent in the quarterfinal round was Louisville St. Xavier. The two teams had split their two regular season games. The Bulldogs edged the Tigers 28-25 in Maysville. St. Xavier won 35-18 when the two teams met again in Louisville. In the state tournament game, St. Xavier beat Maysville 37-26. Chester Tuel had a team high 10 points for the Bulldogs.

In September of 1942, Jones announced that intramural sports would take the place of football. Maysville had switched from 11-man football to six-man football in 1940. Jones cited several reasons for discontinuing football including the lack of bus to transport the team because of World War II, the abandonment of the sport by other schools that had been on the schedule and the fact that football had operated at financial loss which had to be made up by basketball receipts.[396] Maysville High School did not have another football team until 1967.

Maysville's bid for back-to-back trips to the state tournament ended with a 33-24 loss to Berry in the championship game of the 1942 10th Region Tournament.

The Bulldogs lost to MMI 26-24 in the semifinals of the 10th Region tournament in 1943.

Prior to the 1943-44 season, Coach Jones wrote this letter to his players:

In a few days now, school will be under way, and I am certain that you are anxious to know our plans for the coming basketball campaign. Inasmuch as the Maysville High Bulldogs have won 16 or more games per season for the past 10 consecutive years, we have a bit of tradition to uphold. Sixteen victories may seem to be too large an order for an inexperienced varsity squad, but I have a great deal of confidence in you boys. Insofar as I know now, there is not a single smoker among the boys to whom I am sending this letter. Smoking may not be such a bad habit, but ANY OLD "PLUG" CAN SMOKE. It takes a fellow with a little BACKBONE to resist the temptation, and think of the savings$$$.

The most important phase in training for basketball lies in the proper rest and sleep. There is where you get that extra last quarter drive which is so necessary to a great team. We didn't have that last year. Grantland Rice, America's most famous sportswriter, once offered a bit of advice in the form of a poem to young big league ball players and I believe it applies to every sport. The poem ended in these lines:

"For there is not a guy in sight
Who can bat around .300
And bat around all night !"

In line with the war effort, long trips are naturally out. The Mt. Sterling trip is likely to be our longest but we will have an attractive 20 game schedule. By the way, when Tourney Time rolls around, let's forget all about travel restrictions then. WE can go all the way through the District, Regional, Sectional and on to the State Tourney at Lexington if you and I have the "STUFF".

We again will offer a scholarship trophy to the letterman with the highest scholastic standing providing he has at least an "1.5" average. In the event that several lettermen have good class records, we shall give an award to each letterman whose standing is "2" or better. Of course, the boy with the highest marks will receive a larger and more attractive trophy. Arrange your schedule so that the 8th period is free and, by all means, keep up your studies from the very first day. An ineligible player can't do the team any good.

Sincerely,

The letter was signed by Coach Jones.[397]

The Bulldogs won their fourth consecutive district title in 1944 but lost to Brooksville 18-16 in the first round of the regional tournament. Three of Maysville's six losses that season were to Brooksville.

Maysville closed out regular season play in 1945 with a five-game winning streak. Due to war time travel restrictions, Orangeburg, Minerva and Maysville were in the 76th District, while Fleming County and May's Lick were in the 77th District. Orangeburg walloped Minerva 68-15, and then Maysville routed Orangeburg 60-20 in the championship game.

The Bulldogs earned another trip to the state tournament with wins over Brooksville (28-25), North Middletown (30-16) and

Cynthiana (27-21) in the regional tournament.

Maysville drew Louisville Male in the first round of the state tournament. The Purples had defeated the Bulldogs 49-29 in a regular season game in Maysville on February 10. The state tournament was played at the Jefferson County Armory in Louisville. Maysville had a 9-8 lead at the end of the first quarter. Male rallied to lead 25-20 at halftime. The Bulldogs were up 28-27 midway through the third quarter, but Male was back on top 35-32 at the end of the quarter. The Purples went up 43-36 in the final quarter. Maysville cut the deficit to three at 44-41 with 1:30 to play. That ended up being the final score after Male froze the ball to secure the win. Both teams shot poorly from the field- Male was 18 of 62 for 29 percent and Maysville made just 16 of 57 for 28.1 percent. The Purples were 8 of 11 on free throws, while the Bulldogs made 9 of their 17 foul shots.[398] Male went on to win the state championship.

Maysville closed out the 1945-46 season with a home game against Male. The Bulldogs jumped out to an 8-0 lead and led 14-5 at the end of the first quarter, 21-7 at halftime and 26-15 after three quarters. Male made just 8 of 43 shots from the field in the game and Maysville won 41-25. Male star Gene Rhodes was held to four points, all on free throws.[399]

The Bulldogs entered the district tournament with a 17-6 record. Maysville routed Fleming County 64-31 in the semifinals and cruised past Orangeburg 67-32 in the championship game.

Maysville drew Brooksville in the opening round of the 10th region tournament. The two teams had split their two regular season games. Brooksville won 34-29 at home on January 25. A crowd estimated at 2,000 packed the Maysville gym for the rematch on February 18. Kenny Reeves scored 29 points to lead the Bulldogs to a 57-40 victory. Reeves was 10-of-14 from the field and 9-of-10 from the free throw line.[400]

Reeves scored 14 points in Maysville's 44-27 win over Brooksville in the regional tournament. The Bulldogs beat Cynthiana 44-26 in the championship game. Reeves led the way again with 19 points.

Odds-makers listed Breckinridge Training of Morehead as the 5-2 favorite to win the state tournament. Male was second at 4-1 and Maysville was third at 6-1. The Bulldogs' first round opponent, Campbell County, was one of the long shots at 40-1.[401]

Maysville led Campbell County 15-6 at end of the first quarter, 24-13 at the half and 39-22 on the way to a 50-34 victory.[402] Reeves had his second straight 19-point game.

The Bulldogs met Ft. Knox in the quarterfinal round. Ft. Knox upset Inez in the first round.

"That was a big shock to me," Jones said. "I thought we were going to play Inez, and that was the team I really scouted, but Ft. Knox upset 'em."

The first quarter ended with Ft. Knox leading Maysville 13-11. The Eagles outscored the Bulldogs 15-8 in the second quarter to lead 28-19 at the half. Maysville had trimmed the deficit to five at 35-30 by the end of the third quarter, but Ft. Knox won, 46-38. Ed LeForge was Maysville's leading scorer with 13 points. Reeves added 12 points

"We were awful disappointed because that was a good team in '46," Jones said.

Maysville closed the season with a 22-7 record.

Reeves was the first Maysville player to be named to the Kentucky All-Star team for the annual series against the Indiana All-Stars. Reeves played at the University of Louisville. He was a starting guard on the Cardinals' 1948 NAIB championship team. Reeves had 1,245 career points at the University of Louisville. He is a member of the school's Hall of Fame and his jersey is retired.[403] Reeves was drafted by the Boston Celtics in 1950 and signed a $4,500 contract.[404] Reeves never played for the Celtics. He became a dentist. "I have fond memories of Maysville High and 10th Region basketball, Coach Jones in particular and what a great coach he was," said Reeves. "And what fundamentals he taught."[405]

Chapter 9 St. Patrick's First Team

The 1945-46 season marked the return of basketball at St. Patrick, the Catholic school in Maysville. St. Patrick had had a team in the 1938-39 season. William "Teence" Ryan, a member of Coach Earle D. Jones' first team at Maysville, was the St. Patrick coach.

The team played its first game on the road against Sandy Hook and lost 30-10. St. Patrick picked up its first win in the second game of the season- a 28-18 victory over St. Catherine in the Maysville gym.

St. Patrick beat Orangeburg 24-20 in the first round of the district tournament and lost to Washington 28-24 to finish with a 6-13 record.

Members of the first team included Jack Brannen, Paul Mitchell, Bob Higgins, George Guilfoyle, Jim Sullivan, Phil McGuire and John McCarthy.[406]

When basketball returned to St. Patrick in 1945, another former Maysville Bulldog, Morris "Mert" Blanton, was the coach. Blanton, a 1937 graduate of Maysville High School, had been an amateur featherweight boxer.[407]

Laurence Caproni, who played at Maysville in the 1920s, assisted Blanton in the first part of the season.[408]

Maysville Coach Earle D. Jones furnished St. Patrick with basketballs and outfitted the team early in the season when the uniforms were late in arriving.[409]

In a preseason story on St. Patrick, the *Public Ledger* wrote "those who have seen them in practice sessions are of the opinion that the aggregation has possibilities of developing into a fast, aggressive outfit."[410]

St. Patrick played its home games in the Maysville gym.

In the first few seasons, newspaper reports referred to the team as "Fighting Irish",[411] "Paddys"[412] or "Paddies".

More than 400 people turned out for St. Patrick's first game of the 1945-46 season-a 40-16 victory over the Minerva Maroons. More fans might have attended the game had it not been on the night of the election for city and county offices.[413]

St. Patrick lost to Fleming County 36-21 in the first round of the district tournament to close the season with an 8-16 record.

Members of the 1945-46 team were James O'Hearn, Jack

Pat McKay of McKay's Studio

Front row (L-R): Jimmy Williams, Ed Comer, M.J. Brannen, John T. Larkin, Jim Stahl, Jack McDough, Jimmy O'Hearn, Ginny O'Neill, Pat McKay Jr. and George Mitchell. Middle row (L-R): Tommy Collopy, Kirby Collins, Paul Tierney, Jimmy Heffernon, Bobby Buckley, Pat Sheridan, Ralph Higgins and Francis (Fanny) Stahl. Back row (L-R): George Burrows, Reverend Leo B. Casey, Dick Brannen and Coach Mert Blanton.

McDonough, Jimmy Stahl, George Mitchell, John Larkin, Pat McKay, Bernard O'Neill, Jimmie Williams, M.J. Brannen, Eddie Comer and Ralph Higgins.[414]

St. Patrick hosted Lexington Latin on February 23, 1947 in the first game played on Sunday in Maysville.[415] St. Patrick won 49-16.

St. Patrick won 19 games in the 1946-47 season but drew Maysville in the opening road of the district tournament. It was the first time the two schools had faced each other. Maysville won 35-13. It was St. Patrick's sixth loss of the season.

St. Patrick was even better in the 1947-48 season. A 35-34 victory over Fleming County in the first round of the district tournament ran St. Patrick's record to 20-7. The Paddies beat Orangeburg 57-34 in the semifinals. St. Patrick lost to Maysville 51-32 in the championship game, but was headed to the 10th Region Tournament for the first time.

St. Patrick drew the Buena Vista Cardinals in the first round of the regional tournament at Paris. Jack McDonough was back in the lineup for the Paddies after being sidelined for all three district tournament games with an ankle injury.[416]

St. Patrick led 10-8 at the end of the first quarter. Buena Vista was up 26-16 at the half and led 30-16 in the third quarter. The Paddies had cut the deficit to seven at 32-25 at the end of the third quarter. St. Patrick continued to chip away at the Cardinals' lead, and with 10 seconds to go, the Paddies were within two points. George Mitchell hit a foul shot to cut it to one.[417] Then, Fanny Stahl stole the ball. He recalls what happened next:

"The official was a guy named Dan Tehan. Well, Dan Tehan was one of the strong supporters of Xavier (University). He was a football player there, and he was also the sheriff of Hamilton County (Ohio) for years and years and years. And I took the ball away from the guy I thought cleanly and made the layup to win the game, and damned if he didn't call a foul on me, we lost the game. The final score was Buena Vista 38, St. Patrick 37.

St. Patrick came so close to winning its first game in the 10th Region Tournament. The school would have to wait 34 more years before getting its first win in the regional tournament.

Stahl averaged 19.6 points a game (and scored a season-high 32 points vs. Augusta) in the 1948-49 season. But he was more than a scorer. Stahl was an exceptional dribbler. He honed his ball handling skills by dribbling a basketball up and down the old U.S. 68 hill.

"I kept a basketball pretty much with me all the time," Stahl says. "That did happen, yes, because I used to run up and down the hill almost every day in and out of the summer, basically."

After beating Minerva in their first two games of the 1948-49 season, St. Patrick only won two more games and finished the year with a 4-20 record.[418]

Chapter 10 Bulldogs Win State

In the fall of 1946 Coach Jones heard that a testimonial dinner was going to be held for him at the end of the season.

"I asked my friend Dr. John I. McDowell if that was so?" Jones recalled. "He said 'yeah,' I said 'How did you happen to pick out this year? I'm glad you're doing it.' Well, he said 'You've been having good teams, but you're not going to have a very good team this year, and we thought it would be good for your morale.'"

"And I thought about that, good gracious, I didn't know it was going to be that bad. It looked to me as though we were going to have a fair team. But sometimes you can be so close to a thing you can't see it. Anyhow then it occurred to me if I have a bad season and they have a testimonial dinner nobody will come. Bad coaches that lose don't draw many people."

Jones said he just went to work with the players and told them "There was one thing we're going to try to do, we're not going to try to win the state tournament, (we're) just gonna get there."

Two eighth graders - George Cooke and Bobby Ormes- made the varsity team.

Maysville opened the season at home against the Orangeburg Tigers. The Bulldogs' starters were Harold Walker and Gus Stergeos at the forwards, Buddy Shoemaker at center and Ed LeForge and Bobby Williams at the guards. Maysville led 8-0 at the end of the first quarter and 21-7 at halftime en route to 30-17 victory. Not everyone was impressed by the by the team's performance. The *Public Ledger* wrote: "It was generally agreed after the game that Coach Earle D. Jones has a tough job cut out for him in ironing out the kinks in his present team to make it a smooth-working formidable outfit."[419]

Ten Bulldogs scored in a 73-26 blowout road victory over Morgan. The Bulldogs scored 28 points in the third quarter. LeForge led the way with 17 points. Stergeos followed with 16, and Shoemaker added 13. Cooke started in place of Williams and scored five points.[420]

Ormes started instead of Cooke against the Vanceburg Lions in Vanceburg. The Bulldogs were up 19-3 at the end of the first quarter, 29-9 at the half and 45-15 after three quarters. The final score was Maysville 59, Lewis County 25.[421]

The Bulldogs beat Fleming County 40-24 in the first of three straight home games. Next was a 47-24 win over Carrollton. Maysville ran its season-opening winning streak to six games with 74-12 rout of Augusta.

The winning streak was snapped when the Bulldogs traveled to Lexington and lost to Coach Ralph Carlisle's Lafayette Generals 45-34. Carlisle had played for Jones at Kavanaugh.

Maysville reeled off another six-game winning streak by beating Dayton 47-38 at home, Augusta 54-28 on the road, defending state champion Breckinridge Training 38-30 at home, Breckinridge Training 40-38 in overtime in Morehead and Mt. Sterling 67-21 at home.

Maysville hosted Bracken County (formerly Brooksville) on January 23. Bracken County was up 34-26 with 4:30 left in the game. The Bulldogs closed to within two at 36-34. In the closing seconds, Stergeos was fouled as he missed a crip shot. He sank both free throws to tie the game and force overtime. The Bulldogs scored the first three points in the extra period, but the Polar Bears answered with a 3-0 run. Maysville edged back in front 41-39 only to see Bracken County tie it again. The second overtime was sudden death. The Polar Bears controlled the tip, and Charles Stapleton hit a crip shot to win the game 43-41.[422]

A crowd estimated at 1,600 packed the Maysville gym for the Bulldogs' game against the Olive Hill Comets. Maysville was without LeForge who had a cold. Olive Hill roared out to a 9-0 lead. Maysville rallied and the game was tied at 15-15 at the half. Cooke fouled out in the third quarter. Olive Hill led 30-28 at the end of the third quarter. Shoemaker fouled out in the fourth quarter, and the Comets defeated the Bulldogs 44-34.[423]

LeForge was back in the lineup when Maysville made the long trip to Inez. The Bulldogs had a two-point lead after three quarters, but Shoemaker and Cooke fouled out in the fourth quarter. Inez outscored Maysville 13-3 in the fourth quarter to win 42-26.[424]

Next up was a home game against Lafayette. The game was tied 32-32 with 1:30 to play. The Generals went ahead 35-32 on a foul shot and a field goal and sent the Bulldogs to their fourth straight loss by freezing the ball for the final 30 seconds.[425]

Maysville ended the losing streak with a 62-22 road win over the Mt. Sterling Trojans. Cooke scored a game-high 17 points.

A crowd estimated at 2,100 squeezed into the Maysville gym to watch the Bulldogs play the top ranked team in the state, Inez. Several hundred fans were turned away. Only season ticket holders were admitted after 7:30 p.m. The *Public Ledger* wrote "The game was played before the largest crowd in the history of basketball in Maysville." The Indians, coached by Russell Williams, lived up to their No. 1 ranking by jumping out to an 11-1 lead at the end of the first quarter. Inez was up 29-7 at the half and won 54-32.[426] It was Maysville's fifth loss in six games.

Maysville traveled to Brooksville looking to avenge the double overtime loss to the Bracken County Polar Bears. Buddy Gilvin took Cooke's spot in the starting lineup. No overtime periods would be needed as the Bulldogs had a double digit lead at the end of each quarter and won by the score of 54-39.[427]

Gilvin started against Louisville Male and scored 10 points to lead Maysville to a 39-33 home court victory.

The Bulldogs played their final road of the regular season at Orangeburg. Shoemaker had the flu and did not play. Gilvin moved to center, and Orme started at forward. The Tigers took a 7-0 lead, but the Bulldogs answered and the game was tied 7-7 at the end of the first quarter. Maysville led 13-9 at the half and 17-15 after three quarters. The Bulldogs were able to hang on for a 26-24 win.[428]

Shoemaker was back in the lineup for the final game of the regular season, a home game against Louisville Manual. Coach Jones had settled on a starting five of LeForge, Stergeos, Shoemaker, Gilvin and Walker.[429] The Bulldogs won 56-48 to run their record to 17-6 heading to postseason play.

Maysville defeated the St. Patrick Paddies 35-13 in the first round of the district tournament.

The Bulldogs had an even easier game against the Minerva Maroons in the semifinals. Maysville led 21-0 at the end of the first quarter and 39-8 at halftime on the way to a 68-17 victory. The Maysville starters only played the first quarter and three minutes of the third quarter.[430]

Maysville defeated Orangeburg 34-24 in the championship game. The Tigers only had five field goals.[431] LeForge had a game-high 16 points.

Maysville drew Orangeburg in the opening round of the 10th Region Tournament at Paris. Stergeos had a cold and did not play. Cooke started in place of Stergeos and scored 16 points to lead the Bulldogs to a 47-25 win.[432] It was Maysville's fourth win of the season over Orangeburg.

Stergeos was still sick when Maysville played Morgan in the semifinals. The Bulldogs got off to a fast start and led 18-3 at the end of the first quarter and 34-12 at the half. Maysville won, 61-31. Cooke started again and scored 12 points.[433]

It was Maysville vs. Bracken County in the championship game. Stergeos was able to return to action, but he came off the bench as Cooke was in the starting lineup for the third straight game. Bracken County led 13-11 at the end of the first quarter. Cooke's field goal just before the second quarter ended gave Maysville a 22-20 lead at halftime. The Bulldogs were up 28-23 after three quarters. The Polar Bears got to with two points in the fourth quarter, but the Bulldogs won, 34-31, after freezing the ball in the last two minutes.[434] Maysville was headed back to the state tournament for the third straight year.

Gilvin had a cold and an earache and missed practice on Monday, March 17 – three days before the start of the state tournament. Gilvin was able to take part in the Bulldogs' practice the next day. That was the team's final workout before leaving for the state tournament.[435]

The 10 players who made the trip to the state tournament were LeForge, Walker, Stergeos, Orme, Gilvin, Shoemaker, Elza Whalen, Herman Tolle, Ed Taylor, Ferdie Case and Walter Maher.[436]

Maysville drew the Corbin Redhounds in the first round. Jones' scouting system included compiling a scrapbook with scores of games and comments from throughout the state. He subscribed to several Kentucky newspapers, but the Corbin newspaper was one of the few he didn't sign up for during the 1946-47 season.[437]

Gilvin was well enough to start against the Redhounds. Cooke started in place of Stergeos. Corbin led 8-5 at the end of the first quarter and 17-15 at halftime. The Bulldogs took the lead at 18-17 two minutes into the third quarter and never trailed again.[438] The final score was Maysville 39, Corbin 30.

"We just played terrible," Jones said, "and Corbin did too."

Maysville's opponent in the quarterfinal round was Magnolia, the champion from the 6th Region. Maysville was up 10-9 at the end of the first quarter. Magnolia led 23-22 at the end of the first half and 36-32 after three quarters. Maysville outscored Magnolia 16-7 in the fourth quarter to win 48-43.[439]

"We beat Magnolia, but we had a hard time doin' it," Jones said.

Owensboro upset Clark County 61-43 in the quarterfinal round.

"That shocked everybody," Jones said. "Clark County was supposed to go to the finals against Brewers (the tournament favorite)."

Maysville wasn't given much of a chance against Owensboro in the semifinals.

"Everybody said 'well it's all over now, it'll be Owensboro and Brewers, and probably Owensboro is gonna win it,'" Jones said. "Well, you know how they set the odds, and they had us [as a] 15-point underdog."

Walker made a long shot to give the Bulldogs a 2-0 lead and they never trailed. Maysville was up 10-7 at the end of the quarter, 28-19 at the half and 42-36 after three quarters.[440] The Bulldogs won, 56-41. Gilvin led Maysville in scoring with 13 points. Cooke and Shoemaker added 12 points apiece.

The Brewers Redmen defeated Hazard 52-44 in the other

semifinal. Brewers, located in Marshall County, in western Kentucky, had survived a scare in the first round of the state tournament. After trailing Bowling Green 35-32 with six minutes to play, the Indians rallied to win 43-36. Brewers beat Louisville Male 49-43 in the quarterfinals.

Jones recalled getting ready to make the trip from the hotel to the Jefferson County Armory for the championship game.

"All the boys had gone over to dress, and George Cooke and I were on the elevator, we were the only two on there," Jones said. "And I said 'George, you've had a real good season, and, can you make it one more time?' he says 'Coach, Brewers can't beat us.' That was a kid in the eighth grade."

Brewers took a 2-0 lead. Shoemaker hit a crip shot to tie it at 2-2. The Bulldogs took a 4-2 lead on a short shot by Shoemaker. Maysville was up 10-9 at the end of the first quarter. After a tie at 15-all, the Bulldogs went on an 11-2 run to lead 26-17. Brewers scored the final two points of the half to make it 26-19. Maysville had its biggest lead of the game at 37-27, but the cushion was down to seven at 43-36 at the end of the third quarter. Three Brewers players fouled out - Van Mathis in the third quarter and Barney Thweatt and Jim Owens in the early in the fourth quarter. Despite losing those three players, Brewers got to within 44-43. Then LeForge hit a free throw, a crip shot and another free throw to give the Bulldogs a five-point lead at 48-43. Gilvin fouled out with four minutes left in the game. Coy Creason hit a free throw for Brewers to cut it to 48-44. Two free throws by Stergeos and one by Walker pushed the Bulldogs' lead back out to 51-44. Back-to-back field goals by Tom Mathis and Wright trimmed Maysville's lead to three at 51-48 with two minutes to play. Walker made one of two free throws, Shoemaker made a free throw and Walker followed with a crip shot and was fouled. Walker missed the free throw, but the Bulldogs were up 54-48. Arnett hit a long shot for Brewers with one minute go, but that would be the final basket of the game as Maysville was able to freeze the ball and win, 54-50. The Bulldogs were the state champions.[441]

"We were right in there all the way, just nip and tuck," Jones said. "And we got ahead in the second half and kept it, and Brewers couldn't overcome us."

LeForge led Maysville in scoring with 14 points. Shoemaker followed with 12 and Walker added 10.

The two seniors-LeForge and Walker-received the championship trophy from KHSAA secretary Ted Sanford, and each Maysville player received a miniature gold basketball.[442]

Shoemaker was the only Bulldog named to the all-tournament team.

Coach Jones was carried into the lobby of the Kentucky Hotel on the shoulders of the fans. When people back in Maysville heard of the victory on the radio, many began to parade about downtown.[443]

"It was a real exciting thing, you can't beat winning the state tournament," Jones recalled 40 years later.

A motorcade of 100 cars drove to Washington to escort the team to Maysville Sunday afternoon. The procession toured the city with car horns blowing and sirens blaring.[444]

"When a community wins a state championship, they really celebrate," Jones said. "And it's a lot of fun."

The procession stopped at the Market Street esplanade where the fans got to see Coach Jones and his championship team.[445]

The city schools observed a half-holiday on Monday in celebration of the championship.[446]

The district, region and state championship trophies along with Shoemaker's all-tournament team statuette were displayed in the east window of Merz Brothers department store on West Second Street.[447]

The Maysville Rotary Club gave an honor dinner for the state champions. Coach Jones and the two seniors, Walker and LeForge, spoke at the meeting.[448] The Maysville Lion's Club gave billfolds to Jones and the players.[449]

When *The Courier-Journal* announced its postseason awards, Jones was named Coach of the Year, Shoemaker was named first-team all-state, LeForge was selected to the third-team and Cooke and Walker earned honorable mention.[450]

Walker and LeForge were named second-team all-state by the Herald-Leader. Stergeos received honorable mention recognition from the *Herald-Leader*.[451] LeForge was later named to the Kentucky All-Star team.

The testimonial dinner for Jones, first talked about the previous fall, was held at First Christian Church.

"That turned into a championship dinner," Jones said. "And it didn't have any trouble getting a crowd for that, it was sold out."

University of Kentucky Coach Adolph Rupp was the guest speaker at the dinner.

In a letter to Jones, Rupp wrote "I really enjoyed being with you and I think that Masyville (sic) pulled a number one affair for you. Naturally, I was glad to be a part of it. I don't see how it could have been nicer."[452]

Jones was asked to write articles for two publications- *Southern Coach* and *Athlete*. The pay for the article in *Athlete* was $5.[453]

Jones was offered the job of basketball coach and physical education teacher at Canton High School, a three-time champion in Georgia, at a salary of $3,000 per years.[454]

Public Ledger

Front row (L-R): Gus Stergeos, Walter Maher, Ferdinand Case, Ed Taylor, Harold Walker, Buddy Shoemaker, Allie Gilvin, Joe Hinson and Ed LeForge. Back row (L-R): Manager Winn Thomas, Manager Chad Christine, Coach Earle D. Jones, Herman Tolle, Bobby Ormes, Ervin Knapp, George Cooke, Elza Whalen and Manager Billy Perrine.

Canton had to look elsewhere for a coach. Jones stayed in Maysville, and the Bulldogs were looking to win back-to-back state titles.

Chapter 11 Runner-up Finish for the Bulldogs

Maysville opened the 1947-48 season at home with a 58-37 victory over Morehead. The Bulldogs suffered back-to-back losses to the Clark County Cardinals-37-32 in Winchester and 42-26 at home.

Maysville then reeled off 12 consecutive wins including a 55-20 rout of the Lafayette Generals in Lexington.

The Bulldogs made the long trip to Inez to play the Inez Indians. Buddy Shoemaker, Buddy Gilvin and Bobby Ormes fouled out in the third quarter. The game was tied at the end of the third quarter, but the Indians outscored the Bulldogs 11-1 in the fourth quarter. The winning streak was snapped with a 43-33 loss.[455]

The Bulldogs closed out the regular season with an eight-game winning streak beginning with a 53-49 home court victory over Lafayette. The streak included two victories over Ashland. Maysville also avenged the loss to Inez with a 57-41 win at home. The Indians were missing two starters due to injuries.[456]

The Bulldogs headed to postseason play with a record of 22-3.

Maysville breezed through the district tournament with lopsided wins over May's Lick (71-34), Minerva (71-29) and St. Patrick (51-32). Shoemaker had a cold and sat out all three games.[457]

Even with Shoemaker back in the lineup, Maysville had a tougher than expected game against Cynthiana in the first round of the 10th Region Tournament. Cynthiana led 19-17 at the half. Maysville rallied to lead 38-31 at the end of the third quarter and won, 50-44.

The Bulldogs trailed Buena Vista by the score of 21-20 at the end of the first half in the semifinals, but outscored the Cardinals 38-14 in the second half for a 58-35 win.

Maysville met Paris in the championship game. The Bulldogs took a 2-0 lead on a basket by Shoemaker. Paris went on a 13-0 run, and the Greyhounds were up 15-6 at the end of the first quarter. Paris scored the first four points of the second quarter and had a 29-21 lead at the half. Maysville opened the third quarter on an 8-0 to tie the game at 29-29, but Paris closed the quarter on a 9-2 run to lead 38-31. The Greyhounds increased the lead to nine points at 41-32 with 6:42 left in the game. Maysville scored 10 unanswered points to take a 42-41 lead. The go ahead basket was scored by George Cooke. Paris center Bob Blake along with Shoemaker and Ormes fouled out in a span of 15 seconds. Paris tied the score on a free throw. Herman "Shotsie" Tolle, who had entered the game when Ormes fouled out, hit a field goal to put Maysville back in front at 44-42 with 2:30 to play. Elza Whalen, who had replaced Shoemaker, sank two fouls shots to make it 48-42. Paris made a basket to get to within two at 48-44 with 45 seconds remaining, but the Bulldogs held the ball and won their fourth consecutive 10th Region title.[458]

The *Public Ledger* called it "one of the greatest and most spine-tingling finishes ever witnessed by Maysville fans."[459]

Acting captain Gus Stergeos received the championship trophy and was carried off the floor by his teammates.[460]

Brewers was ranked No. 1 and Owensboro No. 2 in *The Courier-Journal* Litkenhaus rankings. Maysville was ranked 7th.[461]

Maysville drew Scottsville in the first round. The Bulldogs led 7-4 at the end of the first quarter, 15-14 at halftime and 26-21 after three quarters before pulling away for a 52-39 victory. Stergeos led Maysville in scoring with 14 points. Cooke added 13 points.[462]

Maysville upset the Owensboro Red Devils 55-45 in the quarterfinal round. Three Bulldogs scored in double figures- Stergeos with 16, Cooke with 14 and Gilvin with 11.

Maysville met Carr Creek in the semifinals. The Bulldogs led 16-12 at the end of the first quarter and 32-29 at the half. Carr Creek led 45-42 after three quarters and was up 54-51 with 30 seconds left in the game. In the closing seconds, Gilvin made a lay-up and was fouled. He hit the free throw to tie the game at 54-all and force overtime. Gilvin scored the only basket in the overtime period to Maysville a 56-54 victory.[463]

It was Maysville versus Brewers in the championship game for the second straight year.

Brewers entered the state tournament with a 32-0 record. The Redmen had a tough first opponent - the Clark County Cardinals. With three minutes to play, Brewers had a five-point lead. But Clark County outscored Brewers 6-1 and the game was tied at 57-all at the end of the regulation. Clark County took a 59-57 in the overtime before the Redmen scored the final six points to win 63-59. Brewers routed Shelbyville 57-34 in the quarterfinals. The Redmen edged Male 38-36 in the upper bracket semifinal and had three hours more rest than Maysville heading into the championship game.

The championship game was tied 11-all at the end of the first quarter. Maysville led 29-26 at the half. The score was tied 36-all after three quarters.

Whalen hit two straight field goals to give the Bulldogs a 40-36 lead. The Redmen scored five straight points to go back in front 41-

40. Maysville regained the lead at 42-41 on a basket by Ormes. Coy Creason made a shot to give Brewers the lead at 43-42. Whalen hit a field goal to put the Bulldogs back on top at 44-43 with just under five minutes to play. Stergeos had fouled out, and Shoemaker was playing with four fouls. Brewers hit five free throws, and the Redmen led 48-44 with 3:30 to go. Gilvin hit a hook shot to cut it to 48-46. Creason answered with a one-handed shot for a 50-46 Brewers lead. Cooke hit a short shot to slice to the deficit to two again at 50-48 with 2:45 to play, but Brewers scored the final five points to win 55-48.[464] The Redmen were undefeated state champions.

The Courier-Journal reporter Johnny Carrico wrote "Maysville had nowhere near the strength of the determined Redmen and faded badly in the final three minutes."[465]

In the fourth quarter, Maysville had six goals to five for Brewers, but the Redmen made nine free throws. For the game, Brewers had one more free throw (19) than field goals (18).[466]

The loss snapped the Bulldogs' 14-game winning streak. Maysville's record was 31-4.

Stergeos, who fouled out in the first 90 seconds of the fourth quarter of the championship game,[467] and Shoemaker were named to the all-tournament team.

A motorcade of several hundred cars waited for the team near Washington for more than three hours Sunday afternoon. A police car and a fire truck led the team to the esplanade. Congratulatory remarks were given, and WFTM radio announcer Lou France interviewed Jones and the players.[468]

Shoemaker and Stergeos were named to *The Courier-Journal* All-State Team.[469]

The Bulldogs received certificates of achievement from the Maysville Junior Chamber of Commerce. The ceremony was broadcast on WFTM radio.[470] The Maysville Lions Club entertained the players and Coach Jones,[471] and a community banquet was held for the team at First Christian Church.[472]

The members of the 1947-48 squad were Buddy Gilvin, Buddy Shoemaker, Gus Stergeos, Herman "Shotsie" Tolle, Walter Maher, Ferdinand Case, Eddie Taylor, George Cooke, Bobby Ormes, Emory Lacy and Elza Whalen.[473]

Maysville opened the 1948-49 season with five consecutive victories including a 40-39 road win over Clark County. That was the longest winning streak of the season.

A crowd estimated at 2,200 packed the MHS gym for the rematch against Clark County in February. The Cardinals were ranked number one in the state. Maysville led 36-25 after three quarters and won 49-45.[474]

Public Ledger

Front row (L-R): Emery Lacey, Herman Tolle, George Cooke, Ed Taylor, Buddy Shoemaker, Buddy Gilvin, Bobby Ormes, Elza Whalen, Gus Stergeos. Middle row (L-R): Bobby Ritchie, J. Weaver, Ferdy Case, Walt Maher, R. Higgins, F. Ormes, Nick Pitakis, W. Tolle. Back row (L-R): Coach Earle D. Jones, James Hardymon, Lawrence Porter and Jack Perrine.

The next day the *Public Ledger* had a front page editorial with the headline Maysville Needs Bigger Gym.[475]

The Bulldogs beat Catlettsburg and lost to Louisville Manual to end the regular season with a 17-7 record.

Maysville routed May's Lick 67-35 in the semifinals of the district tournament and won its ninth consecutive district championship with a 58-38 victory over Orangeburg.

The Bulldogs drew the Paris Greyhounds in the first round of the 10th Region Tournament at Paris. The Greyhounds had won both regular season games against Maysville and were favored to win the region.

Maysville led 27-26 at the end of the third quarter and scored the first four points of the fourth quarter to lead 31-26. Paris went on a 10-5 run to tie the game at 36-all. Whalen made a free throw with seven seconds to play to put the Bulldogs back in front at 37-36. William Hudnall sank a free throw to tie the game at 37-all with five seconds remaining. Cooke made a one-handed shot that would have given Maysville the win but the official timer ruled that the buzzer had sounded before the shot, and the basket was nullified. Both teams scored five points in the overtime period. Paris forward Eugene Cain scored on a putback five seconds into the sudden death overtime to give Paris a 44-42 victory.[476]

The *Public Ledger* wrote: "After the game Maysville fans were unanimous in the belief that the Bulldogs had won the game, claiming that Cooke's shot not only had left his hands but was at the bankboard before the buzzer sounded. The two referees appeared to hold this belief too but decided to consult the official time-keeper, Claude Thompson of Paris, and he contended the game ended before the shot was made. The officials then agreed to accept his decision."[477]

The *Public Ledger* story continued "Many Paris fans also were heard to remark that Maysville had won the game."

The heart breaking loss snapped Maysville's streak of four consecutive 10th Region titles.

Chapter 12 MHS 1950-1956

Maysville had a terrific run in the 1940s-nine district titles, five regional championships, one state championship and one state runner-up finish.

The winning ways continued in the 1950s. The 1949-50 team compiled a 20-7 regular season record with George Cooke and Bobby Ormes leading the way. The Bulldogs won their 10th consecutive district championship.

Maysville beat Morgan 50-37 in the first round of the regional tournament. Ormes suffered a sprained ankle in the fourth quarter and was not expected to play in the semifinal game against Augusta.[478]

Ormes did not play in the first half, but Coach Earle D. Jones sent him into the game near the middle of the third quarter. Augusta led 38-36 in the fourth quarter. Herman "Shotsie" Tolle hit a field goal to tie the game, and Ormes sank a foul shot to give the Bulldogs a 39-38 lead. Maysville outscored Augusta 8-1 the rest of the way to win 47-39. The final eight-point margin was the largest of the game.[479]

It was Maysville versus Paris in the championship game at Paris.

Advance ticket sales were scheduled to begin at 12:15 p.m. Saturday at the Maysville gym. Fans began arriving at the gym at 9 a.m. By 11 a.m., a long line had formed. With rain failing, the decision was made to allow the fans to go inside the gym and sit in the bleachers in the order in which they had arrived. Once the ticket sales began, groups of five to 10 people were allowed to leave their seats and go to the ticket window. The ticket sales were conducted in an orderly manner for about the first half hour. Then, without warning, several people, rushed from their seats and ran toward the ticket booth causing a stampede. One woman was knocked to the floor and a number of children were caught in the stampede, but no injuries were reported.[480]

All of the tickets were sold soon after order was restored. Many people who had been at the gym for two hours lost their place in line and were unable to purchase tickets. No tickets were available at the Paris gym, the game was sold out.

Ormes was able to return to the starting lineup. With three minutes to go in the second quarter there was some rough play under the Paris goal. After a conference with the officials, Cooke and Paris' Gayle Rose were taken out of the game by their respective coaches. Both players were allowed to reenter the game at the start of the third quarter. Cooke scored a game-high 19 points and the Bulldogs pulled out a 45-41 victory for their fifth regional championship in six years.

There was a huge demand for state tournament tickets (262 fans applied for tickets and only 142 were allotted to Maysville) but there was no stampede when the tickets went on sale Monday morning.[481]

Maysville received an additional 32 tickets and they were sold to fans in the order in which the applications were received.[482]

Maysville drew Owensboro in the first round. Owensboro star Cliff Hagen had graduated at the end of the first semester and was playing for the University of Kentucky freshmen team.[483]

The Bulldogs led 10-9 at the end of the first quarter and 21-18 at halftime. Even though Ormes spent most of the third quarter on the bench with three fouls, Maysville was up 32-28 at the end of the third quarter. Ormes scored 14 points in the fourth quarter and the Bulldogs outscored the Red Devils 24-12 to win, 56-40. Ormes ended up with 22 points. Cooke added 17 points.[484]

Jones and all the players except for Ormes and Cooke came down with food poisoning after dining on cream chicken at the hotel Thursday evening. Ormes and Cooke had not eaten with the team. The rest of the players were up all night. Dr. Harry Denham was called at 3 a.m. to care for the players and Coach Jones.[485]

The Bulldogs were weak when they faced the Clark County Cardinals in the quarterfinals. Cooke left the game with 4:45 to play in the second quarter. He had a badly inflamed instep on his right foot that was attributed to a tight shoe. Cooke did not play anymore in the first half.[486]

Clark County, which had a huge height advantage over Maysville, led 25-22 at halftime. The Cardinals increased the lead to six at 41-35 at the end of the third quarter and defeated the Bulldogs 52-43. Harlan "Fatso" Tolle was Maysville's leading scorer with 15 points. Cooke tossed in 14 points.[487] The Bulldogs ended the season with a 26-8 record.

Maysville won district titles the next four seasons, but lost in the regional tournament each year. The 1950-51 team won 24 games. That was Cooke's senior year. He is Maysville's all-time leading scorer with 2,316 points. Cooke played in four games at the University of Kentucky during the 1951-52 season[488] and later left UK.

Gerry Calvert was the Bulldogs' star in the 1951-52 and 1952-53 seasons. The concern of one of his teachers led to a moment of serendipity that resulted in Calvert becoming a basketball player.

"Little Miss Patterson is the one that made me what I am today because she decided that I wasn't going to come to school with no paper, no pencils and not read. So at first she started out making me dust the blackboards. And then she decided that she had to grade papers so we had to go over and watch basketball practice. And then one day Coach Jones looked up there and said 'Miss Patterson, who is that with you?' And she said 'Well, that's a little guy staying after school here.' And he said 'Well, I need somebody down here, can I borrow him?' And she said 'yes.' So I go down and I still had my street shoes on, and I started to walk out on his floor, and he said 'hey boy, take them shoes off.' So I'm out there in my sock feet, and these other kids got tennis shoes. And so he said to one of the managers at that time was named Jackie Perrine or Jimmy Hardymon, I can't remember which, he said 'go get this boy a pair of tennis shoes.' So that's how I got started playing (at) Maysville."

Calvert says he thinks he was in the seventh grade at the time. He honed his skills playing against players from St. Patrick and Fee High Schools.

"We didn't realize that the schools were segregated. We knew there was a Fee High School, (a) Catholic high school and Maysville High School. But we all played together, we all went places together. And behind the Catholic school, St. Patrick's, they had some basketball goals ... and we all played together. A lot of my friends, Gene Bluford for instance from Fee High School, great basketball player."

Calvert led the Bulldogs in scoring his junior and senior seasons and is 16th on Maysville's all-time scoring list with 1,172 career points.

He signed to play at the University of Louisville but had a change of heart after a brief appearance in the Kentucky-Indiana All-Star Game. The Kentucky All-Stars were coached by University of Louisville head coach Peck Hickman and his assistant, John Dromo.

"We got ready to start the game and they threw the ball up and I ran down the floor with the ball, went to shoot a crip and got knocked about 10 rows in the bleachers and just about got knocked out." said Calvert. "And so Coach Hickman pulled me out and sat me on the bench. I never played another second. And I was really hurt. I was crying and really upset. And Earl Adkins came up to me and Charlie Tyra and said 'you know you guys, why don't you all come to Kentucky with me?' And I told Charlie, I said 'Charlie, I'm going.' And he said 'please don't.' I said 'you come with me, we'll go to Kentucky and we'll be National Champions.' And so he said 'I know you're mad, I know you're mad at Coach Hickman, but' he said 'Coach Hickman did what was best for you.' 'Cause they thought I was really hurt. And I said 'no, I'm going to Kentucky, if I get a scholarship.'"

University of Kentucky assistant coach Harry Lancaster offered

Calvert a scholarship the next day, and he accepted it. Calvert tried to convince Tyra to join him at UK, but Tyra went to Louisville and was a two-time All-American and played five seasons in the NBA.

Calvert played baseball and basketball at UK. He was an elected co-captain his senior season.

Maysville ended the regular season in 1955 with a 13-10 record. The Bulldogs beat Minerva 50-33 in the first round of the district tournament. The very next night, the Maysville Board of Education accepted Jones' resignation as coach.

Jones, who had also served as principal of Maysville High School since the 1949-50 school year, had submitted his resignation to Superintendent Ted C. Gilbert on December 6, but it was held in confidence until the March 2 school board meeting.[489]

In his resignation letter, Jones wrote: "The rapid increase in enrollment at the Maysville Center building has brought with it such added responsibilities, I now feel it wise to request that I be relieved of the basketball coaching duties effective at the termination of the present season."[490]

The season ended with the next game – a 47-45 loss in the district semifinals to the Tollesboro Wildcats. Tollesboro was coached by Jones protégé William "Teence" Ryan. The loss snapped Maysville's streaks of 13 consecutive district championships and 13 straight trips to the regional tournament.

Jones' record at Maysville was 470-180.[491] He guided the Bulldogs to 19 district titles and nine regional championships. Jones also won 71 games at Kavanaugh. He had 19 coaching victories in state tournament play-a record he held until 2006 when Dale Mabry of Pleasure Ridge Park won his 20th game.

Woodrow "Woodie" Crum, the assistant coach at Maysville for three seasons, was named as Jones' successor the same night Jones' resignation was accepted. Crum was a star athlete at Jenkins High School and Union College. He was the head coach at May's Lick High School in the 1951-52 season.

It was a smooth transition for the Bulldogs and Crum. When the 1955-56 regular season came to an end, Maysville had a record of 19-7. Sophomore Allen Smith, who had played on the varsity since the eighth grade, was the leading scorer.

The Bulldogs had lopsided victories over May's Lick (77-23) and Orangeburg (68-28) in their first two games in the district tournament. It was a different story in the championship game as the Fleming County Panthers intercepted a pass with 17 seconds to play and scored to beat the Bulldogs 42-41.[492]

Maysville beat the Scott County Cardinals 53-49 in the first round of the 10th Region Tournament. The Bulldogs faced Fleming County in the semifinals and avenged their loss to the Panthers in the district finals with a 55-48 victory.

Maysville went up against the heavily favored Nicholas County Blue Jackets in the championship game. Nicholas County, led by center Ned Jennings, had defeated the Bulldogs' twice in the regular season- 59-53 in Maysville and 59-43 in Carlisle. Jennings scored 28 points in the game at Carlisle.

A crowd of 3,500 was on hand for the region finals at Harrison County. Nicholas County was up 55-54 with two minutes left in the game. Bobby Mills sank two free throws, and Marvin Tucker made one of two foul shots to give Maysville a two-point lead at 57-55. Jennings hit a 10-foot turn around shot to send the game into overtime.

In the first overtime, Jennings made a layup to give the Bluejackets a 59-57 lead. Mills hit two free throws to tie the game and force a sudden death overtime.

In the sudden death overtime, Jennings missed a free throw, his teammate, Leo Lynam, got the rebound and was fouled. Lynam missed his free throw. Mills got the rebound and passed the ball to Tucker, who hit a 15-foot jump shot to give Maysville a 61-59 win.

It was Tucker who had thrown the bad pass in the closing seconds of the district championship game. Tucker went from being the goat to the hero.

Fans hoisted Tucker on their shoulders and carried him around the gym. Another group of fans lifted Crum up on their shoulders and carried him around.[493] The Bulldogs were going to state for the first time since 1950.

Maysville faced the Bell County Bobcats in the first round of the state tournament. It was a high scoring game. Bell County led 23-22 at the end of the first quarter, 46-40 at halftime and 67-54 at the end of the third quarter. With three minutes left in the game, Maysville cut the deficit to two at 74-72. Bell County scored three straight points to lead 77-72. Smith hit a field goal and a free throw to make it 77-75. Murph Slusher's basket put the Bobcats back up by four at 79-75. Tucker made a field goal to cut it to 79-77, but Bell County hit three free throws and won, 82-77. Smith hit 11 straight free throws and scored 23 points. Tucker followed with 22 and Dickie Breeze added 12. The Bulldogs ended the season with a 24-9 record.[494]

An announcement in 1956 brought a historic change in high school basketball beginning with the 1956-57 season.

Chapter 13 Fee's Final Season

Maysville, Mason County and Fleming County school officials, including Earle D. Jones, who had moved up to superintendent of the Maysville Independent Schools, announced in February 1956 that school integration would begin in the fall of 1956.

John G. Fee High School students in grades 10-12 who resided in the Maysville district would attend Maysville High School. Students outside the Maysville district would attend the county high schools. Students in grades one through nine would continue to attend Fee.[495]

That meant the 1955-56 season would be the final one for the Fee Wildcats.

Fee, under the guidance of Coach John Fields, had had continued success in the 1950's.

The Wildcats opened the 1949-50 season with five straight wins. The streak was snapped by a 58-31 loss to Lincoln-Grant.[496]

Fee won several games by double digit margins that season including 48-38 over Lexington Douglass, 66-45 over Ashland and 49-30 over Georgetown Ed Davis.

Fee met Somerset in the first round of the district tournament at Paris. The score was tied at the end of each of the first three quarters. The Wildcats outscored Somerset 14-2 in the fourth quarter to win 54-43. Joe Cunningham scored 20 points.[497]

Dunbar routed Fee 72-33 in the semifinals, but the Wildcats bounced back to beat Richmond 47-39 in the third place game. Norman Warner scored 21 points against Richmond and was named to the All-District Team along with Cunningham. The top four teams advanced to the regional tournament.[498]

Fee lost to Dunbar 49-31 in the opening round of the regional tournament. Cunningham scored 13 points and Warner tossed in 10.[499]

In the final game of the 1950-51 regular season, George King scored 33 points, and Warner added 15, but it was not enough as Paris Western edged Fee 60-58 in double overtime.[500]

The Wildcats lost to Frankfort 57-56 in the regional tournament. Fee was scheduled to play Lexington Douglass in a consolation game, but there was no report on the game.

Fee hosted the 1952 Blue Grass District Tournament at the

Maysville High School Gym. Warner scored 15 points and King followed with 14 to lead the Wildcats past Cynthiana 45-31 in the semifinals.[501]

Fee met Paris Western in the championship game. The Wildcats had won both regular games against Paris Western but were upset 45-36 in the district finals. Joe Haley was the leading scorer for Fee with 12 points.[502]

The regional tournament was held at Paris. Fee beat Danville 61-36 in the first round and edged Lexington Douglass 59-58 in the semifinals. The Wildcats faced Lexington Dunbar in the championship game. Fee led 12-9 at the end of the first quarter, 21-19 at the half and 31-24 after three quarters. It was 40-all at the end of the fourth quarter. Dunbar won 44-42 in overtime. Warner led the Wildcats with 16 points.[503]

Fee routed the Somerset Trojans 75-47 in the first round of the sectional tournament. The game was played at Fee. Four Wildcats scored in double figures. Humphrey led the way with 19 points, William Johnson added 15, Haley followed with 14, and King tossed in 12.[504]

The final two rounds of the sectional were played at Lexington Dunbar. Fee beat Hazard 48-38 in the semifinals. In the championship game, the Wildcats outscored Dunbar 15-4 in the fourth quarter to win 49-32. Fee was led in scoring by Jackson Bennett with 13 points. Johnson scored 11 and Warner added 10. The Wildcats were going to the state tournament for the first time since 1947.[505]

Fee played the Bowling Green Mustangs in the first round of the state tournament. It was 15-all at the end of the first quarter. Bowling Green led 26-22 at the half and 39-37 at the end of the third quarter. The Wildcats outscored the Mustangs 14-9 in the fourth quarter to win 51-48. King led Fee in scoring with 22 points.[506]

The Wildcats slipped past Paris Western 49-47 in the semifinals.

Fee lost to Louisville Central 71-44 in the championship game. Central led 15-7 at the end of the first quarter, 34-13 at halftime and 49-31 at the end of the third quarter. King was the only Wildcat in double figures with 15 points, King and Warner, both seniors, were named first-team all-state. Bennett, a junior, was named second-team all-state.[507]

"One of the best players I ever saw was Norman Warner," says Laurnie Caproni, former *Ledger Independent* sports editor. "Norman couldn't been much more than 5-8, 5-9; he was just so smooth."

Fee opened the 1953 district tournament with a 75-42 rout of Cynthiana. All five starters scored in double figures. Robert Humphrey led the way with 19 points, Jackson Bennett followed with 14, Leonard Owens and Vincent Alexander scored 12 points apiece and George Jones added 11.[508]

The Wildcats played Paris in the district championship game, but there was no report on the game.

Fee lost to Somerset Dunbar 52-38 in the first round of regional tournament. All five Fee starters fouled out. The Wildcats bounced back to beat Frankfort 50-45. Humphrey scored 18 points and Jones added 14. Fee defeated Stanford 74-42 in a consolation game.[509]

Fee lost to Somerset Dunbar 75-68 in the sectional tournament at Somerset. Bennett scored 21 points and Humphrey had 12.[510]

Fee had a couple of freshmen- Robert Jones and Eugene Peters – in the starting lineup in the 1953-54 season.

The Wildcats beat Cynthiana 58-54 in the semifinals of the district tournament. William Rice scored 15 points, Jones followed with 14 and Joe Franklin added 10.[511]

Fee lost to Paris Western 78-31 in the championship game. Jones was named to the all-tournament team. Wendell Greene was named to the second team.[512]

The Wildcats lost to Somerset Dunbar 66-45 in the first round of the regional tournament. Fee defeated Frankfort Mayo Underwood 54-52 in the first round of consolation play, but the Wildcats' season ended with a 53-38 loss to Danville Bate in the consolation finals. Jones was named to the all-region team. Greene received honorable mention.[513]

Fee hosted the 1955 district tournament at the Maysville High School gym. The Wildcats beat Ashland in 64-59 in the semifinals. Jones scored 28 points but Fee lost to Winchester Oliver 64-55 in the finals. Greene scored 12 points.[514]

Fee lost to Danville Bate 62-61 in semifinals of the regional tournament. Paris Western edged the Wildcats 69-65 in the consolation game. Jones scored 18 points, Greene had 14 and William Hendrix added 11 in the consolation game.[515]

The 1955-56 season was winding down when the school integration was announced. Fee closed out the regular season by edging Booker T. Washington 58-57 in Ashland to run its record to 19-3. Jones scored 33 points and Franklin added 10 points.[516]

Fee was the runner-up in the Blue Grass Conference in 1956. In seven years in the conference, Fee won two championships and was the runner-up three times.[517]

Four Wildcats scored in double figures as Fee ran past Mt. Sterling 71-44 in the semifinals of the district tournament. Cornell Lofton led the way with 19 points, Jones and Franklin scored 14 points apiece and Peters added 10.[518]

Fee outscored Winchester Oliver 14-6 in the third quarter en route to a 56-53 victory in the championship game. Jones scored 22 points,

Lofton followed with 11, and Franklin added 10.[519]

The Wildcats lost to Lexington Dunbar 54-48 in the semifinals of the regional tournament and then beat Winchester Oliver 62-51 to take third place. Jones had another big game with 26 points. Peters scored 15, and Franklin added 13.[520]

Franklin fired in 20 points, and Jones and Peters each scored 10 as Fee cruised past Harlan 56-34 in the semifinals of the sectional tournament to earn a berth in the state tournament.[521]

Fee was fortunate a trip to state was not on the line in the sectional finals because the Wildcats lost to Lexington Douglass 63-57. Jones scored 17 points.[522]

Fee drew undefeated Louisville Central in the first round of the state tournament. Central was the defending national champion.[523]

Central led 8-6 at the end of the first quarter, 24-14 at the half and 37-27 after the three quarters. Central outscored Fee 18-9 in the fourth quarter for a 55-36 victory. Jones scored 12 points and Franklin added 10.[524] Jones was named to the all-state team.[525]

Fee ended its final season with a 23-6 record.

While giving a brief greeting at the Fee's banquet, Maysville Schools Superintendent Earle D. Jones mentioned the pride the community felt in the team. There was a tribute to Coach Fields. The players on Fee's last team included seniors Winifred Black, Cornell Lofton and Joe Franklin, juniors Robert Jones and Eugene Peters, sophomores James Smith and Alfred Thomas, freshmen Paul Jones, Charles Stewart and Ulysses Greene, and 8th grader Eugene Moore.[526]

Chapter 14 Integration and a Heartbreaking Loss

Twenty-three former students of Fee High School enrolled at Maysville High School on September 5, 1956. The *Public Ledger* wrote that "local integration worked smoothly."[527]

A little over a month later, 22 prospective players showed up for the first day of basketball practice. The group included six returning Maysville lettermen - Dickie Breeze, Kenny Downing, Allen Smith, Jackie Allison, Bobby Reetz and Bobby Hutchison - and two starters from Fee's last team - Robert "Bobby" Jones and Eugene "Gene" Peters.[528]

Jones was nicknamed "Toothpick" because he kept a toothpick in his mouth, even when he played basketball.

Coach Woodie Crum announced his starting lineup on the day before the season opener. Breeze and Downing were the forwards, Jones was the center, and Allison and David Curtis were the guards.[529]

The Bulldogs opened the season against the Minerva Maroons in Minerva. Maysville led 20-5 at the end of the first quarter, 39-7 at halftime and 68-16 after three quarters. The final score was Maysville 83, Minerva 29. Jones scored 17 points, Curtis tossed in 15, and Breeze added 14.[530]

Smith started over Curtis, and Charles Stewart took Downing's place in the starting lineup for Maysville's home opener against Tollesboro. Jones scored 24 points to lead the Bulldogs to a 70-49 victory. Smith scored 13 points and Allison followed with 10.[531]

Despite the 21-point win, Crum told the *Public Ledger* "[the Bulldogs] did not turn in as good a game as expected." Crum added that "Breeze and Jones though very good, should improve their rebounding." The coach did praise a couple of players. "Allison did a good job of long shooting the first quarter, and the improved play of Charlie Stewart shows he's really worked for a starting position," Crum said.[532]

All five starters scored in double figures in a 73-58 road win over the Clark County Cardinals. Smith and Jones scored 18 points each, Allison had 12 and Breeze and Stewart scored 10 apiece.

A 79-60 win over Olive Hill was followed by a 98-66 rout of Paris. The Bulldogs beat Harrison County 66-45 and Fleming County 60-38.

Jones scored 36 points in a 91-73 victory over Inez.

Smith scored 22 points to lead the Bulldogs past Erlanger Lloyd 59-48.

Nicholas County's six-foot-eight center Ned Jennings scored 29 points, but it wasn't enough as the Bulldogs defeated the Bluejackets 58-53. Maysville was 10-0 heading into the Christmas break.

Jones scored 32 points to lead Maysville to an 89-52 win over Ashland Holy Family in the Ashland Invitational Tournament. It was Maysville's first appearance in the AIT, which was the most prestigious holiday tournament in Kentucky.

Maysville played the Ashland Tomcats in the semifinals. After trailing 70-60 in the fourth quarter, the Bulldogs rallied and led 79-78. But Ashland forward Dale Griffith hit two free throws with four seconds to play to give the Tomcats an 80-79 victory that snapped Maysville's 11-game season-opening winning streak. Allison scored 30 points, Smith tossed in 19 and Jones added 18.[533]

The Bulldogs defeated Russell 90-61 in the third-place game. Jones poured in 31 points, Peters followed with 19 and Smith scored 14. Jones, Smith and Allison were named to the all-tournament team.[534]

Maysville opened the 1957 portion of the schedule by crushing Mt. Sterling 75-37.

The Scott County Cardinals gave the Bulldogs a good game, but Maysville prevailed by the score of 78-70.

Jones scored 35 points as Maysville beat Ashland 74-55 in Ashland to avenge the loss in the AIT.

The Bulldogs topped the Berea Pirates 88-46. The Pirates were coached by former Maysville star Ed LeForge.[535]

Maysville and Newport Catholic were tied at 66-all at the end of regulation. With the Bulldogs trailing by two in the overtime period, Jones sank two free throws to force a second overtime. Maysville outscored Newport Central 3-0 in the second overtime on a free throw by Jones and a field goal by Peters to win, 71-68. Jones scored 37 points.[536]

The Bulldogs, led by Jones' 31 points, cruised past Breckinridge Training 101-45 in the MHS gym. It was the first time a Maysville team had hit the century mark. The *Public Ledger* wrote: "With 1:30 remaining, Maysville had racked up a total of 94 points, and the fans were screaming for the 'Dogs to make an even hundred points, which they did with one to spare."[537]

Smith and Jones combined for 36 of Maysville's 42 first half points in a 74-57 blowout of Inez.[538] Smith, despite suffering a broken jaw in the game, ended up with 23 points, and Jones added 22. Smith was expected to be out three weeks.[539]

Smith missed the next four games, but the Bulldogs continued to win. Jones scored 34 points in a 77-51 victory over Meade Memorial ran the Bulldogs' record to 20-1.

Jones scored a career-high 38 points including 22 of Maysville's 24 second half points in a 57-51 road win over the Olive Hill Comets.[540]

When Maysville and Nicholas County met in Carlisle, the Bulldogs double teamed Bluejackets center Ned Jennings, and Nicholas County kept two defenders on Jones. Jennings scored 23 points, but Maysville had four players in double figures, and the Bulldogs won, 68-63. Peters led the way with 18 points, Jones followed by 17, Breeze tossed in 11 and Stewart added 10.[541]

Jones was 15 of 20 from the field and scored 32 points to lead the Bulldogs to an 85-70 victory over Paintsville. Jones made seven straight shots in the third period.[542]

Smith returned to action when the Bulldogs hosted the Fleming County Panthers. Smith came off the bench to score 2 points, and Maysville won, 64-53.[543] Jones had a game-high 25 points.

Smith was back in the starting lineup and scored 10 points in Maysville's 62-60 overtime victory over the Clark County Cardinals.[544] The win ran the Bulldogs' record to 25-1.

Maysville posted a 66-47 road win over Frankfort and remained sixth in *The Courier-Journal's* Litkenhous ratings.[545]

Jones was kept out of the lineup for a rest when the Bulldogs played the Harrison County Thoroughbreds in Cynthiana. Peters started at center and scored 21 points to lead Maysville to a 56-45 win. It was Harrison County's first home loss of the season.[546]

The Bulldogs romped past the Mt. Sterling Trojans 62-31 in their final home game of the regular season. Smith sprained his ankle in the game[547] and missed the final game of the regular season[548]- a 72-44 road victory over Boone County. Maysville was headed to the district tournament with a 29-1 record. It was considered an undefeated regular season because the only loss was to Ashland in the Ashland Invitation Tournament.[549]

Win No. 30 came in the first round of the district tournament as the Bulldogs trounced the Orangeburg Tigers 103-53. Maysville led 37-12 at the end of the first quarter, 64-12 at the half and 88-29 after three quarters. It was the first time a team had scored 100 points in a 39th District Tournament game. Five Bulldogs scored in double figures. Peters scored 24 points, Jones followed with 21, Downing had 14, Allison with 12 and Stewart added 10. Smith's sprained ankle kept him out of the game.[550]

Smith returned to the starting lineup for the semifinal game against Tollesboro. The Wildcats kept the game close for a little more than a half. Tollesboro had a one-point lead early in the third quarter, but the Bulldogs ended the third quarter on a 17-5 run to lead 43-32.

Maysville took a 20-point lead after holding Tollesboro to just two free throws in the first four minutes of the fourth quarter. The final score: Maysville 60, Tollesboro 44. Jones had a game-high 30 points. Allison scored 12 points, and Breeze added 10.[551]

Maysville outscored Fleming County 29-7 in the second quarter and won the district championship game, 80-50. Jones led the way with 28 points. Peters tossed in 20 points, and Downing came in off the bench to add 11.[552]

Jones scored 25 points to lead the Bulldogs past the Paris Greyhounds 84-62 in the first round of the 10th Region Tournament. Peters scored 15 points, and Allison added 12.[553]

Maysville defeated the Scott County Cardinals 74-68 in the semifinals. Jones scored 27 points, Peters followed with 14, Allison had 12 and Breeze added 10.[554]

It was Maysville (34-1) vs. Nicholas County (18-7) in the championship game.

"The toughest team in the region for anyone to beat will be Nicholas County," Crum told the *Public Ledger* before the district tournaments started. "The Bluejackets have 6-8 Ned Jennings and- if that isn't enough- 6-3 Jack Guy, recent transfer from Paris and 6-3 Rose."[555]

Nicholas County jumped out to a 10-2 lead and was up 18-11 at the end of the first quarter. The Bluejackets led by as many as 10 in the second quarter, but the Bulldogs cut the deficit in half at 33-28 at the end of the first half.

Jennings and Leo Lynam fouled out in the third quarter, but Nicholas County had a 45-41 lead at the end of the quarter. Jones fouled out with about three minutes left in the game, and Peters fouled out with 47 seconds left. Nicholas County defeated Maysville 62-60. The loss snapped the Bulldogs' 23-game winning streak.

Jennings led Nicholas County in scoring with 20 points. Donnie Hillock stepped up his game after Jennings fouled out and ended up with 17 points. Guy added 13 points for the Bluejackets.[556] Jones had a game-high 26 points. Smith tossed in 15 points. Peters added 11.

"There's no doubt that was the best team I ever had," Crum told *Inside Kentucky Sports* magazine in 1974. "They were 34-2 and had all it takes to win."[557]

Maysville ended the year with a 34-2 record. Jones was named to the Kentucky All-Star team. He played one varsity season at the University of Dayton.

Smith led the 1957-58 Maysville team in scoring with an average of 21.4 points per game. The Bulldogs won the district tournament but lost to Paris Western 75-64 in the semifinals of the regional tournament.

The top individual performance of the 1957-58 season was a

46-point game by Orangeburg senior Henry O'Cull in the Tigers' 102-46 victory over the St. Patrick Paddies. Yes, O'Cull matched St. Patrick's team total and set the scoring record for the St. Patrick gymnasium.[558] The record would not be broken until 1974. O'Cull scored 34 points before fouling out late in the fourth quarter in a 66-65 overtime win over May's Lick in the 1958 district tournament.[559]

The Maysville baseball team, coached by Woodie Crum, won the 1958 state championship. Allen Smith was the winning pitcher in all three games in the state tournament.[560]

Maysville had a new player for the 1958-59 basketball season. Alan Bane transferred from Tollesboro to play his senior season for the Bulldogs.

After opening the season with six straight wins, Maysville was No.1 in the United Press International ratings.[561]

In their first game as the state's top rated team, the Bulldogs routed Harrison County 70-28.

Maysville was 10-0 heading into a home game against the Louisville Male Purples. Male, coached by Guy Strong, beat the Bulldogs 66-64 in double overtime.[562]

The Bulldogs dropped to No. 4 in the UPI ratings.[563]

After back-to-back wins over Paris and Scott County, Maysville lost four straight games against tough competition- Newport Catholic, Louisville Manual, Louisville St. Xavier and Olive Hill.

The four-game skid dropped the Bulldogs to No. 10 in the UPI poll.[564]

Maysville bounced back with six consecutive victories. Bane scored 39 points in a 78-64 win over Pikeville during the streak.

The Bulldogs ended the regular season with three straight losses to Hazard, Ashland and Newport.

Maysville cruised through the district tournament with victories over May's Lick (95-36), Tollesboro (70-49) and Fleming County (71-51). Charles "Chuck" Hall scored 30 points in the district championship game against Fleming County.

The Bulldogs defeated the Falmouth Red Devils 81-60 in the first round of the 10th Region Tournament. That set up a semifinal showdown against the Nicholas County Bluejackets. Former Maysville star Gerry Calvert was the Nicholas County coach.

Nicholas County led 13-10 at the end of the first quarter, 23-20 at halftime and 39-32 after three quarters. The Bulldogs took their first lead at 43-42 with 1:12 to go on a basket by Jimmy Hart. The Bluejackets regained the lead on a set shot by Leo Lynam. Hart hit a field goal with two seconds to play to give Maysville a 45-44 win.[565]

Hall led the Bulldogs in scoring with 13 points. Hart and Bane scored 10 points apiece.

Bane took a bad fall late in the game and spent the night at Hayswood Hospital. He was released the next morning, but did not play in the championship game against the Scott County Cardinals.[566]

Even without Bane, Maysville got off to a quick start in the championship game. The Bulldogs led 16-6 at the end of the first quarter, 33-18 at the half and 50-26 after three quarters. The final score: Maysville 80, Scott County 52.[567]

"There was no stopping them," Crum told the *Public Ledger*. "They had too much defense and rebounding, and the team effort was the finest I have ever seen since I have been coaching in Maysville. It was a 'dream night.'"[568]

Robert Alexander scored a game-high 19 points. Jimmy Calvert followed with 17 points, Hart tossed in 12 and Roy Gilbert added 10.

Maysville drew LaRue County in the first round of the state tournament. Gilbert fouled out in the second quarter. Bane went out on fouls late in the third quarter, and a short time later Herman Smith fouled out. The Bulldogs led by as many as 19 at 48-29 in third quarter. The lead was cut to eight in the fourth quarter, but Maysville held on to win, 78-67. Calvert scored a career-high 21 points. Alexander and Bane each scored 18 points.[569]

The Bulldogs ran into a hot shooting North Marshall team in the quarterfinal round. The Jets shot 53.6 percent from the field in the first half and led 47-23 at halftime.

North Marshall was up 66-41 after three quarters and defeated Maysville 75-62. The Jets shot 46.4 percent for the game compared to 30 percent for the Bulldogs. Hall led Maysville in scoring with 23 points. Bane had 13, and Hart added 10.[570]

The Bulldogs ended the season with a 25-9 record.

Maysville won eight district titles and four region championships in the 1950s. Consolidation of the county schools in 1960 would end the Bulldogs' domination of the district tournament.

Chapter 15 Basketball Returns to St. Patrick

St. Patrick began the 1950s with a new coach. Former Morehead State College football and basketball star Joe Lustic was named to succeed Mert Blanton who resigned in August 1949 to return to college.[571]

Fanny Stahl continued to pour in the points for St. Patrick in the 1949-50 season. Stahl scored 40 points in the Paddies' 50-43 victory over Ashland Holy Family in a consolation game of the Diocesan Tournament in Ashland. Stahl was believed to be the first local player to score 40 points in a game. Stahl scored 84 points in three tournament games and was named the Most Valuable Player.

Stahl remembers a funny story from the trophy presentation:

"The priest who gave me the trophy happened to baptize me. I was born in May's Lick, and he baptized me," says Stahl. "He was on the speaker and says 'here's my good friend.' He says 'I baptized him, and now I wished I drowned him.'"

Stahl and Tommy Purdon were named to the all-tournament team.[572]

Stahl followed up his 40-point game with a 30-point performance in a 46-37 win over the Orangeburg Tigers.

St. Patrick closed out the regular season with a 49-35 overtime victory over the May's Lick Cardinals.

St. Patrick and May's Lick met in the first round of the district tournament and the Paddies won, 41-36, to run their record to 20-9.

The Paddies beat Minerva 53-35 in the semifinals and lost to Maysville 50-38 in the championship game.

St. Patrick's season came to an end with a 55-38 loss to Paris in the first round of the 10th Region Tournament. Stahl scored 20 points in his final game. He scored 20 or more points in 14 games that season.

Laurnie Caproni, former *Ledger Independent* sports editor, says Stahl "was just terrific."

Stahl was named to *The Courier-Journal* All-State Second Team[573] and received a scholarship to Villanova University in Philadelphia. Villanova coach Al Severance came to Maysville to award the scholarship to Stahl.[574]

Severance and Maysville resident Frances Comer had been college roommates. Comer told Severance about Stahl.

Stahl says he would have never received a scholarship to Villanova if wasn't for Comer.

After a season and a half at Villanova, Stahl joined the Army and served in Korea. When he got out of the Army, he finished his basketball career at Xavier University in Cincinnati.

St. Patrick went 3-20 in the 1950-51 season, and Lustic left to become the coach at Tollesboro.

Don Grove, who played at Michigan State, was hired as the Paddies' coach. After four losing seasons, (including a 1-20 record in 1954-55) Grove stepped down.

Less than two months before the start of the 1955-56 season, all five St. Patrick starters-seniors Daniel Ryan Jr. and John Buckley, juniors James Whaley and Danny Grove, and sophomore Kearn McHugh-were injured in a car wreck.[575] Whaley was St. Patrick's leading scorer the previous season and had a 40-point game against St. Agatha. Ryan, Whaley and Grove were still hospitalized when the Paddies played their season opener-a 65-25 loss to Minerva. Only McHugh and Whaley returned to action.

Even though he was junior at Xavier, Stahl coached at St. Patrick in the 1955-56 season.

"That turned out to be a total mistake that I made," Stahl said.

Stahl coached the Paddies on the weekends and even drove home sometimes after practice during the week.

"It just didn't make any sense why I did it," Stahl says. "I look back at it now and said 'My God I needed to see somebody to examine me.' The senior year I realized and (St. Patrick pastor) Father Casey realized, hey, this is not working."

Rev. Eugene P. Wagner, assistant pastor at St. Patrick Church, coached the Paddies during the 1956-57 season. Wagner was assisted by Fanny Stahl's brother, Jimmy Stahl.[576]

St. Patrick finally had its own gym in 1956. Jimmy Hart scored 21 points to lead the Paddies to a 46-15 victory over St. Mary's in the first game in the new gym. It was the 1956-57 season opener. The Public Ledger wrote: "With a seating capacity of 600, many of the overflow crowd witnessed the game from the floor."[577] The seating capacity was listed at 500 in a later newspaper story about the gym.[578]

Despite losing the final four games of the 1956-57 season, the Paddies ended up with a 12-11 record- their first winning season since 1949-50.

Fanny Stahl was once again named the coach at St. Patrick in May 1957.[579]

St. Patrick had losing records in the final two seasons of the 1950s.

Chapter 16 1959-60 Season

The 1959-60 season was the final year for May's Lick, Minerva and Orangeburg. The three small schools were going to be consolidated into the new Mason County Central High School in the 1960-61 school year.

Maysville was coming off a trip to the state tournament, but the Bulldogs had been hit hard by graduation.

"Our success will depend on how well the young players develop between now and tournament time," Maysville coach Woodie Crum told the *Public Ledger* before the start of the season.[580]

The Bulldogs only had four returning lettermen - seniors Chuck Hall, Herman Smith and Robert Alexander, and Larry Jacobs, a junior.

"Although we lost six players, we should make a good showing this season as Hall, Smith and Alexander are being counted on to form the nucleus we'll build around," Crum told the *Public Ledger*.[581]

Laurnie Caproni, former *Ledger Independent* sports editor, says Hall "was a man playing a boys' game."

Maysville's junior varsity team was undefeated the previous season.

"Some of these boys should help a lot," Crum told the *Public Ledger*.[582]

The Bulldogs outscored Augusta 89-61 in the season opener, but lost to Clark County, 74-67, in the second game of the season.

After four straight wins, the Bulldogs lost to Louisville Flaget 58-52 at home.

A three-game winning streak was snapped by a 62-46 loss to Louisville St. Xavier in the Cincinnati Invitational Tournament.

The Bulldogs bounced back with a 63-55 road win over Scott County and were set to host Louisville Manual, the 1959 state runner-up.

"The Bulldogs played rather listlessly against Scott County but have shown a lot of spirit and hustle this week in practice," Crum told the *Public Ledger*. "Larry Jacobs has been moved back to his old guard spot and is showing improvement."[583]

Alexander scored 19 points to lead a balanced attack as Maysville beat Manual 65-57. Smith had 16 points. Jacobs tossed in 12, and Darrel Hill added 11. It was Maysville's first win over a team from Louisville since the 1954-55 season.

The Bulldogs continued to win. Hall scored 29 points and Alexander added 28 in an 80-63 victory over the Ashland Tomcats-Maysville's 12th consecutive victory and the 20th win of the season.

The winning streak was snapped by a 67-66 loss to the Clark County Cardinals at home in the next to last game of the regular season. Maysville closed out the regular season with a 74-61 road victory over the Newport Wildcats.

The Bulldogs were headed to postseason play with a 21-4 record.

"The tournaments are going to be rough because we are a marked team," Crum told the *Public Ledger*. "But nevertheless we are ready, and with the team effort we have, we are going to get to work and prove that we are a good outfit."

Maysville, No. 8 in the Litkenhous ratings, breezed past the Fleming County Panthers 57-31 in the opening game of the 39th District Tournament. Hall and Smith scored 14 points apiece, and Jacobs added 11.[584]

Donnie Simms scored 20 points, and Tommy Bean added 15 to lead Orangeburg to 58-52 victory over May's Lick. Carl Mitchell came in off the bench and scored 25 for the Cardinals. James Warner tossed in 12 points.[585]

St. Patrick had a 43-33 lead over Minerva at the end of the third quarter. The Maroons got to within four points in the final period before the Paddies pulled away for a 60-44 victory. Tommy Donovan led St. Patrick in scoring with 17 points. Joe Greenwell followed with 16, and Bill Gilkey added 10. Philip Davis was Minerva's leading scorer with 14 points, while Tony Wenz and Monroe "Butch" Forman scored 10 points apiece.[586]

Prior to the game, St. Patrick coach Fanny Stahl had told his players they could toss him in the shower if theybeat Minerva. After the game Stahl, fully clothed, was thrown into the cold shower in the locker room. He had to send home for a change of clothes.[587]

St. Patrick played the Tollesboro Wildcats in the semifinals. With 1:51 to play in the game, Donovan missed an outside shot, but Tommy Pfeffer tipped the ball in the basket to put the Paddies ahead 52-50. Larry Breeze sank a 20-footer to tie the game at 52-all. Donovan answered with a 20-foot shot to put St. Patrick back in front at 54-52. Tollesboro cut the deficit to one by making the first of two free throws. The second shot missed, and St. Patrick got the rebound. The Paddies called a time out with 11 seconds to go. When play resumed, St. Patrick held the ball until the buzzer sounded. The Paddies won, 54-53, and were headed to the district championship game and the regional tournament for the first time since 1950. Donovan was St. Patrick's leading scorer with 18 points. Gilkey had 12, and Greenwell scored 11.[588]

Stahl was doused in the cold shower once again and had to send home for dry clothes before he could leave the gym.[589]

Maysville routed Orangeburg 80-35 in the other semifinal game. The Bulldogs led 16-6 at the end of the first quarter, 41-12 at halftime, and 69-19 at the end of the third quarter. Four Maysville players scored in double figures - Smith with 19 points, Hill had 18, and Hall and Alexander each had 13. Simms was Orangeburg's leading scorer with 13 points.[590]

The three county schools saw their final season come to an end in the district tournament. The returning players would be teammates at the new Mason County Central High School the next season.

Maysville Superintendent and former coach Earle D. Jones coached the Bulldogs in the district championship game while Crum was on a scouting trip. Maysville breezed past St. Patrick 83-43. All five Maysville starters scored in double figures. Jacobs led the way 16 points. Smith tossed in 15, Alexander and Hill scored 14 apiece, and Hall added 12.[591] Donovan led St. Patrick scoring in with 15 points. Jim Collins added 14 points.

Maysville and St. Patrick drew each other in the first round of the regional tournament. Despite the 40-point win in the district finals, Crum was not looking past the Paddies.

"At the present time we are not looking ahead to the state tournament, Scott County or any other opponent but have as our single current goal the defeat of St. Patrick," Crum told the *Public Ledger*. "Many people are talking about the Bulldogs in the state tournament, and some publicity already has us playing in the classic. It doesn't take much thinking to remember that our 1957 team was good enough to win the district championship but didn't get to state primarily because of overconfidence.

"The members of the Bulldogs team are smart enough not to look ahead, but to play one game at a time. Our team is good enough to win the regional tournament, but it takes a little luck along with skill."

Maysville led St. Patrick 12-2 at the end of the first quarter. Crum went to his bench early in the second quarter and alternated his subs the rest of the game except in the third quarter when St. Patrick, after trailing 30-15 at halftime, got to with 11 at 38-27. The Bulldogs ended the third quarter on 9-2 run and lead 47-29. The final score was Maysville 63, St. Patrick 34. Hall led Maysville in scoring with 15 points. Smith scored 12, and Jacobs added 11. Pfeffer was St. Patrick's top scorer with 10 points.[592]

Maysville outscored Scott County 22-9 in the third quarter to win the semifinal game by the score of 74-51. Alexander fired in 25 points and Hill followed with 11.[593]

The Bulldogs played the Pendleton County Wildcats in the championship game. There were four ties in the first quarter before Maysville ended the quarter on an 8-2 run to lead 20-14. Pendleton County closed the gap to two early in the second quarter, but the Bulldogs led 34-29 at the end of the first half. Maysville was ahead, 52-40, after three quarters, and the Bulldogs won, 73-60. Alexander led the way with 19 points. Jacobs tossed in 16, Smith tallied 15, and Hill chipped in 11.[594]

Maysville was headed to the state tournament for the second straight year and the third time in Crum's five seasons as the head coach.

Ashland was Maysville's first round opponent in the state tournament.

"I think we have the toughest placement of any team in the tournament," Crum told the *Public Ledger*. "Every team we may meet has class. But we had the toughest draw in the region, too. We won there, and we can win at Louisville. I honestly think we're as good as any club in the tournament. But you have to get the breaks to go all the way."[595]

Crum had a word of caution about what the Bulldogs were up against in the opening round game with Ashland.

"You just don't kick those Tomcats around when the blue chips are down," Crum told the *Public Ledger*. "Sure we licked them good early in the season. But this is another game. And Ashland will be playing it for keeps."[596]

There were four ties in the first quarter. Maysville led 18-16 at the end of the first quarter. Ashland tied the game at 20-all, but the Bulldogs enjoyed a 33-27 lead at halftime. Maysville was up 47-44 at the end of the third quarter and led by seven at 55-48 in the fourth quarter. The Tomcats narrowed the gap to one at 55-54. The Bulldogs upped the lead to four at 60-56. In the final minute, Ashland hit a field goal, and Maysville made a free throw, and the Bulldogs won 61-58. Hall led a balanced scoring attack with 20 points. Smith scored 13, Hill 12 and Alexander 10. Ashland had two more field goals than Maysville, but the Bulldogs outscored the Tomcats 17-10 from the free throw line.[597]

Louisville Flaget, the team that had handed the Bulldogs their first loss of the season, was Maysville's opponent in the quarterfinal round. Flaget led 23-12 at the end of the first quarter, but the Bulldogs cut the deficit to four at 34-30 at the end of the second quarter. The Braves pushed their lead back out to 10 at 54-44 at the end of the third quarter. Maysville opened the fourth quarter with a 10-0 run to tie the game at 54-54. John McGill hit two free throws to put Flaget back up by two. Hall made a basket to tie the game at 56-56. Flaget hit two more free throws to lead 58-56. The Braves gained possession and held the ball. Maysville committed a foul with eight seconds to play. Flaget missed the free throw, and Hall got the rebound for the Bulldogs. When Maysville put the ball into play, Buddy Weihe came up with a steal and was fouled as the horn sounded. He made the free throw to make the final score Flaget 59, Maysville 56. All five of the Braves' fourth quarter points were on free throws. Hall and Hill led Maysville in scoring with 16 points apiece. Smith, who fouled out with 2:08, left in the game, having scored 12.[598]

The Bulldogs ended the season with a 28-5 record. Flaget went on to win the state championship. Hall was named to the all-tournament team. He was a First Team All-State selection by the *Herald-Leader*[599] and a Second Team All-State selection by *The Courier-Journal*.[600]

Chapter 17 Mason County High School's First Team

The three small county schools - May's Lick, Minerva and Orangeburg - that were consolidated into the new school had not had a lot of success on the hardwood.

Minerva had won back-to-back district titles in 1927 and 1928 and advanced to the state tournament both years by being the runner-up in the regional tournament.

Minerva defeated Augusta 17-12 in the championship game of the 1933 district tournament.

The only other two district championships for county schools happened under unique circumstances.

Minerva beat May's Lick 51-30 in the championship game of the district tournament in 1940,the year Maysville was ineligible for postseason play.

May's Lick, coached by Clark Chesnut, defeated Fleming County 37-27 to win the 77th District Tournament in 1943. May's Lick and Fleming County were the only two teams in the district due to wartime redistricting.[601]

William "Teence" Ryan was hired to teach physical education and coach the basketball team at the new Mason County High School. It would be Ryan's fifth school in five years. After two coaching stints at Tollesboro, Ryan coached Minerva in the 1957-58 season, Mt. Orab, Ohio, in 1958-59 and New Richmond, Ohio, in 1959-60.

A county-wide committee was formed to come up with a nickname for the sports teams at the new high school. The board of education accepted the committee's recommendation of Royals. Royal blue and white were selected as the school colors.[602]

Mason County played its home games in the Washington School gymnasium. The Royals' first game was at home against Owingsville on November 8, 1960. That was Election Day with John F. Kennedy being elected President of the United States. Richard Nixon carried Mason County and the state of Kentucky. The Royals rallied from a 12-point deficit and won, 44-43. The *Public Ledger* wrote "the team exhibited far better coordination, than had been anticipated."[603] Larry Jones led Mason County in scoring with 14 points.

Mason County lost to Bracken County 56-52 in Brooksville and defeated Augusta 84-64 at home. The Royals lost to the Deming Black Devils 70-49 in Mt. Olivet. Deming was coached by Jesse Amburgey, the last coach at May's Lick. Amburgey had resigned from Mason County soon after Ryan was hired.[604]

Larry Jones scored 34 points to lead Mason County to a 79-58 win over Tollesboro – the first of 13 consecutive victories.

The winning streak included several close games. The Royals edged Pendleton County 54-53.

St. Patrick led 16-11 at the end of the first quarter and 30-28 at halftime, but Mason County rallied to win 64-59 in the first game between the two schools. Jones scored a game-high 20 points, while Joe Greenwell was St. Patrick's leading scorer with 16.[605]

In the next game, Mason County and Bracken County were tied at 60-all at the end of regulation. Both teams scored four points in the overtime period. Rusty Ryan, the coach's son, made a field goal in the sudden death overtime to give the Royals a 66-64 victory. Ryan scored 28 points and Jones added 22. David Hause scored 28 for Bracken County.

Gerald King, a transfer from Maysville, became eligible for the January 24th game against the Augusta Panthers in Augusta. King scored 17 points in the Royals' 84-44 victory.

Mason County was 15-2 heading into the much anticipated game against the Maysville Bulldogs.

Maysville had played a difficult schedule and had a record of 11-5. The Bulldogs' losses were to Clark County, Louisville Flaget, Harrodsburg, Louisville St. Xavier and Ashland. Maysville was coming off a 92-58 victory over Olive Hill.

The Maysville gym was packed for the first game between Maysville and Mason County. The *Public Ledger* reported that fans were standing several deep long before the game started. Maysville led 19-13 at the end of the first quarter, 45-27 at halftime and 64-49 after three quarters. The Bulldogs' biggest lead was 20 points. The final score was Maysville, 82, Mason County 72. Maysville hit 33 of 54 from the field for 61.1 percent. Dwight Murphy scored a game-high 28 points for the Bulldogs on 14 of 18 from the field. Jones was Mason County's leading scorer with 21 points.[606]

Maysville won five of its last eight regular season games to run its record to 17-8.

Mason County bounced back from the loss to Maysville by closing out the regular season with seven straight wins including a 71-58 victory over St. Patrick. The Royals headed to postseason play with a 22-3 record.

The Bulldogs and Royals were in opposite brackets in the district

Public Ledger

Mason County's 1961 39th District champions.

tournament. Maysville defeated Tollesboro 66-32 in the first round and Fleming County 63-47 in the semifinals. Mason County drew a first round bye. The Royals routed St. Patrick 72-44 in the semifinals. The Paddies had a 13-13 record.

All tickets for the championship game between Maysville and Mason County at the Maysville gym were sold in advance.[607]

Mason County led 13-10 at the end of the first quarter and 21-17 at the half. The Bulldogs outscored the Royals 17-7 in the third quarter to lead 34-28. Maysville increased its lead to nine at 40-31 with less than six minutes left in the game. Mason County went on an 8-0 run to cut the Bulldogs' lead to one at 40-39. Maysville ended its scoring drought with two free throws to lead 42-39. Arlie Mitchell hit two free throws with 17 seconds left to get the Royals to within a point at 42-41. King intercepted a pass and made a layup to put Mason County ahead 43-42 with nine seconds on the clock. Maysville was unable to score in the closing seconds.[608] Mason County had pulled off the upset and won the district championship in its first season.

"The people in Maysville, who were hardcore basketball fans, almost to a person would have told you that there is no way that kids from Minerva, May's Lick and Orangeburg would ever beat Maysville," says Laurnie Caproni, former *Ledger Independent* sports editor. "That's exactly what they thought. They learned different quickly."

Larry Jones scored a game-high 16 points. Darrel Hill scored 12 points for Maysville before fouling out in the fourth quarter. Ryan also fouled out in the final period.[609]

Mason County played Bracken County in the first round of the 10th Region Tournament. The game was tied 55-all with 2:35 to play. Bracken County scored five straight points to lead 60-55. Ryan hit a long shot, and King made a free throw to cut the deficit to two, but James Linville sank two free throws with nine seconds to go to make the final score Bracken County 62, Mason County 58.[610]

The Royals ended their first season with a 24-4 record.

Rusty Ryan remembers how his dad molded that first Mason County team:

"He took a group of young men who the year before were, I wouldn't say hated rivals, but they didn't necessarily like each other… he had boys from Minerva, Orangeburg and May's Lick as his beginning, and then Jerry (King) and some of the people that couldn't make the team down in Maysville came out to be on our first team. So he took that group and our group, put 'em together, and we were competitive from day one. I mean we were good in the beginning; we were excellent at the end."[611]

Maysville rebounded from the loss in the district finals with a 71-53 victory over Scott County in the first round of the regional tournament. Hill scored 29 points, including 12 in the fourth quarter.[612]

Hill had another 29-point game in the Bulldogs' 59-50 victory over North Middletown in the semifinals. Hill scored 19 points in the first half.[613]

Maysville met Harrison County in the championship game on the Thoroughbreds' home court. Harrison County led 16-6 at the end of the first quarter. Maysville rallied to tie the game at 27-all and 29-all in the second quarter. The game was tied at 36-all in the third quarter and the Bulldogs went ahead at 38-36. The Thoroughbreds ended the quarter on a 6-1 run to lead 42-39. Maysville rallied once again and tied the game at 48-all. Harrison County answered with five straight points to lead 53-48. The Bulldogs cut the deficit to three at 57-54. Murphy hit a shot as time ran out to make the final score: Harrison County 57, Maysville 56. Donnie Tucker was the Bulldogs' leading scorer with 16 points. Hill was held to 12 points.[614]

Crum resigned to take the coaching job at Bowling Green. In six seasons as Maysville's head coach, Crum compiled a record of 160-42. He guided the Bulldogs to four district titles and three regional championships. Crum is Maysville's second-winningest coach behind Earle D. Jones.

Chapter 18 1961-62 Season

Former Bracken County High School and Eastern Kentucky State College star Larry Wood was hired to succeed Woodie Crum as the coach at Maysville.

Wood says he happened to be in the right place at the right time when Crum left Maysville.

Wood had ended his military service in April of 1961. He says legendary Maysville Coach Earle D. Jones, who was the Maysville Schools Superintendent at the time, and Wood's coach at Eastern Kentucky, Paul McBrayer were friends, and he thinks that had something to do with him getting the Maysville job.

The only coaching experience Wood had was one season as a graduate assistant at Eastern Kentucky.

After opening the 1961-62 season with a 76-65 road loss to the Clark County Cardinals, the Bulldogs won six straight games. Then, Maysville lost four games in row. The Bulldogs snapped the losing streak with a 78-74 win over Harrison County. Maysville had a record of 7-5 when they hosted the Mason County Royals.

Mason County was 11-2 and had won five straight games.

Maysville defeated Mason County 55-50. Dwight Murphy scored 19 points for the Bulldogs; Gerald King scored 19 for the Royals.

Maysville went 6-4 over the final 10 games of the regular season. George Davis scored 42 points in an 82-74 loss to Wheelwright.

Mason County closed out the regular season with a 10-game winning streak to run its record to 22-3.

Maysville defeated Fleming County 80-62 and Mason County was a 63-46 winner over St. Patrick in the semifinals of the district tournament. St. Patrick ended the season with an 8-21 record. Tom Donovan was the Paddies' leading scorer for the season. He had a career-high 32 points in a win over Vanceburg.

For the second straight year, Mason County avenged a regular season loss to Maysville by beating the Bulldogs in the championship game of the district tournament. King and Curtis Slater scored 20 points apiece to lead the Royals to a 56-46 win. George Greene was Maysville's leading scorer with 13 points.

Maysville drew the Bourbon County Colonels in the first round of the 10th Region Tournament. Bourbon County defeated Maysville 53-48 in the regular season. The regional tournament game went down to the wire. Bobby Hiles hit an 18-footer to put the Bulldogs ahead 62-61 with seven seconds left in the game. After a Bourbon County timeout, Jim Lemaster missed a long shot at the buzzer. Murphy scored a game-high 29 points.

Mason County, behind 22 points by King, defeated Paris 79-58 for the school's first win in regional tournament play.

Greene scored 23 points to lead Maysville past Scott County 71-53 in the upper bracket semifinal.

If Mason County could get past Harrison County in the lower bracket semifinal, the Royals and Bulldogs would meet in the championship game.

Freddy Warner hit two free throws to give Mason County the lead at 52-51. Keller Works made a layup to put Harrison County on top 53-52. The Royals had one last chance to regain the lead but committed a turnover.[615] Mason County ended the season with a 24-4 record.

It was Maysville vs. Harrison County in the 10th Region championship game for the second straight year. Maysville trailed 52-43 late in the third quarter. In the last two minutes of the quarter, the Bulldogs went on a 14-5 run to tie the game at 57-all. Harrison County went up 68-57 with 5:56 left in the game. The Bulldogs rallied to within two points- the last time at 76-74 on a crip shot by George Davis with nine seconds left. Bobby Jenkins hit two free throws to give Harrison County a four-point lead with three seconds to play. Harrison County Coach Charles "Jock" Sutherland made his players sit on the floor in the center circle so they would not commit a foul. The long inbounds pass went to Hiles who made a shot for the final two-point margin: Harrison County 78, Maysville 76. Works scored 32 points for the Thoroughbreds. Davis had 25 for the Bulldogs.[616]

Maysville had a record of 17-11 in Wood's first season as coach.

Chapter 19 Bulldogs Return to State

Maysville opened the 1962-63 season with 15 consecutive victories. The winning streak included victories over McDowell, Harrison County and Ashland in the Ashland Invitational Tournament. The Bulldogs, under second year coach Larry Wood, edged Ashland 78-76 in the championship game.

Wood says people in Ashland couldn't believe that a team like Maysville won the tournament.

"We went back two weeks later and beat 'em again," says Wood. "That was something the team and I were very proud of - that fact that we could go to Ashland twice in the same year and beat 'em twice."

Before the Bulldogs won that second game over Ashland, the season-opening winning streak had been snapped with an 88-63 road loss to Harrison County.

Maysville and Mason County both had impressive records heading into their annual regular season showdown. The Bulldogs were 17-1. Mason County was 13-1 and had an 11-game winning streak. The Royals' only loss was to Falmouth in the third game of the season.

Maysville edged Mason County 45-43.

Maysville won six of the last eight games in the regular season. The two losses were to Newport Catholic, 73-69 at home, and to Newport, 74-67, at Newport in the final game of the regular season.

Mason County bounced back from the loss to Maysville with five consecutive victories. The winning streak was snapped by a loss to Owingsville. The Royals closed out the regular season with back-to-back wins over St. Patrick and North Middletown.

Mason County drew a first round bye in the 39th District Tournament. The Royals' season came to an end with a 55-43 loss to the Fleming County Panthers in the semifinals. Teddy Purcell, a member of Mason County's first team in 1960-61 before transferring to Fleming County, scored a game-high 24 points for the Panthers.

Maysville also drew a first round bye. The Bulldogs played the St. Patrick Saints in the semifinals. St. Patrick's nickname was changed from Paddies to Saints during the season. The Saints had defeated Tollesboro 45-39 in the first round.

Maysville outscored St. Patrick 29-13 in the fourth quarter to win 81-51. George Davis led the Bulldogs with 21 points. Don Butler had 22 points and Robin Berry added 19 for the Saints who ended the season with an 8-17 record.

Maysville defeated Fleming County 74-50 in the championship game.

The Bulldogs played the Deming Black Devils in the first round of the 10th Region Tournament. Deming led 30-28 at halftime, but the Bulldogs outscored the Black Devils 21-10 in the third quarter and 25-17 in the fourth quarter for a 74-57 victory. All five starters scored in double figures with Davis leading the way with 17 points. Bill Breeze had 16, Greene 15, and Hiles and Murphy 13 apiece.[617] Breeze had moved into the starting lineup after Mike Hall was diagnosed with hepatitis in January.[618]

Maysville used another big second half to beat Scott County 76-53 in the semifinals. After leading by just a point at halftime, the Bulldogs outscored the Cardinals 17-9 in the third quarter and 29-15 in the fourth quarter. Murphy scored 25 points.[619] Hall returned to action for the first time since the win over Mason County on January 16.

The Bulldogs played the Bourbon County Colonels in the championship. The score was tied at 40-all at the end of the third quarter. With 2:07 left in the game, Maysville was up 47-45. The Bulldogs pulled away with eight straight points on a layup and four free throws by Davis and two free throws by Murphy. As the game wound down, Murphy made four more free throws, and Bourbon County hit four free throws to make the final score: Maysville 59, Bourbon County 49. Davis scored 21 points, Murphy 11 and Greene 10.[620] After two straight region runner-up finishes, Maysville was headed back to the state tournament.

The team rode atop a fire engine in a mile-long parade. Mayor Thomas "Tex" McDonald named Wood "Honorary Fire Chief" for the day and gave each player a tie clasp adorned with a symbolic key to the city.[621]

Maysville played the Clay County Tigers in the first round of the state tournament. The Bulldogs jumped out to leads of 12-3 and 18-6. Maysville was up 37-33 at the half, but the Tigers outscored the Bulldogs 22-11 in the third quarter to lead 55-48. Clay County led 65-52 with 4:46 left in the game. Murphy made two field goals, and Greene added a basket to cut the deficit to seven with 2:54 to play. Murphy hit a long shot to bring Maysville to within five. Clay County missed a couple of free throws, and Murphy scored again to cut the Tigers' lead to three at 65-62 with 1:08 remaining. Murphy came up with a steal, made a layup and was fouled with 1:08 to go. Murphy stepped up to the line with a chance to tie the game, but he missed.

Murphy fouled out with 46 seconds to play. Clay County missed the free throw. Hiles missed twice from the field. Clay County missed another free throw with 12 seconds to play. Hiles was fouled with five seconds showing on the clock. He made the front end of the one-and-one to tie the game at 65-all. After a Clay County timeout, Hiles sank the bonus free throw to give Maysville the lead. Clay County missed two shots in the closing seconds. The Bulldogs scored the final 14 points of the game to win 66-65. Murphy led the way 18 points, Greene had 15, Breeze 13 and Hiles 10. Pearl Hicks scored a game-high-31 points for Clay County, including 20 in the second half before fouling out with 3:36 left in the game.[622]

Hiles caught the eye of at least one college coach by making those pressure packed free throws.

"[An] assistant coach from Georgia Tech came to us after the game and said 'I'll take that kid right now,'" says Wood.

Maysville lost to eventual champion Louisville Seneca 78-60 in the quarterfinals. Seneca had a front line of six-foot-two and a-half, Mike Redd, six-foot-five Tom Duggins and six-foot-seven Wes Unseld. Redd scored 41 points against the Bulldogs. Unseld scored 15. Davis had 26 points for Maysville.

Wood says the Bulldogs were a very good team, "but we just didn't have any size to compete with that kind of size (Seneca) had."

Maysville ended the season with a 30-4 record. Davis was named to the all-tournament team.

Chapter 20 A Big New Gym

It would be a long wait for a return trip to the state tournament following Maysville's 10th Region championship in 1963. The rest of the decade brought a number of coaching changes for the local schools, several outstanding players and the construction of a huge gymnasium for Mason County High School that would add to the lore of the game.

The first coaching change took place at Mason County. The school's first coach, William "Teence" Ryan, resigned in 1963. In three seasons as the Royals' coach, Ryan compiled a record of 68-12 for a winning percentage of 85 percent. He guided Mason County to two district championships.

Mason County hired 26 year old Herb Childers Jr., a native of Burnside in Pulaski County. Childers began his teaching and coaching career at Burnside. After one year at Burnside, he was hired as the coach at Ferguson where he compiled a record of 87-35 in four seasons.[623]

Former Maysville baseball and basketball star Allen Smith was hired as Childers' assistant coach at Mason County.[624] Smith was a star pitcher at Louisiana State University. He was LSU's first All-America and was named All-Southeastern Conference in 1961 and 1962.[625]

Childers guided Mason County to the district championship in his first season. The Royals beat the St. Patrick Saints 56-34 in the first round of the district tournament. The Saints ended the season at 8-18. Mason County defeated Tollesboro 51-23 in the semifinals. The Royals beat the Fleming County Panthers 63-53 in the district finals, but former Mason County player Teddy Purcell scored 20 points to lead the Panthers to a 47-45 victory over the Royals in the first round of the 10th Region Tournament. Mason County ended the season with a 20-6 record.

The Maysville Bulldogs lost to Fleming County 74-48 in the semifinals of the district tournament to end the season with a 10-15 record – Maysville's first losing season since 1939-40 when the Bulldogs had to forfeit all of their wins because they had played an ineligible player.

The Mason County Fieldhouse opened during Childer's second

Mason County school officials wanted a big gymnasium, and the new high school Fieldhouse fit the bill: It had seating for 5,200 and could seat an additional 1,000 fans on the stage.

season as the Royals' coach. Voters in the Mason County school district approved a special annual school building tax by a mere 135 votes in a special election on Feb. 24, 1961. Voters had rejected the tax in four previous elections in less than seven years.[626]

Mason County school officials wanted a big gymnasium. Walter Worthington was chairman of the Mason County Board of Education at the time. He said the state wanted Mason County to build a gym with a capacity of 2,500, but Mason County fans and school officials wanted the new facility to be bigger than Harrison County's gym, which hosted the 10th Region Tournament.

After the special tax was approved, the school board voted three to two to use a seating capacity of 4,500 in the preliminary plans. Worthington and Vice-Chairman Ivan Mason voted against the motion. They thought the capacity should be 5,000.

"I figured if we didn't get bigger than 45-hundred, [the regional tournament]) would go back to Harrison County every other year," Worthington said.

Bids were advertised after the Maysville and Mason County school boards adopted a prevailing wage scale from $1.25 for common labor to $4.25 for bricklayers.[627]

The first bids for construction of the gym were rejected.[628] East

End Construction Company of Maysville was the winning bidder the second time around.[629]

The cost of the project, including the construction of an Industrial Arts building ended up costing $1.5 million dollars.

An open house was held on Jan. 10, 1965. Worthington cut the ribbon and more than 2,000 people toured the new gym[630] which became known as the Mason County Fieldhouse the following season.

"I thanked the school board, I thanked the people," Worthington said. "I thought [the gym] was one of best assets that's ever come to Mason County."

The gym had seating for 5,200, and 1,000 additional seats could be placed in the stage.[631]

A crowd estimated at between 2,000 and 2,500 attended Mason County's first game in the new gym on January 15, 1965. The Royals defeated Ripley, Ohio 82-63.[632]

Four nights later, Mason County defeated the Maysville Bulldogs 70-58 in front of a crowd estimated at 3,900.[633]

Maysville avenged the loss by beating Mason County 70-56 in the first round of the district tournament in the new gym. Maysville defeated Tollesboro 57-47 in the semifinals. University of Kentucky Coach Adolph Rupp attended the game to watch Hiles who scored 24 points and grabbed 18 rebounds.[634] The Bulldogs beat Fleming County 69-61 in the championship game. Maysville Coach Larry Wood says winning the first district tournament played in the new gym was one of the highlights of his time as the Bulldogs' coach.

The new Mason County gym hosted the 1965 10th Region Tournament.

Maysville and Fleming County met in the first round. Eugene Morton scored 22 points to lead the Bulldogs to a 76-60 victory. Maysville lost to Lexington Bryan Station, 86-61, in the semifinals. The Bulldogs ended the season with a 19-11 record.

Hiles led Maysville in scoring with an average of 20.8 points a game. He went to the University of Kentucky. After playing on the freshman team at UK, Hiles transferred to Morehead State University.

The St. Patrick Saints were winless (0-21) in 1964-65, and Fanny Stahl was fired as the coach. Stahl doesn't think it was the winless record that got him fired. He was only making $2,500 as the coach. He had opened a couple of pizza parlors and went into the wholesale beer business. He says whoever was in charge at St. Patrick did not like his business ventures.

"Thank God they got rid of me," Stahl says. "That was the best thing that ever happened to me."

Bill Forman, a 1959 graduate of St. Patrick was hired as the new coach. Forman, who played for Stahl, became a starter his freshmen season when four starters were injured in an automobile accident. For four years, Forman started every varsity game except one-when a knee injury caused him to sit out a game his senior season.

Forman played one season at St. Joseph's College in Indiana before transferring to Morehead State College. Forman says he stayed very close to the St. Patrick program while at Morehead and he accepted the Saints' coaching job when it became available.

"[I] violated all things I'd been taught in college about coaching," says Forman. "No. 1, you should never come back to your home school and coach. And No. 2, you should always start as an assistant coach and work your way up."

While he didn't have any coaching experience, Forman had learned a lot from Stahl.

"I watched what Fanny Stahl had done with defenses," says Forman. "And Fanny, in my opinion, started the match-up zone. I really believe that ... when he showed it to me I was in college. I didn't know what he was doing. He said 'What am I playing, is this man-to-man, is this zone, what is this?' And I couldn't really know. I kept saying 'Well, it looks like man-to-man, cause, you know, they're following the ball.' And then I'd say 'No, no, no, it's zone.' He just was having a ball with me. But I honestly believe that he was the one who really started the match-up zone."

Chapter 21 Marathon Game

Professional basketball came to Maysville for one night in the fall of 1965. The St. Louis Hawks defeated the Cincinnati Royals in an NBA exhibition in the Mason County Fieldhouse. Royals star Oscar Robertson had not signed his contract and did not make the trip to Maysville. Wayne Embry of the Royals and former University of Kentucky star Cliff Hagen, a member of the Hawks, did not play. Player-coach Rickie Guerin led St. Louis with 22 points. Adrian Smith was Cincinnati's top scorer with 21 points. Jack Twyman had 16, and Jerry Lucas scored 15. The crowd was estimated at 2,500.[635]

Less than two months later, the 1965-66 high school season got under way. The Mason County Royals beat the St. Patrick Saints 77-39. It was St. Patrick's 23rd consecutive loss going back to the first round of the 1964 district tournament.

The Saints snapped the losing streak with a 71-66 win over Belfast, Ohio. The players celebrated by throwing first-year coach Bill Forman into the shower.

St. Patrick made it two straight wins with an 81-52 victory over Sinking Springs, Ohio. John Stahl scored 41 points on 19 field goals and three of four from the free throw line to break the St. Patrick scoring record of 40 set by Stahl's uncle, Fran "Fanny" Stahl,[636] in 1950 and matched by James Whaley in 1954.

John Stahl didn't hold the record for long. Six games later, Bob Garey scored 42 points to lead St. Patrick to a 97-66 win over Belfast, Ohio. That win snapped a five-game losing streak.

The Saints won four of their next six games to run their record to 6-8. But St. Patrick had lost five straight games when they hosted the Millersburg Military Institute Cadets on February 9, 1966. That game turned out to be a nine overtime marathon.

Two things stand out for those who played in the game - the length of time it took for the game clock to wind down between the overtime periods and how the crowd got bigger as the game kept going.

The old clock in the St. Patrick gym had a sweep hand that started at eight minutes.

Steve Gallenstein, who scored 22 points in the game for St. Patrick, says the MMI coach wanted the horn to go off automatically when time expired instead of relying on the St. Patrick timer to sound the horn after three minutes. So the clock had to run down from the eight minute mark to the three minute mark before each overtime period began. That was a total of 45 minutes of down time.

"In between [the overtime periods], we not only sat on the bench and listened to instructions," said Gallenstein, "But sometimes I remember carrying on just conversations with the MMI players."

When the game started, there wasn't a very big crowd, but that changed as people who were listening to Don Stahl call the play-by-play on WFTM radio started showing up at the gym.

"MMI didn't bring much of a crowd, and we had several of our parents there, that was about it," says Forman. "By the time it was over, the gymnasium was full. People were standing, [it was] standing room only."

It was a long night for everybody. Stahl recalled that he got to the gym at about 6:15 p.m. and didn't get home until around midnight. He had to fill the five minutes between each overtime period in addition to doing the play-by-play of 59 minutes of game action.

John Stahl, who scored 25 points before fouling out in the third overtime, also remembers how the crowd kept getting bigger.

"In the overtimes, the place was just packed," said John Stahl.

Mike Walton was a sophomore sub for St. Patrick. He said he was at the end of the bench when the game started, and he kept moving up as his teammates fouled out. He eventually ended up sitting next to Coach Forman. Walton said he was "praying not to get in."

Garey led the Saints with 37 points before fouling out in the seventh overtime.

"I just absolutely loved to play," said Garey. "I could have played all night. I think [I would have] been a little tired, but it was fun. Our whole team just enjoyed playing."

The score was tied 74-74 at the end of regulation. Neither team scored in the third and fifth overtimes. The scores at the end of each of the first eight overtimes were: 78-78, 84-84, 84-84, 92-92, 97-97, 101-101, and 103-103. In the ninth overtime, Sonny James hit one of two free throws to give MMI the lead at 104-103. With one minute to play, Gordon Fields made a basket to give the Saints a one-point lead. Van Davis made a field goal to put the Cadets back in the lead at 106-105. St. Patrick missed its last three shots. The game was finally over at 11:30 p.m.

Gary Kidwell, a former coach and athletic director at Lewis County, was an assistant coach for MMI. He said the team had ordered hamburgers from the White Light restaurant, which was just down the street from the gym, and the managers picked up the order at the end of the third quarter. Needless to say, the burgers were cold by the time the game ended.

St. Patrick had a knack for playing long games. The Saints beat Fleming County 54-53 in a five-overtime game in 1963 and defeated MMI 86-84 in five overtimes in 1968.

Two nights after the nine-overtime game, St. Patrick snapped the six-game losing streak by beating Hazel Green Academy 77-75.

The Saints lost three of their last four regular season games and closed out the season with a 79-59 loss to the Lewis County Lions in the first round of the district tournament for a record of 8-18.

The Maysville Bulldogs lost to the Fleming County Panthers 51-41 in the semifinals of the district tournament to finish the season with a 10-15 record.

The Mason County Royals won the district tournament but lost to the Pendleton County Wildcats 69-58 in the first round of the regional tournament. Mason County's record was 15-12.

Maysville Coach Larry Wood resigned in March. In five seasons as the Bulldogs' coach, Wood had a record of 86-56. He guided Maysville to two district titles and one region championship.

Mason County Coach Herb Childers and his assistant coach, Bob Hall, both resigned in April. Childers had a record of 51-30 and the Royals won two district championships in his three seasons as the coach.

Chapter 22 New Coaches for MHS & MCHS

Both Mason County and Maysville hired new coaches in May 1966.

Jim Mitchell, a 36-year-old native of Lexington, was named the new coach of the Mason County Royals. Mitchell, a graduate of Eastern Kentucky State College, had coached at Vevay, Indiana, for three seasons. He had previously coached at Berea and Harrodsburg.

Maysville hired former Bulldog standout, 33-year-old Harlan "Fats" Tolle, as its new coach. Tolle was a senior on Maysville's 1950 10th Region championship team. He was a four-year varsity basketball player at Morehead State College and played one season of minor-league baseball. Tolle was the head coach at Tollesboro High School for three seasons. He says he had finished his third season as the coach at Lewisburg Elementary School when he got a call from his high school coach, Maysville Schools Superintendent Earle D. Jones.

"He called me one day and asked me if I would come talk to him, which I did," says Tolle. "And he asked me if I would be interested in coaching there, and I said, 'Yeah, I sure would.' So, he had me to come down to the board meeting one night with him and all the board members. So, they talked to me, and they asked me if I had anything to say. And I said a few words, and they hired me that very night."

Tolle's nickname during his youth and his playing days at Maysville was "Fatso." It was later shortened to "Fats." He says the nickname was a misnomer.

"When I was born, I was just a fat baby, a fat kid, and my uncle came in the hospital one day, and he saw me [and] said, 'There's O' Fatso,'" says Tolle. "And for some reason, it just stayed with me all of my life. I haven't been fat at all, [I've] never been fat."

Maysville opened the 1966-67 season with an 81-73 victory over Lewis County and then lost three straight games. The Bulldogs bounced back to win four consecutive games and seven of the next nine games for an 8-5 record heading into the game against Mason County.

The Royals were on a seven-game winning streak after going 3-5 in their first eight games, including a four-game losing streak.

Mason County beat Maysville 60-47. The Royals ran their winning streak to 16 games before losing to Bourbon County 59-58.

Mason County closed out the regular season with a win over Newport and a loss to Newport Catholic for a 20-7 record.

Maysville was 10-9 after a 75-54 loss to Pendleton County on February 4, but ended the regular season with five straight wins.

Mason County routed St. Patrick 98-59 in the first round of the 39th District Tournament. St. Patrick closed out its season with a 4-23 record.

Maysville topped Lewis County 82-62 in the first round.

In the semifinals, Mason County beat Fleming County 92-50, and Maysville was a 79-73 winner over Tollesboro.

Mason County defeated Maysville 80-60 in the championship game.

Maysville lost to Harrison County 64-53 in the first round of the 10th Region Tournament to end the season with a 17-11 record.

Mason County played the Pendleton County Wildcats in the first round of the regional. Pendleton County had defeated Mason County 75-70 in double overtime in the regular season game at the Mason County Fieldhouse, the same venue for the regional tournament.

The Royals got off to a fast start in the regional tournament game and led 20-12 at the end of the first quarter, 38-26 at the half, and 49-43 after three quarter. A fast break basket by freshman guard Ronnie Lyons gave Mason County a 63-60 lead with 50 seconds to play. But Pendleton County scored six straight points to lead 66-63. Mason County senior Fred Hester, who scored a game-high 29 points, made a shot at the buzzer to make the final score: Pendleton County 66, Mason County 65.[637] The Royals ended the season with a 23-8 record.

Mason County opened the 1967-68 season with six straight wins. After a 19-point loss to Tates Creek, the Royals reeled off nine consecutive victories including a 68-52 win over Maysville. Mason County averaged 83.3 points a game during the streak, which ended with a 60-56 loss at home to Harrison County.

The Royals put together another winning streak. A 77-55 victory over Meade Memorial was Mason County's fifth straight and ran the Royals' record to 20-2. But senior guard Tommy Corde, the team's leading scorer, suffered a back injury with only two minutes left in the game. Corde scored a game-high 27 points before getting hurt.[638]

Laurnie Caproni, former *Ledger Independent* sports editor, says Corde "Was another one of those players ... the best player people never heard about. Good lord, he was good."

Mason County's hopes for its first trip to the state tournament suffered a serious blow when senior center Gary Rosser fractured his right kneecap and tore ligaments in his right knee[639] in the first quarter of the next game- a 52-51 loss to Monticello. Rosser, who was averaging 10.8 points per game, would miss the rest of the season.

Corde was unable to play against Monticello, and he was still sidelined when the Royals lost to the Clark County Cardinals 57-55 in Winchester.

Corde returned to action against Bourbon County and scored 17 points to lead the Royals to a 54-46 victory.

Mason County beat Newport Catholic 82-69, but closed out the regular season with a 75-60 loss to Newport.

Mason County drew St. Patrick in the first round of the district tournament. The Saints had two eight-game losing streaks during the season and entered the game with a 6-20 record. Mason County had routed St. Patrick 83-43 back in December.

The Saints tried to hold the ball against the Royals in the tournament game. Mason County led 7-3 at the end of the first quarter, 15-5 at the half and 22-10 after three quarters. The Royals won 37-15. St. Patrick took only 16 shots from the field and made just four. The Saints were 7-of-8 on free throws. Mason County was 13-of-24 from the field and 11-of-14 on foul shots.[640]

Mason County played Maysville in the semifinals. The Bulldogs had drawn a first round bye.

Maysville won 10 of the first 11 games of the season. The Bulldogs scored 90 or more points in seven games including a 111-75 victory over Deming in the final game of the regular season.

Mason County led 36-25 with 2:32 left in the second quarter. Maysville scored the last eight points of the half to cut the Royals' lead to 36-33. Mason County was up 59-53 with 5:11 to play in the game. The Bulldogs rallied again to tie the score at 63-63. The Royals led 66-64 with 37 seconds to go and hit three free throws to win 69-64.[641]

Maysville ended the season with a 17-6 record.

Mason County defeated the Tollesboro Wildcats 84-59 in the championship game.

Lyons scored 23 points to lead the Royals past the Bourbon County Colonels 65-51 in the first round of the 10th Region Tournament.

Corde and Earl Black scored 19 points apiece as Mason County beat the Mt. Sterling Trojans 74-61 in the semifinals to set up a showdown against the Clark County Cardinals in the championship game.

Mason County led 18-12 at the end of the first quarter. Corde went to the bench in the second quarter with his third foul, but the Royals were up 35-31 at the half. Corde started the second half but picked up his fourth foul and went back to the bench with 6:50 left in the third quarter. The Royals were able to keep the lead and were up 48-44 heading into the final period. Corde checked back with 6:23 left in the game but fouled out 43 seconds later when he tried to stop six-foot-seven Ernest Gentry on drive. Mason County's lead was down to one at 54-53 with 5:01 to go. Clark County went ahead 56-54 on a three-point play by Mike Poer. Fred Overly tied the game at 56-56 with 3:12 left. Clark County answered with a 9-0 run to lead 65-56 with 26 seconds remaining. Mason County guard Wayne Burns hit a shot just before the buzzer to make the final score: Clark County 65, Mason County 58.[642]

The Royals and their fans were left to wonder what if Rosser had not suffered that season-ending injury and what if Corde had not been plagued by foul trouble in the championship game. He only played 13 minutes and 24 seconds. Mason County's record was 27-6.

Corde played at Ohio University. He was selected by the New York Knicks in the 8th round of the 1972 NBA Draft, but never played in NBA.

After two seasons as the Maysville coach, Tolle left to take the coaching job at Ripley, Ohio. Tolle's record at Maysville was 34-17.

Tom Creamer was hired to succeed Tolle. Creamer began his coaching career as an assistant football coach and an assistant basketball coach at Russell.

After two seasons at Russell, Creamer became the head football coach at Beechwood. He also served as the assistant coach for the basketball team. When the head coach of the basketball team moved to Cincinnati, Creamer took over as the head coach. He coached both the football and basketball teams for two seasons.

Creamer says a big postseason victory by Beechwood led to him coming to Maysville.

"We upset Covington Holmes in the district tournament [and] went to the region for the first time in a long time, and Earle Jones, the superintendent at Maysville, saw that in the *Kentucky Post* and called me and asked me to come up and interview for the job. And one of his statements was 'But I don't want you to have anything to do with football anymore.'"

Creamer says he was elated when he got the call because he knew about the Bulldogs' program, but his wife, Brenda, asked "Why Maysville?" "And I said 'Well, Maysville's been to the state tournament about as many times as anybody,'" says Creamer. "And she said, 'Let's go.'"

Maysville had a veteran team for the 1968-69 season. "That was a great bunch of kids, and they accepted me," says Creamer.

The Bulldogs had an 11-3 record and were on a nine-game winning streak heading to the game against Mason County. The Royals had opened the season with a 10-game winning streak and had a 15-2 record.

Harry Brooks and Gary McNutt scored 24 points each to lead the

Bulldogs to a 75-66 victory. It was Maysville's first win over Mason County since March of 1965. Lyons had a game-high 30 points for the Royals.

Maysville won its next three games. The 13-game winning streak was snapped by a 73-55 home loss to the Ashland Tomcats. The Bulldogs closed out the regular season by winning four of its last five games.

Two nights after losing to Maysville, Mason County hosted the Clark County Cardinals and lost 70-58. The Royals then reeled off four consecutive victories before losing to Monticello 87-69 despite a 31-point performance by Lyons. Mason County went 3-3 over the final six games of the regular season.

Maysville drew St. Patrick in the first round of the 39th District Tournament. The Saints had won 10 games. In the second win of the season, an 82-77 overtime victory over Augusta, St. Patrick senior Ward Blakefield scored 21 points and grabbed 34 rebounds.[643] Jim Joe Stahl had a game-high 29 points. In the next game, Blakefield had eight points and nine rebounds before suffering a badly sprained ankle in the second quarter of a 64-50 loss to St. Thomas.[644]

Jim Joe Stahl and Jim Sullivan were St. Patrick's leading scorers that season. Sullivan scored 36 points in a win over Deming in January.

Maysville beat St. Patrick 70-43 in the first round of the district tournament game. The Saints ended the season with a 10-20 record.

Maysville advanced to the semifinals to play Mason County. The Royals had a first-round bye.

Lyons scored 46 points to lead Mason County to a 72-66 win. Maysville closed out the season with a 20-5 record.

Mason County defeated the Lewis County Lions 79-59 in the championship game.

Mason County would not have home court advantage in the 10th Region Tournament. Kentucky High School Athletic Association Commissioner Ted Sanford approved Clark County as the site for the regional tournament. It was an unpopular decision in Mason County. The tournament had been held in the Mason County Fieldhouse since the big gymnasium opened 1965.

Mason County edged Mt. Sterling 65-64 in the first round and defeated Paris 76-59 in the semifinals.

The Clark County gymnasium was not big enough for the crowd that showed up for the championship game between Mason County and Clark County. 4,632 tickets were sold, and about 600 passes were used. Two-hundred people had to watch the game on closed circuit televisions.

Lyons was held to 16 points, and Mason County lost 85-57. The Royals ended the season with a 26-9 record.

Chapter 23 Ronnie Lyons Scorches the Nets

Ronnie Lyons poured in points for very good Mason County teams in his first three seasons on the varsity. He was the fifth leading scorer his freshmen season (8 points per game), the second leading scorer as a sophomore (12.1 ppg), and was the leading scorer his junior year (23.5 ppg). He took his scoring to a new level his senior season-1969-70.

Lyons scored 22 points in each of the Royals' first two games - a win over Lee County and a loss to Pendleton County.

He scored 33 points in each of the next two games - a victory over Tollesboro and a loss to Clay County.

Lyons pumped in 38 points to lead Mason County to an 84-79 win over Tates Creek.

He was held to six points in a loss to Bath County. That would be the last time he failed to score in double figures. In the next 10 games, he scored 37, 40, 31, 18, 24, 30, 31, 37, 25 and 38 points. Mason County's record was 9-7.

The Royals traveled to Winchester to play the Clark County Cardinals. Clark County had won the prestigious Louisville Invitational Tournament. Lyons scored 36 points, but Bobby Newell had 32 and Dale Cosby 21 to lead Clark County to a 95-68 victory over Mason County.

Lyons scored 30 points in a 10-point loss to Franklin County and 20 in a 40-point win over Raceland.

Mason County had a 10-9 record heading into the game against the Maysville Bulldogs. Maysville had a 3-11 record. The Bulldogs opened the season with a 94-58 win over Lewis County, then lost eight straight games.

Mason County jumped out to a 19-10 lead at the end of first quarter. Lyons hit five field goals in the first period, but he went from the 1:41 mark of the first period to 2:48 in the third quarter without a field goal. Maysville rallied and led 27-25 at the half and 42-36 after three quarters. The Bulldogs went on to win by the score of 59-55. Maysville had balanced scoring with four players in double figures. James Smith had 23 points, Homer Cablish and Paul King with 11 each and Ken Cunningham with 10. Lyons, with 26 points, was the only Mason County player in double figures.[645]

The Royals bounced back with a 61-52 win over Bracken County. Lyons led the way with 36 points.

Lyons fired in 45 points in an 83-57 victory over Fleming County. It was standing room only in the Fleming County gym, and many fans were turned away.

The Royals returned home for the next game, and Lyons had another 45-point game in a 77-66 loss to Portsmouth.

He scored 26 points in a 61-52 victory over University of Breckinridge.

In home games on back-to-back nights, Lyons scored 44 points in an 80-71 win over Middlesboro and broke his own Fieldhouse scoring record with 47 points in a 66-64 loss to Monticello. He hit 23 field goals in the Monticello game, including eight in a row in the second quarter and 10 in the fourth quarter.[646]

Lyons scored 38 points in a 71-63 win over Mt. Sterling and 45 in a 75-73 overtime loss to the Harlan Green Devils.

"He's by far the best guard I've seen," Harlan Coach George Francis said. "And it's not only shooting either. He plays defense, can handle the ball with best and for a little man he can go to the boards."[647]

Four nights later, Lyons fired in 60 points to lead the Royals to an 82-76 victory over the Bourbon County Colonels at Bourbon County. Lyons was 15-of-19 from the field in the first half. He had eight field goals in the first quarter, seven in the second, six in the third, and seven in the fourth. Mark Vice scored 10 points. Wayne Burns returned to the starting lineup for the first time January 6.[648]

Lyons scored 21 points in a 76-72 loss to Montgomery County.

The Royals closed out the regular season against Newport Catholic. Prior to the game it was announced that Lyon's jersey would be retired at the end of the season. He scored 35 points, but the Royals lost 90-66.

Mason County and Maysville were in opposite brackets in the district tournament.

Lyons scored 37 points to lead the Royals past Fleming County 70-47 in the first round.

Mason County played the Tollesboro Wildcats in the semifinals. The first quarter had a strange ending. The ball went out of bounds off Tollesboro. There was no time showing on the clock, and the teams headed to their respective benches. But it was decided that the buzzer had not sounded, so there was a fraction of a second remaining in the quarter. Lyons received the inbounds pass behind the center line and quickly launched a hook shot that hit nothing but the net. Lyons ended up with 40 points, and Mason County won 82-64.

Lyons fired in 37 points to lead the Royals past the Fleming County Panthers in the semifinals.

The Maysville Bulldogs, who had finished the regular season with a 7-18 record, defeated St. Patrick 77-56 in the first round of the district tournament. St. Patrick ended the year with a 9-14 record. The Bulldogs beat Lewis County 78-67 in the semifinals. It was Maysville vs. Mason County in the championship game.

The Mason County Fieldhouse was packed with 55-hundred fans. Mason County led 20-17 at the end of the first quarter and 24-21 early in the second quarter. The Royals pulled away when, during a six-minute stretch, Lyons hit 10 of 13 field goal attempts, including nine in a row and scored 25 points. Mason County led 55-34 at halftime. Maysville cut the deficit to 11 with 6:10 left in the game, but the Royals answered with 10 straight points and went on to win 87-68. It was Mason County's fifth straight district title. Lyons scored 48 points. He was 20 of 41 from the field. James "Skeet" Smith led Maysville with 25 points. Ken Cunningham added 20.[649]

The 10th Region Tournament returned to the Mason County Fieldhouse. Maysville lost to Paris 76-53 in the first round to end the season with a 9-20 record.

Mason County drew the Harrison County Thorobreds in the first round. Harrison County led 52-45 with 6:50 left in the game. But Mason County went on an 18-4 run to lead 63-56. The Thorobreds would get no closer than four as Mason County won 72-63. Lyons, who sat out the final 6:38 of the second quarter after picking up his third foul, scored 14 points in the fourth quarter and ended up with a game-high 27. Mike Corde had 19 and Wayne Burns added 17.[650]

Mason County faced tournament favorite and two-time defending champion Clark County in the semifinals. Clark County was up 36-29 with 2:50 to play in the second quarter. But Lyons scored 12 points on four consecutive free throws and four straight field goals during a 14-7 run, and the Royals went to the locker room at halftime with a 43-39 lead. Mason County led by as many as nine in the third quarter, but the Cardinals closed the gap to 62-59 at the end of the quarter. Clark County opened the final quarter with a 17-7 run to lead 76-69 with 4:10 left. Mason County scored six straight points to get to within one.

Clark County scored on an offensive follow, but Burns hit back-to-back shots to give the Royals a 79-78 lead with 2:12 to go.

Two consecutive baskets by Lynn Hopewell and Bobby Newell gave the Cardinals a three-point lead. Tommy Greene scored on an offensive follow and Mason County was only down one at 82-81 with 56 seconds left.

Danny Neely made one of two free throws to give Clark County a two-point lead with 50 seconds showing on the clock. Denny Barbour sank a 15-footer to tie the game at 83-all with 38 seconds left.

Newell was fouled with 19 seconds to go and sank both free throws to put Clark County up 85-83.

Lyons did not get to take the potential game-tying shot. Corde received the inbounds, drove into front court and missed a shot in the lane. Hopewell grabbed the rebound and Clark County ran out the clock.

Mason County's season and Lyons' illustrious high school career were over. Mason County's record was 20-16. Lyons scored 1,216 points in his senior season and had 2,621 career points.

Lyons scored 14 points, as the U.S. All-Stars, coached by Mason County coach Jim Mitchell, beat the Pennsylvania All-Stars 87-81 in the Dapper Dan Classic in Pittsburgh.[651] At the time, the Dapper Dan Classic was the most prestigious high school all-star game in the country.

Lyons was named to every all-state team, but the Mr. Basketball Award went to Robert Brooks of Richmond Madison.

Brooks and Lyons were teammates on the Kentucky All-Star team in the annual series against the Indiana All-Stars. Lyons played less than five minutes and scored two points on one of two shots in the first game in Louisville.[652]

A week later in the rematch in Indianapolis, Lyons scored 22 points on 9 of 17 from the field and four of six from the free throw line. Indiana won both games.[653]

Lyons was a three-year starter at the University of Kentucky. He was a sophomore when the career of Coach Adolph Rupp came to end with a 73-54 loss to Florida State in the NCAA Tournament.

Chapter 24 1970-71 Season

As the 1970-71 season approached the Maysville Bulldogs and Coach Tom Creamer were looking to bounce back from a losing season. The team's two leading scorers from the previous year, James Smith and Paul King, were now juniors. The Bulldogs also had a sophomore by the name of Fred "Bubbles" Walker. "His talent was unlimited," says Creamer.

The question at Mason County was how would the Royals fare after the graduation of Ronnie Lyons, Wayne Burns and four other players from the 1969-70 team.

Maysville had a record of 11-3 and Mason County sported a 12-5 mark when the rivals met at the Mason County Fieldhouse in January. The crowd was listed at 4,500. Denny Barbour scored a game-high 25 points to lead Mason County to a 69-67 victory.

Maysville routed Lewis County 83-55 in the first round of the district tournament. The Bulldogs breezed past St. Patrick 80-30 in the semifinals. The Saints closed out the season with a 9-18 record. Mason County defeated Fleming County 98-63 in the other semifinal.

A crowd of 5,000 was on hand for the championship game. The score was tied at 43-43 at halftime. The Bulldogs outscored the Royals 18-5 in the third quarter and went on to win 84-66. It was Maysville's first district title since 1965. Smith scored 36 points on 13 of 18 from the field and 10 of 13 from the free throw line. He scored 25 points in the first half.[654]

Smith scored 30 points as Maysville routed Bourbon County 74-46 in the first round of the 10th Region Tournament. Mason County beat Bracken County 69-65 in the first round. In the semifinals, Mason County edged Harrison County 63-61, and Maysville was upset by Pendleton County 69-68. Maysville closed out the season with a 23-7 record.

Once again, Mason County was just one win away from that elusive first trip to the state tournament.

Mason County led Pendleton County 44-36 at halftime, but lost 80-79. The Royals missed the front end of the one-and-one, a technical free throw, and a field goal attempt in the closing seconds.[655] Mason County was the region runner-up for the third time in four years. The Royals closed out the season with a 26-10 record.

Chapter 25 Bulldogs Pull Off Huge Upset

Maysville and Mason County both had the nucleus of their teams back for the 1971-72 season.

Maysville opened the season with a 103-28 romp over the Augusta Panthers. The Bulldogs beat Clark County 71-57 and Paris 83-52 and were tied with Hazard for sixth place in the first Associated Press poll of the season.[656]

Maysville ran its season-opening winning streak to five games with lopsided victories over Fleming County (90-71) and Mt. Sterling (65-41), and moved up from seventh to third in *The Courier-Journal* Litkenhous ratings. James Smith scored 30 points in the win over Fleming County.

The winning streak came to end with a 58-54 road loss to Newport Catholic.

Maysville won its next two games and headed to the Ashland Invitational Tournament with a 7-1 record. The Bulldogs were No. 4 in the AP poll.[657]

Smith scored 29 points to lead the Bulldogs to an 80-67 win over Betsy Lane in the first round of the Ashland Invitational. The Bulldogs edged Russell 66-64 in the semifinals. Maysville was No. 2 in the Litkenhous ratings, No. 3 in the AP poll and No.5 in the United Press International poll.[658]

Maysville lost to the Ashland Tomcats 70-55 in the championship game. Smith and Fred Walker were named to the all-tournament team.

The Bulldogs won their next three games and were 12-2 when they headed up the U.S. 68 hill to play Mason County.

The Royals had won 11 straight games and had a 14-2 record. During one six-game stretch, Mason County averaged 93 points a game.

In a 97-89 win over Covington Catholic, Mike Corde scored 35 points and the Royals made 45 of 54 free throws including 25 of 27 in the fourth quarter (12 in the final two minutes).[659]

Maysville lead 21-20 at the end of the first quarter and 45-36 at halftime. Mason County was up 56-54 after three quarters. Walker's tip-in tied the game at 56-56. Mason County scored six straight points to lead 62-56. Smith suffered a knee injury and was carried off the floor with 1:03 to go and Mason County up 74-65. The Royals went on to win 77-67. Walker had a game-high 24 points. Kenny Ross was Mason County's leading scorer with 18.[660]

Smith sat out Maysville's next three games but the Bulldogs defeated Pikeville, West Carter and Rowan County.

Smith returned to action in a home game against Johnson Central. Walker scored 34 points and Smith 31 to lead the Bulldogs to a 92-68 win. Walker and Smith combined for 26 rebounds.[661]

The Bulldogs' four-game winning streak was snapped by an 84-71 road loss to the Ashland Tomcats.

Mason County kept on winning. The Royals followed up the victory over Maysville with wins over Clark County and Bracken County.

Mason County traveled to Newport to play Newport Catholic, the team that had handed Maysville its first loss back in December. The Royals won 82-78 in overtime. Barbour hit 19 of 19 free throws and scored 35 points. Mason County made 32 of 34 free throws.[662]

Mason County beat University of Breckinridge 77-61 in Morehead before returning to the Mason County Fieldhouse for a three-game homestand.

A 61-49 victory over Middlesboro on February 4 ran Mason County's record to 20-2 and the winning streak to 17 games.

The next night Larry Lofton scored 23 points to lead the Royals to a 91-80 win over Monticello. It was the fourth time Mason County had scored 90 or more points in a game that season.

Mason County made its first appearance in the AP poll at No. 9 on February 8.[663] That night, Barbour fired in 25 points in the Royals' 87-53 victory over Mt. Sterling.

The Royals ran their winning streak to 20 games with a 74-50 victory over Portsmouth Clay in Portsmouth. Barbour suffered a slight concussion in the game and did not play in the next game- a 63-60 victory over Estill County.[664]

Bill Harding suffered a knee injury in the Estill County game and was carried off the floor. David Danner had suffered a broken wrist in practice the previous week.[665]

Barbour returned to action against Fleming County and the Royals beat the Panthers 76-61.

Mason County closed out the regular season with wins over Bourbon County, Montgomery County and Hazard for a sparkling 28-2 record and extended their winning streak to 25 games.

Maysville bounced back from the loss to Ashland with a 98-60 win over West Hardin. Smith had a game-high 25 points. It was the fourth game in which the Bulldogs had scored 90 or more points that season.

Walker scored 17 points in the first quarter and 23 of his game-high 25 points in the first half to lead Maysville to an 81-67 victory over Richmond Madison.[666]

The Bulldogs cruised to an 87-41 win over Nicholas County for their third consecutive win and their seventh in the eight games since the loss to Mason County.

The winning streak ended with an 80-66 loss to Holy Cross.

In the final game of the regular season, Smith scored a season-high 33 points to lead Maysville to an 89-82 victory over Covington Catholic. The Bulldogs were headed to postseason play with a 20-5 record.

Maysville and Mason County were in opposite brackets in the district tournament. The Bulldogs routed Tollesboro 107-60 in the first round and advanced to the semifinals to play St. Patrick. The Saints of Coach Bill Forman had won 10 games in the regular season. One of those victories was a 75-59 upset of Bourbon County at Bourbon County. John Schumacher scored a career-high 39 points despite having the flu.

"I didn't think he would play," says Forman. "He warmed up, and I asked him, I said, 'You wanna try it?' and he said, 'Ah let me give it a try.' And he did. And I would take him out and rest him as I could, but he was just on fire, not only from his temperature from the flu, but he was on fire with the basketball."

St. Patrick was no match for Maysville in the district tournament semifinal game. The Bulldogs routed the Saints 95-51. St. Patrick ended the season with a 10-17 record.

Mason County drew a first round bye and breezed past Fleming County 98-63 in the semifinals.

The crowd was estimated at 5,000 for the district championship game showdown between the Royals and the Bulldogs.[667]

Mason County led 51-45 with 3:45 left in the third quarter, but Maysville ended the quarter on a 17-4 run to lead 61-55. The Bulldogs led 79-67 with 3:22 to play. Mason County got to within three at 81-78 with 1:41 to go, but could get no closer. Maysville won 88-80 snapping Mason County's 26-game winning streak. Jay Hall came off the bench to score a career-high 23 points for Maysville. Smith tossed in 22. Corde had a game-high 24 points for Mason County.[668]

Smith scored 24 points and Walker 23 to lead Maysville past Bourbon County 75-59 in the first round of the 10th Region Tournament.

Mason County drew Paris in the first round. Paris led 31-26 with 6:39 to left in the third quarter, but the Royals went on a 30-8 run and won 68-56. Corde scored 14 points in a six-minute stretch in the second half and ended up with a team-high 19 points.[669] It was Mason County's 30th win of the season.

One more win by each team would set up a region championship game between Maysville and Mason County. Maysville played Clark County in the upper bracket semifinal. The upset-minded Cardinals opened the third quarter with a 9-2 run to lead 48-43. Then, Walker picked up his fourth foul with 5:29 left in the period. But Maysville rallied with six straight points to regain the lead. The Bulldogs pulled away in the fourth quarter for an 82-64 victory. Smith led the way with 23 points; King had 20.[670]

The lower bracket semifinal pitted Mason County against its old nemesis Pendleton County. Mason County led 34-19 with 2:45 to go in the second quarter. During one stretch, the Wildcats went 5:43 without a field goal. But Pendleton County put together a furious rally and cut Mason County's lead to 39-34 at the end of the first half. Pendleton County scored the first six points of the third quarter to take the lead at 40-39. The Wildcats led by 14 midway through the fourth quarter. Mason County got to within 81-78 with 1:58, but Pendleton County pulled out an 88-84 win.[671] It was the fourth straight time the Wildcats had defeated the Royals in regional tournament games. Mason County closed out the season with a 30-4 record.

Smith scored 28 points and Walker added 27, including 13 in the first quarter, to lead Maysville to a 93-74 win over Pendleton County in the championship game. The Bulldogs outscored the Wildcats 42-25 in the second half.[672] It was Maysville's first 10th Region title since 1963.

The team traveled to the state tournament in Louisville in cars instead of a bus. Creamer says on the way to the hotel, they drove up to Freedom Hall, and the players got out and looked in the doors.

Maysville faced Christian County in the first round of the state tournament. The Bulldogs trailed by nine early in the game, and Walker went to the bench with three fouls with 1:39 to play in the first quarter. Maysville was behind 19-13 at the end of the first quarter. The game was tied 35-35 at halftime. Christian County led 41-39 early in the third quarter, but the Bulldogs ended the quarter on a 20-8 run to lead by 10. The Colonels drew to 67-61 with four minutes left, but Maysville answered a 7-0 run and won 85-74. King scored a game-high 23 points, Smith added 21.[673]

Maysville was a huge underdog to top ranked Louisville Central in the quarterfinals.

Creamer received a phone call from George Unseld, a high school assistant coach in Louisville.

"He said, 'Tom, I've seen your team play, and if I can tell you a few things, I can help you beat Central.' Well I couldn't believe it. I said 'Sure.'"

Creamer recalls Unseld giving him three tips for beating the Yellowjackets, "He said, 'Central's so quick, that tell your boys that when they're going to pass the ball fake a pass to the right and reverse it to the left because Central is so quick, as soon as you act like you're going to throw it to the right, they move to the right.' Okay, that was one thing. And we just killed them on that. We made a fake, [then] took it up the other side of the floor. Okay, Number two, 'When you cross the over and back line, don't stop. Tell your kids to go right to the basket. Because most teams when they get it across the over and back line, they're so flabbergasted that they beat the press that they let Central get in behind them again and set their defense up. Don't let them do that; go right to the basket.' So we did. And then, the third thing was, 'You got two officials, and most the time when Central scores, the two officials head down the floor - one on the left and one on the right. And they don't see Central trapping you up in the full court and hacking you on the arms. Tell the officials to stay down the floor.'"

"Well, we started the game; Central got three quick fouls, and it just kind of demoralized them. We called it *Reverse;* we took in to the right and took back to the left and took it right to the basket."

Central jumped out to a 5-0 lead, but Maysville was up 23-15 at the end of the first quarter. Even though King was on the bench with four fouls, the Bulldogs had a 10-point lead with 6:25 left in the half. Walker picked up his third foul and joined King on the bench with 4:44 to go in the half. Central pulled to within four at 34-30 with 2:54 remaining in the half. The Bulldogs answered with an 7-2 run on a 10-footer from Tony Humphrey, two free throws by Mark Turner, a tip-in by Jay Hall and foul shot from Steve King to lead 41-32 at halftime. Walker played only 1:42 in the third quarter after picking up his fourth foul, but the Bulldogs had increased the lead to 59-45 at the end of the third quarter. Central would get no closer than 11 in the final quarter. The final score was Maysville 83, Central 70. Walker scored a game-high 21 points. Paul King had 15, Smith 14 and Steve King 11.[674]

Maysville played the Elizabethtown Panthers in the semifinals. Both teams started off with red hot shooting. The Bulldogs made eight of their first 13 shots. The Panthers connected on nine of their first 14 shots. There were four ties and 10 lead changes in the first quarter which ended with the score tied 20-20. E-town led 40-34 at the half and 61-52 after three quarters. There were five ties and 17 lead changes in the game before Elizabethtown moved out to a 71-60 lead with just over five minutes left in the game. Walker fouled out with 4:33 to play. Maysville cut the deficit to two at 73-71 with 2:30 to go. But the Panthers were able to hang on for an 83-79 victory. Elizabethtown shot 62 percent from the field in the game.[675]

"They were good and they had corner shooters, and we played a

The Ledger Independent

Front row (L-R): Steve King, Gary Mallory, Mitch Thomas, Mark Turner, Karl Commodore. Back row: Paul King, Terry Gilbert, Jay Hall, James Smith, Tony Humphries, Fred Walker and Mike Brookins.

1-3-1 [zone] and that hurt us," says Creamer. "And that was the one thing that I think taught me a lesson in coaching basketball – you gotta be prepared for certain things. I could not get my kids to play a 2-3 zone because they were so used to playing the 1-3-1 [zone]. We played that 1-3-1 for two years in a row for these kids because they were good at it and they go out there and trap. And so I tried to change them to a 2-3 zone."

Creamer had not seen Elizabethtown play until the state tournament. He says he watched the Panthers play Russell in an "up and down game."

"I didn't see that much shooting out of them other than short jumpers and layups," says Creamer. "So when we went to a 1-3-1 zone, they kicked it to the corner, and they got some wide open shots, and they really hurt us."

Smith scored a game-high 32-points and was named to the all-tournament team. The Bulldogs ended the season with a 28-6 record.

In a pre-game interview with WFTM radio play-by-play man Don Stahl before the state championship game, E-town Coach Ray Vencil said "I think we beat the best team in the tournament when we beat Maysville this afternoon." [676]

Elizabethtown lost to Owensboro 71-63 in the state championship game.

Chapter 26 A Controversial Loss at State

Bill Forman stepped down as the St. Patrick coach following the 1971-72 season. He had gone back to school at Xavier University and received a master's degree in school counseling. He left St. Patrick to start the guidance counseling program at Maysville High School. He was the baseball coach at Maysville for one season.

The new coach at St. Patrick was twenty-two year old Gary McKinney, a 1968 graduate of Bracken County High School and a 1972 graduate of Morehead State University.

The Saints opened the season with seven straight losses and lost 12 of their first 14 games. St. Patrick sophomore Tim Purdon had four 30-point scoring games including a season-high 36-point performance against Tollesboro.

St. Patrick lost to Fleming County in the district tournament to finish the season at 9-18.

Maysville lost five key players from the 1972 state semifinalist team to graduation-starters James Smith, Paul King and Steve King, and top subs Jay Hall and Mike Brookins.

The Bulldogs opened the season with five consecutive wins as Fred Walker took his game to a new level. He averaged 24.2 points a game in those five games.

The winning streak was snapped by a 78-76 overtime loss to Newport Catholic at home.

Walker scored 37 points in a 69-51 win over Covington Holmes.

The Bulldogs beat Pikeville 67-61 and headed to the Ashland Invitational Tournament with a 7-1 record.

Maysville defeated Breathitt County and Louisville St. Xavier in the first two games in the tournament, but lost to top ranked Bryan Station 68-65 in overtime in the championship game. Walker, Tony Humphrey and Mark Turner were named to the all-tournament team.

Walker only played one and half quarters due to foul trouble and was held to five points in a 61-58 loss to Covington Holy Cross.[677]

Maysville snapped the two-game losing skid with an 87-78 victory over Fleming County.

Harrison County edged Maysville 69-67 in overtime in Cynthiana. Walker scored 24 of his game-high 34 points in the first half. It was the

Bulldogs' third loss in four games.[678]

Maysville bounced back with six straight wins. The winning streak started with a 75-41 rout over the Mason County Royals. It was no contest. The Bulldogs led 19-6 at the end of the first quarter, 33-16 at the half and 44-20 after three quarters. Walker scored a game-high 25 points. The loss dropped Mason County's record to 5-11.

Four nights later, Maysville, playing without Tony Humphrey who had the flu, beat Pendleton County 63-55 in Falmouth. Walker scored 14 of his 29 points in the third quarter.[679]

Walker scored 27 points, and Turner added 24 in a 96-64 win over Rowan County.[680]

The Bulldogs traveled to eastern Kentucky for two games. Walker poured in a school record 43 points in an 82-56 win over Paintsville. Humphrey scored 31 to lead Maysville to a 74-60 victory over Johnson Central.[681]

Walker had a 30-point game in an 81-62 win over Bracken County.[682]

The Bulldogs had a balanced scoring attack in a 69-43 win over Lexington Catholic. Walker scored 22 points, Humphrey 14 and Turner 12.[683]

The winning streak came to end with a 68-56 road loss to Richmond Madison. Walker scored 24 points.[684]

Robert Mayhall scored 33 points to lead Middlesboro past Maysville 72-64 in Middlesboro. Walker had 26 points.[685]

The Bulldogs broke the two-game losing streak with a 77-72 victory over Bath County. All five starters scored in double figures. Walker scored 26 points, Turner 15, Bucky Greene 12, Humphrey 11 and Terry Gilbert 10.[686]

Humphrey scored 34 points including 15 of Maysville's 16 fourth quarter points to lead the Bulldogs to a 67-63 win over Ashland.[687]

Walker scored 26 points as the Bulldogs closed out the regular season with a 100-76 victory over Covington Catholic. It was Maysville's 20th win of the season.[688]

Maysville and Mason County drew first round byes in the 39th District Tournament and met in the semifinals. Mason County had won three of its last five regular season games after snapping an 11-game losing streak.

Walker scored a game-high 26 points to lead the Bulldogs past the Royals 72-52. The loss gave Mason County an 8-21 record- the school's first losing season.

In the other semifinal, Fleming County beat St. Patrick 59-46. The Saints' record was 9-14.

Maysville trailed Fleming County 42-34 with 3:54 left in the third quarter of the district championship game. The Bulldogs went on an

18-0 run on the way to a 76-61 victory. Humphrey scored 30 points, and Walker added 22.[689]

The Bulldogs got off to a fast start against the Clark County Cardinals in the first round of the 10th Region Tournament. Maysville led 23-7 at the end of the first quarter and 29-9 with 6:16 left in the half. Clark County rallied and the Bulldogs' lead was down to six at 37-31 at halftime. There were three ties in the third quarter. Maysville led 55-53 heading into the fourth quarter. The Cardinals tied the game at 55-55. Maysville scored eight straight points to lead 63-55 with 6:12 to play. Clark County cut it to 65-62, but the Bulldogs answered with a 6-0 run and ended up winning, 77-68. Walker had 28 points and Humphrey scored 24.[690]

Maysville played the Harrison County Thorobreds in the semifinals. Harrison County led 14-12 at the end of the first quarter. Maysville was up 30-28 at the half and 50-39 after three quarters. The Thorobreds closed to within three at 62-59 with 2:02 to go and 64-61 with 1:18 left. Bucky Greene pushed the lead back out to five by sinking two free throws with 1:03 remaining. Walker hit a layup with 18 seconds left to make it 68-61. The Bulldogs won 68-63. Walker scored 27 points.[691]

It was Maysville vs. Fleming County in the championship game. Fleming County had upset Bath County 66-64 in the first round and routed Bourbon County 84-62 in the semifinals.

Fleming County missed its first 11 shots from the field and Maysville led 17-10 at the end of the first quarter. The Bulldogs were up 37-30 at the half and 57-52 after three quarters. The Bulldogs led by as many as 18 in the final period and won 82-71. Walker scored 24 points, Humphrey 18, Turner 14, and Greene 10. [692]

Maysville met Lee County in the first round of the state tournament. The Bulldogs trailed by as many as nine in the first half, but rallied to lead 31-29 at halftime.

Maysville had a 45-36 lead with 3:30 to play in the third quarter. Lee County drew to 47-42, but Walker scored five straight points on a free throw and two field goals to push the lead out to 10. Walker went to the bench with four fouls at the end of the third quarter. When he returned to the game, Maysville had an eight-point lead. Walker hit a jump shot and layup to make the score 68-56. Humphrey hit a turnaround shot in the lane to push the lead to 14. The final score: Maysville 76, Lee County 65. Walker fired in 30 points. Humphrey scored 16 and Turner 14.[693]

Maysville jumped out to a 34-17 lead in the second quarter of its quarterfinal round game against Hickman County. The Bulldogs went to the locker room at halftime with a 36-20 lead. But Maysville opened the third quarter with four consecutive turnovers. Hickman County outscored Maysville 17-6 in the third quarter to cut the Bulldogs lead to five at 42-37. Hickman County came all the way back. There were ties at 48, 50, 52, 54, 56 and 58. Hickman County led 60-58 and Maysville had the ball as the fourth quarter was winding down. With 10 seconds left, Turner hit a 20-footer to send the game to overtime. Hickman County, playing for the last shot with the score tied 63-63 in the overtime period, turned the ball over. Maysville got the last shot, but missed. Walker gave the Bulldogs the lead at 65-63 with 2:30 left in the second overtime. Ricky Weatherspoon tied it at 65-all. Both teams had a chance to take the lead but missed the front end of the one-and-one- Maysville with 90 seconds to go and Hickman County with 49 seconds left. The Bulldogs committed a turnover with five seconds remaining. Weatherspoon missed a last second shot, but Greene was called for a foul. It was controversial call. Weatherspoon went to the free throw line with no time left. He made both free throws to give Hickman County a 67-65 win.

Creamer says a week after the state tournament he received a call from a man who captured the final play on film from his seat at midcourt about 10 rows from the floor.

"He said it showed where Bucky Greene was about four or five feet from the man with the ball, and when the man with ball (Weatherspoon) went up to shoot, the ball flipped out of his hand, and the referee down behind Bucky Greene, who could not see the foul, called the foul."

The man with the camera told Creamer that Greene was three or four feet from Weatherspoon when the foul was called.

"Bucky told me he never touched him," says Creamer. "And [of] course, we shouldn't have lost that lead either."

Walker, who was named to the all-tournament team, scored 25 points. Turner scored 16 points on eight of 10 field goals. Greene added 10 points.[694] Maysville ended the season with a 26-7 record. Walker is fifth on the Bulldogs' all-time scoring list with 1,630 points. Creamer says Walker's talent "was unlimited." Walker was a star at Pikeville College.

Chapter 27 Another Heartbreaking Loss for MCHS; Girls' Basketball Returns

The first losing season in school history prompted a coaching change at Mason County in the spring of 1973. Mason County Schools Superintendent Charles Straub recommended that Jim Mitchell be relieved of his coaching duties. The school board voted 3-2 against the recommendation. However, under state law at the time, no one could be hired without the recommendation of the Superintendent. Straub delivered a letter to Mitchell informing him of his dismissal as a coach. Mitchell had tenure and could not be fired as teacher. Mitchell submitted his resignation as coach at a special school board meeting and announced that he would continue teaching at Mason County.[695]

A month later, Mitchell was hired as the basketball coach and Athletic Director at Southwestern High School in Indiana.[696]

In seven seasons at Mason County, Mitchell compiled a 160-74 record. His teams won four district championships.

Twenty-six coaches applied for the Mason County job. Thirty-one year old Gary Jefferson, an assistant coach at Mason County for season years, was hired as the Royals' head coach on June 18.[697]

Mason County had a 14-14 record in the regular season in 1973-74. A highlight of the regular season for the Royals was a come-from-behind win over the Maysville Bulldogs. Mason County trailed by 11 in the first half and by nine in the second half, but rallied to win 58-56.[698]

The Royals beat Tollesboro 73-48 in the first round of the 39th District Tournament.

Maysville and Fleming County drew first round byes and met in the semifinals. Maysville entered the district tournament with a 15-9 record. Kirby Bennett, the fourth leading scorer on the team missed eight of the final 10 games of the regular season[699] with a bad back.[700]

Fleming County had defeated Maysville 74-71 in the regular season game in Flemingsburg.

The Panthers led by as many as 13 in the district tournament game. The Bulldogs rallied and led 55-54 with 2:06 left in the game, but Fleming County answered with eight straight points and won 64-57.[701]

Mason County downed the St. Patrick Saints 60-39 in the other semifinal game. Tim Purdon scored a game-high for the Saints who ended the season with a 14-15 record. Purdon averaged 28.7 points and 14 rebounds a game. He had 14 30-point games during the season, including 38 against Tollesboro.

It was Mason County versus Fleming County in the district championship game. The Panthers had edged the Royals 72-70 in the regular season game in Flemingsburg in December.

Fleming County was trying to win its first district title since 1956. The Panthers led by 11 in the second quarter. Mason County got to within 52-48 with 6:30 remaining in the game. Fleming County pushed the lead out to 61-50. The Royals cut it to 61-54, but the Panthers hit four free throws and a field goal to lead 67-54. Fleming County went on to win 71-59.[702]

Mason County drew the Bracken County Polar Bears in the first round of the 10th Region Tournament and had a 47-33 lead after three quarters. Bracken County rallied to tie the game at 52-52 with 52 seconds to go. The Polar Bears got the ball back and played for the last shot. Bracken County missed a shot and made a putback, but the officials ruled the buzzer had sounded and the basket did not count. Tony Breeze made a driving layup with six seconds to go in overtime to give the Royals a 56-54 victory.[703]

Mason County defeated Bourbon County 58-49 in the semifinals and advanced to the championship game to play Fleming County once again.

Five-thousand, 884 fans jammed the Mason County Fieldhouse for the game.

Fleming County jumped out to a 17-6 lead and was up 17-12 at the end of the first quarter and 34-30 at halftime. Mason County took its first lead at 36-34 with 6:22 left in the third quarter and had a 52-48 lead at the end of the quarter. The Royals were up 60-50 with 6:15 to play. Mason County went into a stall, but it didn't work. Fleming County went on a 16-7 run to cut the Royals' lead to one at 67-66. Tony Brewer became the third Panther to foul out with 19 seconds to play. He was replaced by Bill Brown. Mason County missed the front end of the one-and-one, and Mike Flaugher hit an eight-footer give Fleming County the lead at 68-67 with 11 seconds to play, Dale Horner hit driving layup to put Mason County back in front with three seconds showing on the clock. But Horner was called for a charge. The basket counted, but Brown swished two free throws to give Fleming County the lead at 70-69. Horner's desperation shot at the buzzer missed and Mason County had another heartbreaking loss in the region championship game. The Royals had seven turnovers in the fourth quarter. Their record in the first year under Jefferson was 18-16.

After six seasons as Maysville's coach, Tom Creamer resigned to become the basketball coach and Athletic Director at Danville High School.[704]

"I was principal and basketball coach at Maysville, and it was getting pretty hectic," says Creamer. "Girls' basketball was just coming into play and causing me to have more challenges, so I felt like it was a good time for me [to leave]. And Danville was a tremendous school system, but they were all football, and I knew that when I went there."

Creamer moved from Danville to Shelby County. He guided the Rockets to the 1978 state championship.

Creamer had a 121-56 record at Maysville. His teams won four district titles and two region championships.

Maysville hired 39 year old Lyle Dunbar as its new coach. Dunbar was a graduate of Temple Hill High School near Glasgow. He was a three-year starter at Kentucky Wesleyan where he was a teammate of Kentucky High School basketball legend "King" Kelly Coleman. Dunbar had a 185-72 record in nine seasons as the coach at Scottsville. His teams won three district titles, and the 1973-74 season team was the 4th Region runner-up with a 29-4 record. Before going to Scottsville, Dunbar was the head coach at Fordsville and West Hopkins.[705]

Dunbar says he was going to retire from coaching after the 1973-74 season, but while he was working as an insurance adjuster and attending a tobacco meeting, he heard about the coaching vacancy at Maysville "I went and applied and got the job, so I took it kinda late I guess."[706]

Maysville started three freshmen-Cere Myrick, Eddie Davis and Tim Gilbert-in the 1974-75 season and had a 14-12 record in the regular season.

The Mason County Royals went 14-16 in the regular season.

The St. Patrick Saints had the best record in town- a 19-10 regular season mark.

St. Patrick senior Tim Purdon averaged 29.3 points and 12 rebounds a game. He scored 30 or more points in 17 games. Purdon fired in 47 points in an 81-54 home victory over Nicholas County and 42 points in a 67-61 road win over Bishop Brossart.

In one seven-game stretch late in the season, Purdon averaged 33 points a game.

The 1974-75 season marked the return of girls' high school basketball in Kentucky after a 43-year absence.

Helen Smoot, the Foreign Language teacher at Maysville High School, was named the head coach of the Lady Bulldogs. Phyllis Mahan, a Business teacher at Mason County High School, was the Lady Royals' first coach. Maysville and Mason County met twice during the regular season with the Lady Bulldogs winning both games - 44-28 in the Mason County Fieldhouse and 48-46 in the Maysville Gym.

The boys' and girls' 39th District Tournaments were both played at the Mason County Fieldhouse.

St. Patrick and Mason County met in the first round of the boys' tournament. Purdon was held to nine points and the Royals beat the Saints 50-33. Purdon ended his high school career with 2,315 points. He is St. Patrick's all-time leading scorer. Purdon was named to the All-Catholic All-American Team.[707] He signed to play for Pikeville College but ended up going to Morehead State University and did not play college basketball.

Maysville and Fleming County drew first round byes and met in the semifinals. The Panthers edged the Bulldogs 73-70. There was a brawl right after the game. It started when two adults allegedly led a charge at the game officials as they left the playing floor. The police tried to provide a wall of protection for the officials, but the crowd broke through. The officials escaped unharmed, but fights ensued on the playing floor, in the area to the left of the stage and outside the gym.

"It was mass confusion," said Mason County Sheriff Charles Brodt told *The Ledger Independent*. "I was wedged against the stage and couldn't move." Brodt said the melee, "lasted about 45 minutes."[708]

Two Fleming County female students required medical treatment.

The Maysville and Fleming County girls' teams were scheduled to meet in the girls' district tournament the night after the brawl, but the game was postponed until the next day with special provisions in place.

The game started at 1 p.m., and only the coaches, players, tournament personnel, the press and a crew from radio station WFTM were allowed in the Mason County Fieldhouse.[709]

Fleming County had lost to Mason County 43-20 in the girls' district opener earlier in the week. Mason County senior Paula Fay scored 20 points to match Fleming County's total. There were only three teams in the girls' district and the format called for the first round loser to play Maysville, which drew a bye.

In a shocking upset, Fleming County edged Maysville 32-29. Maysville had routed Fleming County three times during the regular season by the scores of 53-24, 58-24 and 68-29.

Mason County was the district champion by virtue of its win over Fleming County in the opening of game of the district tournament. Fleming County was the runner-up and Maysville's season was over.

Maysville, which won eight of its first 10 games, ended the season with an 11-8 record.

"My girls started the season strong and then, midway through the schedule, they sort of left down and didn't play well together," Smoot said. "It's been all downhill since January."[710]

Mason County defeated Fleming County 58-51 in the championship game of the boys' tournament. It was the Royals' first district title since 1970.

The Royals beat Paris 83-79 in the first round of the 10th Region Tournament, but lost to Bath County 66-59 in the semifinals. Mason County's record was 18-17.

The Mason County girls topped Augusta 50-30 in the first round of the regional tournament, but lost to Clark County 56-32 in the semifinals to end their first season with a 10-6 record.

In April, Kentucky High School Athletic Association Commissioner Billy Joe Mansfield announced that the Maysville boys' basketball program was suspended until January 1, 1976 as a result of the brawl after Maysville's loss to Fleming County in the district tournament. Fleming County received a "severe warning" because of the action of by some of its fans.[711]

Basketball remained in the news throughout the summer as several coaching changes took place before the next season began.

Chapter 28 Mason County Hires Allen Feldhaus

The Mason County Board of Education, following the recommendation of Superintendent Charles Straub, voted unanimously not to rehire Gary Jefferson as the boys' basketball coach in May 1975.[712]

In two seasons as the Royals' head coach, Jefferson had a record of 36-33 with one district championship.

In late May, 46 year old Pete Gill was hired as the Mason County coach. Gill, a graduate of New Albany High School in Indiana and Georgetown College, had 18 years of coaching experience on the high school level including the past four seasons at Georgetown High School. He also coached three years in the service and had a combined record of 400-139.[713]

Gill conducted basketball clinics in the Mason County Fieldhouse that summer, but resigned as the coach in July. Gill had agreed to move his family to Maysville, but personal reasons kept him from doing so. Gill's letter of resignation said the decision was made "in the interests of both parties."[714]

The story about Gill's resignation appeared in *The Ledger Independent* on July 21. That night, Lyle Dunbar resigned as the Maysville coach and former Fleming County Coach Bob Hall was named as his successor.[715]

Dunbar was heading back to western Kentucky to coach at Christian County.

"The job came open at Christian County, and Christian County was in the state tournament that year, [and] had some awfully good athletes. And I wasn't really looking for a job, but it came open, and I was asked to come down and apply for it. And it was just a real opportunity for me to get back to my family, my parents number one, and it [was[such a big program and a good program."[716]

It had been a trying few months for Hall. The Fleming County Board of Education had voted 3 to 1 to dismiss him as the Panthers' coach. But some 3,000 people signed a petition in favor of Hall, and 450 people turned out for the April 23 school board meeting. The school board voted 3 to 1 with one board member abstaining to reinstate Hall.[717]

Then, in June, Hall resigned as the Fleming County coach and appeared to be headed to North Hardin. But Hall, citing personal reasons, turned down the North Hardin job and said he would probably stay out of coaching for a year.[718] He had a change of heart when the Maysville coaching position became available.

The 1975-76 school year was fast approaching and Mason County did not have a coach. Thirty-five year old Allen Feldhaus, a former University of Kentucky basketball and baseball player, first heard about the Mason County job from Sam Grayson of Maysville at a softball game in August. Feldhaus, who had a state job in Frankfort after coaching 10 seasons at Russell County, told Grayson he was not interested. That night Mason County Superintendent Charles Straub called Feldhaus. "I said I don't think I'm interested," recalls Feldhaus. "And he said, 'Would you talk to me?' And I said, 'Well, I tell you, I'm going to Mt. Olivet tomorrow.' I had to go to Mt. Olivet; that was part of my job. And I said, 'How far is Mt. Olivet from Maysville?' He said, 'About 20 or 25 minutes.' And I had to be in Mt. Olivet it was like at noon. And I thought I'll kill the rest of the day. So I just said, 'I'll drive over there."

Feldhaus and Straub met in the board of education offices. Straub offered him the job on the spot. "I said, 'Nah, I don't know," recalls Feldhaus.

When Feldhaus went home that night, his boys said they wished he would get back into coaching. Feldhaus took the job the next day.

Feldhaus, a three-sport star at Boone County High School, played two seasons of minor league baseball in the Washington Senators organization. He had several connections to Maysville and Mason County. Feldhaus played basketball against Maysville in back-to-back seasons. He scored 12 points in a 72-44 loss to the Bulldogs in 1957 and had 36 points in a 66-57 win over Maysville in 1958. Feldhaus hit a home run off Maysville ace Allen Smith in the finals of the 9th Region baseball tournament in 1958. Feldhaus and Smith were roommates for the Kentucky-Indiana All-Star basketball games. Feldhaus says Maysville coach Woodie Crum was responsible for him making the Kentucky All-Star team. Crum was an assistant coach for the 1958 Kentucky All-Stars. Feldhaus brought his Russell County basketball team to the Mason County Fieldhouse in 1970.

There was one more coaching change. Bob Hutchison succeeded Phyllis Mahan as the coach of the Mason County girls' team. Hutchison was a member of Maysville's 1958 state championship baseball team and also played basketball at MHS. He had coached the boys' basketball teams at Lewisburg Elementary School and the Mason County Middle School.

The Mason County girls lost the first two games of the season before reeling off 10 consecutive victories. After back-to-back losses to Harrison County and Bracken County, the Royals ("Lady" had not yet been added to the nickname for the girls' team) closed out the regular season with six straight wins.

Terri Brown scored 31 points to lead Mason County to a 69-63 victory over the Fleming County in the semifinals of the district tournament.

Mason County defeated Maysville 58-38 in the district championship game.

Maysville lost to Bracken County 64-49 in the first round of the 10th Region Tournament at Clark County to end the season with a 7-17 record.

Mason County beat Pendleton County 45-33 in the first round and Bath County 38-35 in the overtime in the semifinals to advance to the championship game against Bracken County.

Mason County and Bracken County had split the two regular season games.

Brown scored 23 points and Mason County beat Bracken County 63-51. The Mason County girls were going to state in just their second season. "They wanted to win," says Hutchison. "They'd done anything to win."

Mason County was ranked 16th in the field of 16 teams in the state tournament at Eastern Kentucky University.[719]

Mason County's starters were Kay Riggs, Marcella Chambers, Susan Hickerson, Terri Brown and Nancy Landers.

Mason County faced a tall Caldwell County team in the first round and led by 13 in the third quarter. Caldwell County rallied to take a 38-36 in the fourth quarter. The game was tied at 38, 40, and 42. Mason County scored the final 10 points of the game to win 52-42. Brown had a game-high 21 points. She scored 10 points in the fourth quarter including six in the final 1:30.[720]

In the quarterfinals against Jenkins, the Royals led 11-9 at the end of the first quarter, but trailed 23-15 at halftime. Mason County drew to 25-22, but Jenkins answered and pushed its lead out to 12 points. The Royals rallied once again, tied the game at 44-all on a basket by Brown with 10 seconds to play to force overtime. Mason County scored the first four points of the extra period, but a 7 to 3 run by Jenkins tied the score at 51-51, and the game went to a second overtime time. Jenkins took a 53-51 lead, but the Royals scored the final six points on two baskets by Brown and one from Chambers to win 57-53.[721] Brown scored 27 points and Hickerson added 15.

Mason County lost to Louisville Butler 62-41 in the semifinals. Butler led 15-6 at the end of the first quarter, 30-12 at the half and 47-25 after three quarters.[722] "We ran into a buzzsaw," says Hutchison.

Brown scored 14 points and was named to the All-Tournament Team. Landers scored 11 points. The loss snapped Mason County's 13-game winning streak. The girls' final record was 23-5.

The Maysville Bulldogs won the 1976 district tournament, but lost in the semifinals of the 10th Region Tournament and had a 17-8 record. The Mason County Royals were the district runners-up and also lost in the region semifinals to finish the season with a 15-19 record. The St. Patrick Saints lost in the first round of the district tournament and had a 5-24 record.

The St. Patrick Saints had a new coach for the 1976-77 season. Lex Turner took over for Gary McKinney. Turner had planned on teaching at Maysville and assisting with the basketball team. "I never really had any thoughts of being a head coach," says Turner. But the teacher Turner was going to replace at Maysville decided not to retire two straight years. When St. Patrick called, Turner took the job. Turner guided the Saints to an 11-10 record in the regular season. St. Patrick edged Tollesboro 73-72 in overtime in the semifinals of the 39th District Tournament to earn their first berth in the regional tournament since 1960.

The winter of 1977 was brutal with heavy snows and temperatures as low as 25 below zero. The Ohio River froze.

Due to a shortage of natural gas, the schools had to turn down their thermostats.

It was about 55 degrees in the Maysville gym when the Bulldogs hosted the Bourbon County Colonels on February 5. The temperature was up to 59 degrees at halftime.[723]

Mason County took the gas conservation measures even farther. The Fieldhouse was closed in early February. The pipes and boilers were drained and cut off.[724] The Royals played their final nine regular season games on the road.

For the first time since the Fieldhouse opened in 1965, Mason County and Maysville faced off in the Maysville gym. The Bulldogs won 69-66.

Maysville went 10-1 in the month of February. Mason County bounced back from the loss to Maysville with a 58-48 win over Fleming County and then lost the last seven games of the regular season.

Maysville beat Mason County 67-53 in the first round of the 39th District Tournament, which was held in the reopened Mason County Fieldhouse. The Royals final record was 7-11.

In the semifinals, Maysville defeated Fleming County 64-56 and St. Patrick edged Tollesboro 73-72 in overtime to earn a berth in the regional tournament for first time since 1960 and just the fourth time in the history of the program.

Maysville beat St. Patrick 85-53 in the championship game.

St. Patrick lost to Harrison County 57-46 in the first round of the 10th Region Tournament to end its first season under Turner with a 12-12 record.

Cere Myrick scored 21 points to lead Maysville past Clark County 62-50 in the first round of the regional tournament.

Myrick scored 25 points, and Timmy Gilbert added 20 as the Bulldogs beat Paris in the semifinals.

The Bulldogs lost to Bath County 72-71 in the championship game. Bruce Jones scored a game-high 37 points for Bath County. Gilbert scored 22 points for the Bulldogs who ended the season at 17-8.

In girls' basketball, Mason County beat Maysville 66-50 in the district championship game, and advanced to the championship game of the regional tournament, but lost to Paris 51-42. The Maysville girls had a 9-12 record. The Mason County girls finished the season at 17-5.

Chapter 29 Back to State for the Bulldogs

Expectations were high for Coach Bob Hall's Maysville Bulldogs heading to the 1977-78 season. Cere Myrick, Eddie Davis and Tim Gilbert, starters since their freshmen season, were back for their senior year and one last run at a 10th Region title. The three veterans were joined in the starting lineup by Barry Kirk and Tony Jones.

The Bulldogs won the Russell Invitational Tournament but ended the 1977 portion of the schedule with a 4-4 record. Two of the losses were to Henry Clay.

Maysville won the inaugural Burley Invitational Tournament at the Mason County Fieldhouse with victories over Paris, Pendleton County and Mason County.

The Bulldogs lost their next three games to Covington Holmes, Bourbon County and Covington Holy Cross. Myrick scored a career-high 35 points in the 86-82 loss to Covington Holy Cross.

Myrick scored 31 points as Maysville snapped the losing streak with an 81-72 win over Virgie. Myrick popped in 29 points in an 81-69 victory Montgomery County. A 71-67 road loss to Covington Catholic dropped the Bulldogs' record to 10-8. Maysville closed out the regular season with five consecutive wins.

Maysville defeated the St. Patrick Saints 73-55 in the first round of the 39th District Tournament. St. Patrick ended the season with a 12-10 record.

The Bulldogs cruised past Fleming County 83-54 in the semifinals to advance to the championship game against the Mason County Royals. Mason County, after going 16-6 in the regular season, drew a first round bye and defeated Tollesboro 75-59 in the semifinals.

Maysville had defeated Mason County 81-73 in the championship game of the Burley Invitational Tournament.

In the district championship game, the Bulldogs led 52-42 with 5:11 to play. The Royals rallied with a 13-3 run to tie the game and force overtime. Mason County took a 61-60 lead with 1:04 left in the extra period - the Royals' first lead since the second period, but Maysville ended the game on a 7-2 run to win 66-63. Myrick scored a game-high 24 points. Dean scored seven of his 10 points in overtime.[725]

Maysville jumped out to a 14-2 lead midway through the first quarter and beat Estill County 71-54 in the first round of the 10th Region Tournament. The Bulldogs shot 70 percent from the field in the first quarter and 60 percent in the first half. Myrick led the way with 21 points.

Mason County edged Pendleton County 59-58 in the first round.

Myrick, who spent most of the first half on the bench, scored 16 of his 18 points in the second half to lead Maysville to a 60-57 victory over Bourbon County in the semifinals. In the other semifinal, the Paris Greyhounds beat the Mason County Royals 74-65. Mason County ended the season with an 18-8 record.

It was Maysville vs. Paris in the championship game. The Bulldogs led 20-18 after the first quarter and 45-34 at halftime on the way to a 94-77 victory. Kirk had a game-high 21 points. Myrick added 19.

Maysville's first round opponent in the state tournament was Bowling Green. There were four ties in the first quarter. Bowling Green led 18-15 at the end of the first quarter. The Bulldogs took their first lead at 21-20 with 6:13 left in the second quarter. Bowling Green went on a 24-6 run to led 44-27 in the closing seconds of the half and led 44-29 at halftime. The Bulldogs rallied to close the gap to 57-54 at the end of the third quarter. Myrick, who scored 13 points in the third quarter, fouled out with 5:33 left in the game. Kirk hit a layup to tie the game at 68-68. Davis gave Maysville the lead at 70-69 with one minute to play. The Bulldogs had the ball and the lead, but Bowling Green junior Danny Carothers intercepted a cross court pass. Carothers drove to the basket, missed a layup, but got the rebound and made the putback to give the Purples the lead. Then, Maysville was called for charge. Carothers missed the free throw, but got the rebound, and Bowling Green killed the final 12 seconds for the win. Kirk was of 11 of 14 from the field and scored a game-high 27 points. Myrick had 17 and Davis added 15.[726]

Maysville ended the season with a 20-9 record.

Myrick is fourth on the Bulldog's all-time scoring list with 1,776 career points. He played one season at Austin Peay University before transferring to Georgetown College.

Mason County defeated Maysville 52-49 in the championship game of the girls' 1978 39th District Tournament. Both teams lost in the first round of the regional tournament. Maysville's record was 8-11. Mason County closed the year at 7-13.

Despite losing three starters to graduation, the Maysville Bulldogs had a regular season record of 22-4 in 1978-79. The Mason County Royals went 19-6 in the regular season. Maysville and Mason County split their two regular season games. The Royals edged the Bulldogs 48-46 in the championship game of the Burley Invitational Tournament. Ten days later, the Bulldogs won 71-70 in overtime.

The St. Patrick Saints, led by senior David Cooney and sophomore Jay Gast, lost eight of their first 10 games, then, won 12 of their last 13 regular season games. Cooney averaged 26.8 points a game and fired in a career-high 41 an 89-53 win over Augusta. Gast averaged 23.6 points and poured in 42 points in a 104-102 double overtime victory over Bishop Brossart. Turner says Cooney and Gast played on opposite wings, and "They were just hard to stop."

Maysville defeated Fleming County 60-53 in the first round of the 39th District Tournament.

St. Patrick drew a first round bye and lost to Tollesboro 72-67 to close out the season with a 14-10 record.

The other semifinal pitted Maysville against Mason County. The Royals had drawn a first round bye.

Mason County won 64-61. Barry Kirk had a game-high 24 points for the Bulldogs who ended the season with a 23-5 record.

Allen Feldhaus Jr. scored 23 points to lead the Royals to a 64-54 victory Tollesboro in the championship game.

Mason County advanced to the championship game of the 10th Region Tournament with double digit wins over Paris and Bracken County, but lost to Harrison County 66-54. It was the fifth time Mason County had lost in the region championship game. The Royals ended the season with a 23-7 record.

The Maysville girls won their first district championship since the return of girls' basketball when they beat Mason County 50-33 in the championship game of the 1979 tournament. It was Maysville's third win over Mason County that season.

Once again Maysville and Mason County lost in the first round of the girls' 10th Region Tournament. Maysville lost to Bourbon County 45-42 to finish with an 18-4 record. Mason County lost to Paris 67-34 and ended the season at 9-16.

Gast, who Turner calls a "once in a lifetime player," raised his scoring average to 33 points per game in the 1979-80 season. He scored 30 or more points in 18 games and 40 or more points in five games. Gast fired in 49 points in a 79-54 win over Augusta. He scored 37 points in a 76-67 loss to Fleming County in the semifinals of the district tournament. The Saints' final record was 11-13.

Maysville opened the season with 13 consecutive losses and finished the year at 4-20. It was the Bulldogs' first losing season since 1969-70.

Mason County went 21-5 in the regular season and won the district tournament with victories over Maysville and Fleming County. The Royals beat Bracken County in the first round of the 10th Region Tournament, but lost to Bourbon County in the semifinals to end the season at 24-6.

Chapter 30 Mason County Finally Goes to State

After back-to-back to 20-win seasons, the Mason County Royals headed into the 1980-81 season with three returning starters- seniors Allen Feldhaus Jr. and Charlie Jackson and junior Kelly Middleton. They were joined in the starting lineup by seniors Terry Jackson (Charlie's brother) and David Orme, the top reserves the previous season. That group had played together for years. Coach Allen Feldhaus was beginning his sixth season at Mason County so his system was in place.

The Royals won five of their first seven games. The two losses were to 10th Region opponents- 58-56 in double overtime to Nicholas County at home and 74-72 to Pendleton County in Falmouth. Allen Feldhaus Jr. scored 31 points in the loss to Pendleton County

Mason County followed the loss to Pendleton County with seven consecutive wins including two wins over the Maysville Bulldogs – 53-49 in the championship game of the Burley Invitational Tournament and 78-54 in the rematch 12 nights later as Middleton scored 28 points and Orme added 27.

The winning streak was snapped by a 60-51 loss to the Clark County Cardinals in Winchester.

The Royals bounced back with an 82-48 victory over Bracken County, but despite a 32-point game from Middleton, lost to Simon Kenton 71-69 in the first round of the 9th vs. 10th Region Tournament at Lloyd Memorial in Erlanger.

In the next game, Middleton scored 38 points to lead the Royals to a 77-55 win over University Breckinridge. Mason County won its next six games to finish the regular season with a 20-4 record.

Mason County and Maysville ended up in the same bracket in the 39th District Tournament. Mason County drew a first round bye, while Maysville drew Tollesboro in the first round,

The Bulldogs had closed out the regular season with three straight wins to improve its record to 15-10.

Maysville, a 92-61 winner over Tollesboro in the semifinals of the Burley Invitational Tournament, pulled out a 59-56 victory over the Wildcats in the district opener to advance to the semifinals against Mason County.

Mason County led 40-23 at the half and 54-37 after three quarters. Maysville rallied to cut the gap to 58-55 with 4:41 left in the game. The Royals pushed the lead back out to seven with 3:12 to go. The Bulldogs hit two shots late in the game, but Mason County held on for a 70-67 victory. Middleton scored a game-high 23 points. Charlie Jackson scored 18, Orme 12 and Feldhaus 11. Maysville, which ended the season at 16-11, was led by Shawn Commodore with 19. Steve Chambers and John Jackson added 18 apiece.

On the other side of the bracket, the St. Patrick Saints and the Fleming County Panthers drew first round byes and met in the semifinals.

St. Patrick, led by senior Jay Gast had compiled a 20-6 regular season record. Gast had continued his torrid scoring pace. He scored 35 points in the season opener, 33 against Tollesboro and 38 versus Bracken County.

Gast poured in 45 against Bishop Brossart. The Saints won the Dayton Invitational Tournament as Gast scored 34 in the semifinals and 31 in the championship game.

Gast scored 45 points in a one-point loss to Ripley. In three straight games against Tollesboro, University Breckinridge and Augusta in January, he scored 35, 32 and 35 points.

In the final two games of the regular season, Gast scored 31 points in a 104-46 victory over Augusta, and 42 in a 63-54 win over Paris.

St. Patrick had two regular season wins over Fleming County. But the Panthers avenged those losses with a 57-55 victory in the district semifinals. Gast scored a game-high 26 points. He finished his high school career with 2,239 points and is second on the Saints' all-time scoring list. Gast was named to the Kentucky All-Star team. He won three letters at the University of Toledo and led the Rockets in scoring his senior season. He was inducted into the University of Toledo Varsity "T" Hall of Fame in 2012.

Four Royals scored in double figures as Mason County routed Fleming County 92-69 in the championship game of the district tournament. Middleton scored 26 points, Charlie Jackson 20, Orme 18 and Feldhaus 15.

Mason County had a tougher than expected time with Deming in the first round of the 10th Region Tournament. Charlie Jackson scored 20 points to lead the Royals to a 53-44. Orme scored 16 and Feldhaus added 10.

The Royals defeated Montgomery County 50-42 in the semifinals. Feldhaus and Charlie Jackson scored 16 points apiece, and Middleton tossed 10.

Once again the Clark County Cardinals stood in the way of Mason County's first trip to the state tournament.

Mason County had won 11 straight games. Clark County had won five-straight and 11 of its last 12 games.

Middleton picked up his third foul and went to the bench with 2:49 left in the first quarter with Mason County leading 8-6. The score was tied at 14-14 at the end of the first quarter. Mason County led 35-28 at halftime and 46-40 after three quarters. The Royals were up 51-42 with 5:52 left. The Cardinals went on a 10-4 run to cut the deficit to three at 55-52 with only 35 seconds remaining. Longtime Mason County fans had too often seen the Royals lose leads in the regional tournament and suffer disappointing losses. That did not happen in 1981. Feldhaus hit two free throws with 24 seconds remaining. Middleton scored on a fast break layup with nine seconds to go, and Orme received a long pass and made a layup in the closing seconds. The final score: Mason County 61, Clark County 52. Mason County, in its 21st season, was finally going to state. Coach Feldhaus says he was "thrilled to death."

Orme scored a game-high 18 points. Middleton had 14 (all in the second half) and Feldhaus and Charlie Jackson added 12 apiece.

A parade was held for the team the next day. Maysville Mayor Bill Boggs proclaimed Wednesday, March 18, 1981 "Mason County Royals Day" in Maysville.[727]

Mason County faced the Shelby County Rockets in the state tournament at Rupp Arena in Lexington on March 18. Shelby County was coached by former Maysville Coach Tom Creamer. He had guided the Rockets to the 1978 state championship.

Mason County led 14-12 at the end of the first quarter. The score was tied at 22-22 at the half. Shelby County led 41-34 after three quarters. That's when Mason County Principal John Branson came out of the crowd waving a pom- pom. He led the cheers and fired up the Mason County crowd which was estimated at 3,000- one of the largest followings at the state tournament in years. The Royals responded to their fans cheers by going on a 9-2 run to tie the game at 43. Shelby County went back in front with a free throw, but Orme scored on an offensive follow, and Charlie Jackson came up with a steal and layup to give the Royals a 47-44. There were ties at 48, 50 and 52. Feldhaus was fouled with 16 seconds to play. He made the front end of the one-and-one to give Mason County a 53-52 lead. After Shelby County took a timeout, Feldhaus missed the bonus free throw. The Rockets got the rebound and quickly got the ball into front court. Shelby County got off two shots in the final seconds, but both rolled off the rimmed. The ball was tipped around and went out of bounds off Mason County. The buzzer had sounded, but it appeared the officials might put a second back on the block. But they quickly ruled the game was over. Mason County had pulled it out. "That ball could have gone in, and you never know how that would have affected your program," says Coach Feldhaus. Middleton led the Royals in scoring with 13 points. Feldhaus, Orme and Charlie Jackson each had 12.

Mason County was a huge underdog in the quarterfinal round against No.1 Bryan Station. The Defenders had routed Allen County-Scottsville 75-44 in the first round.

Bryan Station led 19-17 at the end of the first quarter. Mason County led 33-29 at the half and 47-44 after three quarters. The Defenders used a 12-6 run to take a 56-53 lead. The Royals answered with an 11-4 run to lead 64-60 with 1:21 to play. Bryan Station score to get to with two. Mason County held the ball, and Middleton was fouled with 18 seconds to go. He sank both free throws to make it 66-62. Bryan Station missed two shots; Orme got the rebound and was fouled with 10 second left. He hit both foul shots to give the Royals a six-point lead. The Defenders got a basket with three seconds to play, then, Orme was fouled with one second left. He hit one of two free throws to make the final score: Mason County 69, Bryan Station 64.

In the post game radio interview, Coach Feldhaus said, "It's just hard to believe a guy can be as proud of a bunch of guys as that bunch. But, my gosh, do they believe in themselves! And anything you tell them, they believe. And they can't spell quit."

Middleton led the Royals in scoring with 24 points. Feldhaus Jr. had 20 and Charlie Jackson 10.

Mason County made 31 of 33 free throws in a 79-54 win over the Mayfield Cardinals in the semifinals. Middleton scored 23 points, Feldhaus Jr. 16, Orme 15, and Charlie Jackson 10.

It was Mason County versus the Simon Kenton Pioneers in the state championship game. Mason County had won 16 straight games since losing to Simon Kenton on January 29.

Simon Kenton had won its first three games in the state tournament by a total of four points. The Royals were looking to become the first 10th Region team to win the state championship since Maysville in 1947. The Pioneers were trying to become the first 9th Region team to win a state title.

The paid attendance of 19,776 for the championship game broke the record for a high school crowd.

Mason County led 20-9 at the end of the first quarter and 35-25 at halftime. Coach Feldhaus had no idea intermission for the championship game was longer than usual.

"We go in [the locker room], we go through our same ritual, we go back on the floor and there's still 10 minutes on the clock," says Feldhaus. "And I think it was just a downer. I was dumbfounded. I didn't know what to do with them either. Do you take them back in? Do you restart again or you [do]take them, and you let them watch?

Gerald Orme

Mason County's 1981 team claimed the runner-up spot in the state tournament. The paid attendance of 19,776 for the championship game broke the record for a high school crowd.

What you do? That would be my fault. I should've, I guess, known, but nobody ever said anything to us about that extended halftime."

Simon Kenton started pounding the ball inside in the third quarter and led 47-46 at the end of the quarter. The Pioneers were up 59-48 with 4:15 left in the game. Mason County would get no closer than five. The final score was Simon Kenton 70, Mason County 63.

Middleton scored 20 points, Charlie Jackson 13, Orme 12, Feldhaus Jr. 11, Terry Jackson 6 and Mark Crawford 1.

"I always thought the difference in the ball game was David Dixon got in foul trouble in the first half," says Coach Feldhaus, "and [the] second half he wore us out; he wore us out on the boards and out run us up and down the floor. I remember twice he out run us up and down the floor and got layups. And I think his legs were just a little bit fresher than ours."

Dixon scored 18 points. Simon Kenton's sharpshooter, Troy McKinley, scored 17 points. McKinley's hot shooting in the state tournament earned him a scholarship to the University of Kentucky.

Middleton and Feldhaus Jr. were named to the all-tournament team. Feldhaus Jr. received the Ted Sanford Award. Mason County's record was 28-5. Another parade was held for the team when it returned to town, and a celebration was held at the Fieldhouse.

Allen Feldhaus Jr. was named to the Kentucky All-Star. He played at Eastern Kentucky University.

Chapter 31 25-0 Season for Royals; Historic Win for Saints

Kelly Middleton was the only returning starter from Mason County's 1981 state runner-up team. The new starters were Willie Feldhaus, Jeff Breeze, Gary Beiland and Dale Liles.

The Royals opened the 1981-82 season with an 80-72 upset victory over the Lexington Catholic Knights and kept winning and winning.

A 79-47 win over the Montgomery County Indians in the championship game of the Burley Invitational Tournament ran the Royals' record to 10-0.

In their next game, The Royals held off Paris 60-57 in the Southside Gym in Paris.

Pendleton County guard Talbert Turner fired in 36 points, but Mason County beat the Wildcats 67-61 at the Mason County Fieldhouse.

After a 62-45 victory over the Maysville Bulldogs, the Royals closed out a three-game homestand with a 63-60 win over Clark County.

Mason County won the Harrison County Invitational Tournament with victories over Grant County, Paris and Nicholas County.

Wins over University of Breckinridge, Lewis County and Tollesboro pushed the Royals' record to 20-0.

Middleton scored 22 points, and Beiland added 20 to lead the Royals past Fleming County 76-51.

Mason County traveled to Taylor County and came away with a 64-61 victory. Middleton led the Royals with 20 points.

Middleton scored 26 points and Feldhaus added 23 in a 79-69 victory over Bourbon County.

Feldhaus scored 22 points in a 53-28 win over Harrison County.

Middleton fired in 24 points as the Royals closed out the regular season with an 82-50 rout of Bath County for a 25-0 record- the first undefeated regular season in school history.

The perfect record surprised Mason County coach Allen Feldhaus.

"I thought that we would probably win 60 percent of our games," says Allen Feldhaus. The team was very superstitious. "They even had which one went out first and which one went out last," says Allen Feldhaus. He says he told the team all year long "You guys are not this good; you're not going to keep on winning." Allen Feldhaus says at the end of practice the players would beg him to let them go five more minutes on defense. "They were a unique group," says Allen Feldhaus. "Not many groups were going to do that."

In the opening game of the 39th District Tournament, the Tollesboro Wildcats edged the Maysville Bulldogs 55-52. Maysville ended the season with a 13-13 record.

In the opposite bracket, Mason County and Fleming County drew first round byes and met in the semifinals. Mason County was up by just three points with 2:05 to play. A three-point play by Willie Feldhaus gave the Royals a 48-42 lead. Middleton intercepted a pass and hit two free throws to push the lead out to eight with 1:05 left and Mason County won 57-46.

Kevin Pawsat scored 31 points to lead the St. Patrick Saints to a 74-51 win over Tollesboro in the other semifinal to earn a trip to the regional tournament. Pawsat was the latest prolific scorer for St. Patrick. He scored 30 or more points in six regular season games including 37 against University of Breckinridge.

"Jay [Gast] was probably our best player I ever had," says Turner. "But Kevin was the most dominating player I ever had. I mean teams, including Mason County, had to change their offense, they had to change their defense according to him, [to] try to avoid him one way or the other."

St. Patrick was having a fine season. The Saints had played Maysville in the regular season for the first time on February 11. St. Patrick led 14-12 at the end of the first quarter and 31-29 at the half. Maysville was up 46-43 after three quarters, and had a six-point lead early in the fourth quarter. St. Patrick rallied and led 55-52. Maysville tied it at 55 with 13 seconds to play. J.T. Williams hit a shot with two seconds to go to give the Saints the lead. A Maysville player took a time out, but the Bulldogs were out of timeouts and were assessed a technical foul. Williams hit the technical free throws and St. Patrick had its first-ever win over Maysville. The final score was 58-55.[728]

"There was a heck of celebration that night," says Turner. He recalled that during his first year at St. Patrick the fans had wished him good luck, but they also said "you're never going to beat Maysville."

Less than a month after the win over Maysville, the Saints were in the district championship game against the undefeated Royals.

Mason County led 11-4 at the end of the first quarter and 32-10 at halftime. St. Patrick went on an 18-6 run to close to 44-33 with 6:43 to play. But Middleton hit six free throws, and the Royals went on to win 63-50. Middleton had a game-high 31 points. Pawsat was the Saints' leading scorer with 18.[729] It was Mason County's third win of the season over St. Patrick.

Mason County routed Bracken County 74-26 in the first round of the 10th Region Tournament. The Royals were 10 of 16 from the field in the first quarter and 11 of 16 in the second quarter. Mason County led 43-10 at the half.[730]

St. Patrick played Augusta in the first round and trailed 40-34 after three quarters. The score was tied at 42, 44 and 46. Williams hit a shot to give the Saints a 48-46 lead with 2:01 to go. St. Patrick hit three free throws to extend the lead to five and went on to win 56-50. It was St. Patrick's first-ever win in the regional tournament. Pawsat scored a game-high 27 points.

The semifinal match-ups were Mason County against Clark County and St. Patrick versus Paris.

Mason County led 56-43 with 2:53 to play, but Clark County rallied. Jeff Thornberry hit a half-court shot at the buzzer to tie the game at 63 and force overtime. Clark County was leading 67-66 with 44 seconds left in the overtime period when Liles hit one of two free throws to tie the score. Clark County held the ball before taking a timeout with nine seconds to go. The Cardinals missed a shot in the lane and Middleton was fouled with two seconds remaining. He hit two free throws to give the Royals a 69-67 win.[731]

Paris had a nine-point lead over St. Patrick in the fourth quarter. The Saints closed to within 65-64, but Paris hit eight free throws to win 73-68. Pawsat fired in 38 points.[732] St. Patrick ended the season with an 18-14 record.

Mason County defeated Paris 85-71 in the championship game for its second straight 10th Region title and 30th win of the season. The Royals led 17-8 at the end of the first quarter, 35-22 at the half, and 53-37 after three quarters. Paris had six more field goals than Mason County, but the Royals hit 33 of 39 free throws compared to seven of 13 for the Greyhounds.[733]

Mason County played 13th Region champion Middlesboro in the first round of the state tournament. The Royals led 13-10 at the end of the first quarter, 31-23 at the half and 49-35 after three quarters. Middlesboro closed to within 58-53 with 2:53 left and had a chance to cut two more points off the deficit but missed the front end of the one-and-one. Mason County won 71-63. Middleton scored 29 of his game-high 34 points in the second half.[734]

The crowd of 21,342 for Mason County's game against Virgie was a new record. Virgie's six-foot-eight center Todd May scored 17 first quarter points, and the Eagles led 22-17 at the quarter break. Middleton picked up his third foul in the first quarter and did not return in the first half. Virgie led 31-24 with 5:09 remaining in the second quarter. Breeze picked up his third foul with 3:38 left in the half. Mason County closed the gap to 33-32 at the 2:30 mark, but did not score again until Brian Littleton made a half-court shot at the end of the half. Virgie led 54-45 after three quarters and 56-45 in the fourth quarter. The Royals closed to within 56-51 with 5:41 to play, but could get no closer. Middleton, Breeze and Feldhaus fouled out. The final score was Virgie 68, Mason County 63.[735] The Royals finished the season with a 31-1 record. May ended up with a game-high 34 points. Dale Liles was Mason County's leading scorer with 17 points. Feldhaus added 12. Allen Feldhaus says he knows May was a great player, "But we should have had a little better shot at them than what we did. I'm not saying we could have beat them, but I think if we could have kept out of foul trouble it definitely would have gone down to the end."

Middleton was named to the all-tournament team and received the Ted Sanford Award.

Allen Feldhaus was named Coach of the Year by *The Courier-Journal.*

Middleton played for the Kentucky All-Star team, which was coached by Feldhaus.

Chapter 32 1983 to 1985

Maysville Coach Bob Hall stepped down after the 1981-82 season. Hall had a 115-72 record in seven seasons at Maysville. He guided the Bulldogs to three district titles and one 10th Region championship.

Bill Frey was named the new coach at Maysville. Frey played at Newport Catholic. He came to Maysville after two seasons as the coach at Reading, Ohio. He coached at Covington Holy Cross for five seasons.[736]

Frey's first Maysville team went 18-11 and lost to Mason County in the semifinals of the district tournament. That was Mason County's 20th win of the season, but the Royals' streak of four straight district titles was snapped with a 50-49 loss to Tollesboro in the championship game.

Mason County's quest for three straight 10th Region titles ended with a 43-29 loss to Clark County in the region finals. The Royals ended the season at 22-7.

St. Patrick went 9-17 in the 1982-83 season.

Mason County edged Maysville 65-63 in the championship game of the 1984 district tournament, but was upset by Nicholas County 53-52 in the first round of the regional tournament to end the year at 21-8.

Maysville, appearing in the regional tournament for the first time since 1978, upset Clark County 68-66 in the first round, but lost to Bourbon County 81-65 in the semifinals. With a 21-16 record, the Bulldogs had their first 20-win season since 1979.

St. Patrick had a 5-24 record.

Mason County opened the 1984-85 season with 17 consecutive victories-15 by double digit margins.

The winning streak was snapped by a 57-55 road loss to the Scott County Cardinals.

The Royals bounced back with a 90-66 victory over Tollesboro, then, had back-to-back two-point losses to Bourbon County and Scott County.

Mason County closed out the regular season with a 41-38 win over Harrison County and a 52-51 victory over Bath County to run its record to 20-3.

The Maysville Bulldogs had a new coach for the 1984-85 season. Former Morehead State University player Greg Coldiron took over for Bill Frey.

Maysville lost six of its first 10 games, then, lost 11 straight. The Bulldogs closed out the regular season with back-to-back wins over Augusta and Elliott County.

The St. Patrick Saints had a five-game winning streak snapped by a 55-51 loss to Paris in the final game of the regular season.

St. Patrick beat Tollesboro 72-48 in the first round of the district tournament to advance to the semifinals against Maysville.

There were 10 ties in the game. St. Patrick led by six heading into the fourth quarter. Maysville closed to 45-44 with 3:01 left. That was the last time either team scored until Mark Schumacher hit one of two free throws with two seconds to play to give the Saints a 46-44 victory.[737] It was St. Patrick's second win over Maysville in four seasons. The Saints were headed back to the regional tournament. Maysville ended the season with a 6-18 record.

In the other semifinal, Mason County defeated Fleming County 72-51.

Mason County routed St. Patrick 82-44 in the championship game.

St. Patrick rallied from an eight-point third quarter deficit to edge Estill County 58-57 in the first round of the 10th Region Tournament. Schumacher had a double-double with 23 points and 11 rebounds. He scored 11 points in the fourth quarter.[738]

Chris O'Hearn scored a career-high 32 points to lead Mason County to a 74-51 first round victory over Montgomery County.

In the semifinals, St. Patrick lost to Paris 58-47 to end the season at 16-11, and Mason County beat Pendleton County 62-56.

Paris, trying to win the region title for the first time since 1970, had an eight-point lead in the second quarter of the championship game, but the Royals rallied to lead 30-28 at halftime. Mason County led 42-34 in the third quarter, but the Greyhounds ended the quarter on an 8-2 run to close the gap to 44-42. Mason County scored the first four points in the fourth quarter, but Paris tied the game at 48 with six straight points. The Greyhounds had a chance to take the lead but committed a turnover with 46 seconds to play. Mason County missed the front end of the one-and-one with 24 seconds left. Paris missed two shots, Mason County got the rebound and time ran out. Paris controlled the tip to start the overtime period. The Greyhounds had another turnover with 2:17 to go and Mason County played for the last shot and missed. Paris got the tip in the second overtime and held the ball. The Greyhounds took a timeout with 22 seconds to play. After the timeout, Paris senior Terence Brooks shot a jumper from the left wing that was blocked by Robbie Muse. The ball went to O'Hearn who quickly called a timeout with five seconds left. When play resumed, five-foot-eight junior guard Tony Jackson took the inbounds pass, drove into front court and shot a jumper from near the foul line over the outstretched hand of Myrin Roberts at the buzzer. The shot was good. Mason County won 50-48. Jackson's basket gave the Royals their first points since the 5:26 mark of the fourth quarter.[739] Mason County had a balanced scoring attack. Jackson had 12 points, Deron Feldhaus, Chris Orme and O'Hearn each had 10. Muse tossed in eight points and made one of the biggest defensive plays in the history of the Mason County program. Allen Feldhaus says he tells Muse all the time, "He couldn't jump but three inches, but I said, 'There's one time in your life you almost jumped three feet'".

Mason County played the Lexington Catholic Knights in the first round of the state tournament. Lexington Catholic Coach Tommy Starns had announced he would retire at the end of the season. The Knights took a 22-16 lead in the first quarter and maintained at least a six point lead until early in the fourth quarter. Lexington Catholic's six-foot-eight center Frank Kornet fouled out with 5:55 to play with the Knights leading 60-54. With Kornet out of the game, O'Hearn and Deron Feldhaus started driving to the basket and getting fouled. O'Hearn hit a free throw to give the Royals a 67-66 lead with 1:08 left. Feldhaus made a free throw with 16 seconds left to make it 68-66. Mason County missed the front end of the one-and-one with five seconds remaining, but the Knights could not get off a shot. It was Mason County's eighth straight win. Eight of Mason County's final 14 points were on free throws. O'Hearn scored a game-high 26 points. Feldhaus had 20 points and 18 rebounds.[740]

Mason County went up against the Louisville Doss Dragons in the quarterfinals.

Feldhaus scored 11 points in the first quarter, and the Royals had a 19-8 lead at the quarter break. Feldhaus added eight points in the second quarter, and Mason County went to the locker room at halftime with a 35-32 lead. Doss scored the first eight points of the third quarter to lead 38-35. Mason County ended the quarter on an 8-0 run for a 47-44 lead. There were ties at 48, 49, 53, 55 and 57. Doss took a 59-57 lead with 37 seconds left. O'Hearn rebounded his own miss and made the follow shot to tie the game at 59. Doss shot an air ball, and Mason County got the rebound and took a timeout with three seconds to play. The inbounds pass went through Feldhaus' hands. O'Hearn got the loose ball and missed a shot from the left corner. Chris Orme banked in the putback, but the officials ruled the buzzer had sounded. The two teams were headed to overtime. Doss scored first. O'Hearn hit both ends of the one-and-one to tie the game at 61. Doss regained the lead by hitting two free throws with 40 seconds left. Mason County had a turnover with 14 seconds remaining. Doss sophomore substitute Brandy Monks was fouled with nine seconds to play. He made the first free throw to give the Dragons a three-point lead. Monks missed the second free throw. Feldhaus scored on a putback to cut Doss' lead to 64-63 with three seconds to go. The Royals fouled with two seconds left. Doss missed the free throw, but Mason County missed a desperation shot at the buzzer, and the Royals' season was over. Feldhaus had another double-double with 25 points and 12 rebounds. O'Hearn scored 15 points, and Jackson added 10.[741] Feldhaus was named to the all-tournament team. Mason County's record was 26-4.

Chapter 33 Reitz Rebuilds MHS Program

Former Maysville Coach Woodie Crum was hired to replace Greg Coldiron as the Bulldogs' coach for the 1985-86 season. But Crum stepped down in the summer of 1985 due to health reasons.

"I think Woodie (at) that time in his life, he just didn't have the fire to coaching anymore," says Steve Appelman who was an assistant coach at Maysville. "I think he tried."

Maysville then turned to Bourbon County assistant coach Mike Reitz, who had been a head coach at Deming, Pikeville and Millersburg Military Institute.

Appelman says Reitz was "probably the perfect person for the job because he had a lot of energy, and he worked really hard."

Reitz started rebuilding the Maysville program by starting three talented sophomores - Pat Moore, Chris Wilburn and Mike Case. The Bulldogs compiled an 18-11 record in the regular season.

Mason County opened the 1985-86 season with 15 straight wins. The streak included a 70-64 victory over Romulus, Michigan, in the Hillbrook Classic at Rupp Arena. The winning streak ended with a 78-73 loss to Clark County at home.

The Royals won their next 10 games, including an 86-60 victory over Pendleton County in the championship game of the Burley Belt Conference Tournament.

That winning streak was snapped by a 70-65 loss to Walton-Verona.

Mason County closed out the regular season win a 72-50 victory over Montgomery County to run its record to 26-2.

Mason County defeated the St. Patrick Saints 60-46 in the first round of the 39th District Tournament. St. Patrick ended the season with a 17-14 record.

In the semifinals, the Maysville Bulldogs beat the Tollesboro Wildcats 61-55, and Mason County downed Fleming County 69-51.

Mason County defeated Maysville 58-46 in the championship game.

Mason County drew Estill County in the first round of the 10th Region Tournament. The Royals had a four-point lead heading into the final quarter. Mason County pushed the lead to 10 at 38-28. Jerry

Butler was fouled and headed to the free throw line for the one-and-one when Estill County called a timeout with 3:25 to go. Estill County was slow coming out of the timeout and received a delay of game technical foul. Estill County Coach Bart Rison protested and was assessed three more technical fouls in rapid fashion and was ejected. Butler stepped to the line and made eight of 10 free throws in the one trip.[742] Mason County went on to win 58-32 for its 30th win of the season.

Maysville led Pendleton County 46-27 at halftime. Pendleton County rallied to tie the game at 71-71 with 24 seconds to play. Moore came up with a loose ball and was fouled as he attempted a layup with no time left. Moore missed the first free throw, but made the second one to give the Bulldogs a 72-71 victory.[743] It was Maysville's 20th win of the season.

In the semifinals, Mason County beat Millersburg Military Institute 82-59, and Maysville lost to Clark County 61-37. The Bulldogs' record was 20-13.

It was Mason County versus Clark County in the championship game.

Mason County led 26-15 in the second quarter, but Clark County rallied to within 28-23 at the end of the half. The game was tied at 42-42 after three quarters. The score was tied at 48-48 when Mason County senior point guard Tony Jackson fouled out with 4:01 to go. Clark County went on an 8-2 run to lead 56-50 with 51 seconds to play and won 62-55. Mason County ended the season at 31-3, equaling the school record for wins in a season. "I thought that was possibly our best team," says Allen Feldhaus. "[Clark County's] guards were just so much bigger. We had a hard time keeping their guards from scoring. But that was a good basketball team."

Feldhaus was named Coach of the Year by *The Courier-Journal.*

Chapter 34 Royals Roll Again

Before beginning his senior season at Mason County, Deron Feldhaus signed a national letter of intent with the University of Kentucky. Feldhaus was six-foot-seven and weighed 202 pounds. He and senior guard Jerry Butler were the only two returning starters. They were joined in the starting lineup by seniors Chad Fletcher, Robert Lofton and Rheuben Bluford. Two other seniors, Rodney Jackson and Robbie Jacobs, rounded out the top seven. Jackson started in place of Bluford later in the season.

Mason County opened the 1986-87 season with a 58-51 win over the St. Patrick Saints. The Royals led by as many as 18 in the fourth quarter, but the Saints scored 13 straight points to make it interesting. Feldhaus scored a game-high 25 points.

Mason County lost to Cincinnati Purcell 66-56 in the Blue Chip City Basketball Invitational at Riverfront Coliseum in Cincinnati.

The Royals then reeled off 17 consecutive wins. Feldhaus scored 36 points in a 58-49 win over Pendleton County and 34 in an 81-48 rout of Bracken County.

The winning streak was snapped by a 53-52 loss to Paris in the Burley Belt Conference Tournament.

The Royals won the final seven games of the regular season by an average margin of 30 points.

Mason County and Maysville drew first round byes in the 39th District Tournament and met in the semifinals.

Maysville, under second-year coach Mike Reitz, won its first six games of the season and closed out the regular season with five consecutive victories.

Mason County had defeated Maysville three times during the regular season- 64-54 at the Mason County Fieldhouse, 69-57 in the championship game of the Mason County Invitational Tournament at the Fieldhouse and 66-60 in the Maysville Gymnasium.

With a berth in the regional tournament on the line in the district semifinal, Maysville jumped out to a 17-12 lead at the end of the first quarter. Mason County rallied to lead 28-25 at the half and 46-42 after three quarters. Chris Wilburn hit a long shot from the left side of the court at the buzzer to tie the score at 62-62 and force overtime.

The Royals outscored the Bulldogs 7-2 in the overtime period to win 69-64. Butler scored all seven of Mason County's points in the extra period. "We were very fortunate to win that ballgame," says Allen Feldhaus. Maysville ended the season with an 18-8 record.

Fleming County beat St. Patrick 74-55 in the other semifinal. St. Patrick ended the season with a 12-14 record.

Butler scored 25 points, and Feldhaus added 24 to lead Mason County to a 75-61 victory over Fleming County in the championship game. It was the Royals' fourth straight district title and their eighth in nine years.

Mason County beat Pendleton County 74-52 in the first round of the 10th Region Tournament. Feldhaus led the way with 22 points. Butler and Fletcher scored 16 points apiece.

Feldhaus scored 28 points to lead the Royals past Paris 65-55 in the semifinals. Lofton added 10 points.

The championship game was a rematch of the district finals – Mason County versus Fleming County.

Mason County led 17-14 at the end of the first quarter and 34-33 at halftime. The Royals outscored the Panthers 22-12 in the third quarter to lead 56-45, and led by as many as 16 in the fourth quarter. The final score was Mason County 77, Fleming County 67.

Feldhaus scored 33 points. Butler, Fletcher and Jackson each had 13. Fleming County senior Robbie Graham scored a game-high 38 points including 17 in the fourth quarter. It was Mason County's 30th win of the season.

Allen Feldhaus says while he can enjoy the success of that season now, it was not enjoyable at the time. Opposing fans gave Deron Feldhaus a hard time after he signed with the University of Kentucky. "The pressure just kept mounting and mounting," says Allen Feldhaus. "If anybody ever wanted to win a regional tournament and prove that, you know, he wasn't a fluke, we had to do it. And he handled it great himself too. But we talked a lot about [how] we'll get through this thing."

Feldhaus scored 22 points and Butler 15 to lead Mason County to a 68-49 win over Louisville Doss in the first round of the state tournament. "That did come a lot easier than we anticipated," says Allen Feldhaus.

Mason County played Louisville Ballard in the quarterfinals. Ballard was led by six-foot-five sophomore guard Allan Houston who would go on to star for the University of Tennessee and the New York Knicks.

Ballard led 20-17 at the end of the first quarter and 31-30 at halftime. Feldhaus scored 12 points in the third quarter, and the Royals were up 46-43 at the end of the third quarter.

Mason County led 61-55 with 2:28 to play, but Ballard scored seven straight points to take a one-point lead with 56 seconds left. After taking a timeout with 45 seconds remaining, the Royals held the ball until eight seconds to go when Butler was fouled on driving shot in the lane. Butler made the first free throw to tie the score at 62-62. He missed the second and Ballard got the rebound.[744] Lofton blocked Houston's three-point shot. Ballard senior Chris Riesenberg grabbed the rebound and hit a 10-footer at the buzzer to give the Bruins a 64-62 win.

It was a heartbreaking loss for Mason County. Feldhaus scored a game-high 26 points. Butler scored 13. Houston led Ballard with 24 points.

Allen Feldhaus says that loss "will always sting." But he says there's not anything he would have done differently in the game.

Mason County finished with a 31-3 record for the second straight year.

Deron Feldhaus and Butler were named to the all-tournament team. Allen Feldhaus was named *Kentucky Post* Coach of the Year, and Deron Feldhaus was the *Kentucky Post* Player of the Year marking the first time a father-son duo had won the awards in the same season.[745] Deron Feldhaus was named to the *Herald-Leader* and *The Courier-Journal* All-State teams and played on the Kentucky All-Star team. He is fifth on the Royals' all-time scoring list with 1,937 points. Deron Feldhaus scored 1,231 points at the University of Kentucky. He is one of UK's "Unforgettables," and his retired jersey hangs in the rafters of Rupp Arena. He played professionally in Japan.

Chapter 35 Seniors Lead Bulldogs to State

When Mike Reitz took over as Maysville's coach, the team was coming off a six-win season. Reitz started three sophomores- Pat Moore, Chris Wilburn and Mike Case – his first season and the Bulldogs won 20 games and advanced to the semifinals of the regional tournament. In his second season, Maysville won 18 games and took Mason County to overtime before losing in the first round of the district. Moore, Wilburn and Case were seniors in the 1987-88 season, and Maysville was one of the favorites to win the region.

Moore, a six-foot-three forward, was a consistent scorer and rebounder. Wilburn, a six-foot-five center, Case, a guard, was a sharpshooter who thrived on the new three-point shot.

The other two starters were sophomore forward Jerry King and senior guard J.D. Simpson. The top subs were sophomore guard Jerome Turner and sophomore forward Terry King, Jerry's brother. The King twins are the sons of former Mason County standout Gerald King.

The Bulldogs won their first eight games including a 68-57 victory over the Mason County Royals in the Maysville Gym. That snapped an 11-game losing streak against Mason County.

Bardstown handed Maysville its first loss, 67-65, in the semifinals of the All "A" Classic, a tournament for small schools.

The Bulldogs bounced back to beat Walton-Verona 70-61 in the consolation game. That was the start of a five-game winning streak which included back-to-back victories over Pendleton County - 64-49 in the championship game of the Mason County Invitational Tournament and 72-47 two nights later in Falmouth.

Maysville lost its next three games to Bourbon County, Mason County and Lexington Catholic, all on the road. When the Bulldogs returned to town from the game at Lexington Catholic, Reitz says he crammed the top seven players in his old Cadillac Seville, "And we just rode around the avenue. And they were hollering and screaming. They said 'I live here coach, I live here.' I said, 'No you don't.' And anyway, eventually, [I] took them back to the high school. And I mean those big guys had the windows down, their feet sticking out. And I said, 'Fellas, if we're not this close, we'll never win the region."

The Bulldogs got back on the winning track as Case fired in 32 points to lead Maysville to a 65-47 victory over Mason County in the first round of the Burley Belt Conference Tournament.

Maysville beat Grant County 56-39 in the semifinals and Scott County 73-71 in the championship game. Moore and Case each scored 22 points in the win over Scott County.

The Bulldogs ran their winning streak to five with victories over Bracken County and Fleming County.

Maysville went 3-3 in the final six games of the regular season with wins over Tollesboro, Nicholas County and Newport, and losses to Clark County, Montgomery County and Lexington Bryan Station for a record of 21-7.

Maysville defeated Fleming County 67-60 in the first round of the 39th District Tournament. Moore led the Bulldogs with 24 points; Case had 16 and Wilburn 13.

Maysville advanced to the semifinals to play Mason County for the fourth time that season. The Royals had drawn a first-round bye. The Bulldogs defeated the Royals 50-34. It was Maysville's first win over Mason County at the Fieldhouse since 1979. Case led the way with 16 points; Wilburn had 13 and Moore 10. Mason County ended the season with a 10-13 record- the Royals' first losing season since 1976-77.

Maysville faced the Tollesboro Wildcats in the championship game. Tollesboro had defeated the St. Patrick Saints 62-52 in the other semifinal. The Saints ended the season with a 5-20 record.

Maysville led 28-8 at the end of the first quarter and routed Tollesboro 96-63.[746] The Bulldogs were district champions for the first time since 1978.

Six Bulldogs scored in double figures. Moore scored 18, Case 17, Jerry King and Simpson 15 each, Turner 11, and Wilburn 10.

Maysville drew the Clark County Cardinals in the first round of the 10th Region Tournament. The Bulldogs led 18-14 at the end of the first quarter, 30-25 at the half and 51-41 at the end of the third quarter. Maysville increased the lead to 12 in the fourth quarter, and Clark County never got closer than 10. The final score: Maysville 77, Clark County 65. Case scored 22 of his game-high 29 points in the second half. He hit four three-pointers when Clark County played a zone defense in the third quarter. Case made 10 of 11 free throws in the fourth quarter. Moore scored 21 points and Simpson added 12.[747]

"That was the first time I ever beat Clark County and [Coach] Guy Strong," says Reitz. "Guy Strong came to me after the game, shook my hand and said, 'You just kicked our ass tonight.' And I took that as a big compliment."

Wilburn scored 22 points and Moore added 21 to lead Maysville past Nicholas County 86-47 in the semifinals.

Maysville went up against tournament Montgomery County in the championship game. The Indians had defeated the Bulldogs 73-69 in the regular season game in Mount Sterling.

Montgomery County jumped out to an 11-0 lead over Maysville in the championship game. The Bulldogs answered with an 11-0 run to tie the score. The first quarter ended in a 17-17 tie. Montgomery County was up 36-35 at halftime. Maysville led 56-52 at the end of the third quarter. The Bulldogs pushed the lead out to eight at 63-55. Montgomery County closed to within one point three different times. The last time was at 73-72 with 56 seconds to play, but Maysville scored the final eight points to win 81-72.[748] The Bulldogs were headed to the state tournament for the first time 1978.

Case led Maysville in scoring with 25 points. Moore had 18, Wilburn 17, and Jerry King 10.

Appelman says Reitz "did a wonderful job bringing Maysville back and winning that regional finals."

The state tournament returned to Freedom Hall in Louisville after a seven-year run at Rupp Arena in Lexington. Maysville's first round opponent was Fifth Region champion LaRue County, led by six-foot-eight senior forward Scott Boley.

The Bulldogs led 16-15 at the end of the first quarter, but trailed 35-28 at halftime. Boley scored 14 points in the second quarter. Larue County was up 48-44 after three quarters and led by as many as eight in the fourth quarter. Maysville closed to within 66-62 on a three-pointer by Moore with 29 seconds remaining, but Larue County held on for a 69-62 victory. Boley ended up with 33 points. Moore led Maysville with 21 points. Wilburn added 16.[749]

"That was the year the state tournament was right after the regional tournament," says Reitz. "I believe if we would have had that weekend between to settle down a little bit, I think we might have beat Larue County."

Maysville ended the season with a 27-8 record.

Five months later, Reitz resigned from Maysville to accept the coaching job at Harrison County. Reitz says it was a tough decision, and he calls Maysville "the best place I ever taught."

Reitz has fond memories of the rivalries with Mason County and St. Patrick.

"I called the St. Pat game the battle of Limestone Street," says Reitz. "But you had three schools within five miles of each other. And as soon as basketball was over in March, everybody started talking about the following year. I mean it was the greatest place I've ever been as far as sports goes."

Maysville hired 59 year old Doug Hines as its new coach. Hines a native of Kentucky had spent the past 15 years as the head coach at Mississippi College. He previously coached at Bethel College, Lindsey Wilson Junior College, Crab Orchard High School and Somerset High School. Hines was the freshman coach at the University of Kentucky in 1960. He was not going to coach at Mississippi College in the coming season and was looking to return to Kentucky. Hines had read about the vacancy at Maysville while visiting his twin brother in Lexington.[750]

Maysville beat Mason County 68-53 in the championship game of the 1989 district tournament. Both teams lost in the first round of the regional tournament and finished the season with identical records of 15-14. The St. Patrick Saints closed out the 1980s with an 8-18 record after losing to Tollesboro in the district tournament.

Chapter 36 A Five-Peat for the Lady Royals

Girls' basketball on the local scene in the 1980s included an unprecedented run by the Mason County Lady Royals, the first team at St. Patrick, and numerous coaching changes and the eventual elimination of the sport at Maysville High School.

The Mason County Lady Royals won district titles in 1980, 1981 and 1982, but lost in the regional tournament all three years- in the semifinals in 1980 and 1981 and in the championship game in 1982.

The Lady Royals opened the 1982-83 season with 15 consecutive wins. The streak was snapped by 51-50 road loss to Paris. Mason County won its next game against Lewis County, then, lost to Russell 60-58 at Russell. The Lady Royals closed out the regular season with seven straight victories for a 23-2 record.

Mason County routed Maysville 68-22 and beat Fleming County 68-43 in the district tournament.

In the regional tournament, the Lady Royals defeated Pendleton County 59-50 in the first round, Paris 50-40 in the semifinals and Bracken County 62-45 in the championship game.

Mason County beat Sheldon Clark 55-45 in the first round of the state tournament. Laverne Bluford scored 17 points, Patty Willett 12 and Kay Grayson 10.

Top ranked Warren Central, led by all-state guard Clemette Haskins, defeated Mason County 61-40 in the quarterfinals. Haskins scored a game-high 29 points. Willett, with 10 points, was the only Lady Royal in double figures. Mason County's record was 29-3.

Mason County had a season-opening 11-game winning streak in 1983-84. Tracy Perry scored a career-high 27 points in the season opener against Maysville.

Notre Dame handed the Lady Royals their first loss by the score of 60-50.

A 71-27 victory over Pendleton County was followed by a 61-43 loss to Louisville Male in the Louisville Invitational Tournament.

After back-to-back wins over Lewis County and Russell, the Lady Royals lost to Belfry 55-54 in the first round of the Boone County Invitational Tournament.

Mason County won the last 11 games of the regular season to run its record to 25-3.

The Lady Royals beat Fleming County 79-41 in the district championship game.

Mason County cruised through the regional tournament by defeating Paris 56-38 in the first round, Bracken County 61-44 in the semifinals and Harrison County 59-38 in the championship game.

The Lady Royals played Oldham County in the first round of the state tournament. There were six ties and 10 lead changes in the game. Oldham County led 39-33 with 3:30 to go. Mason County scored five straight points to close the gap to one. Oldham County increased the lead to three at 41-38 with 52 seconds left. Bluford's putback cut the deficit to one again. Oldham County went to the free throw line with only two seconds play. The Lady Colonels made the first free throw, but missed the second one. Mason County got the rebound, but turned the ball over, and Oldham County won 42-40.[751]

The Lady Royals ended the season with a 29-4 record.

There was no long winning streak for Mason County at the start of the 1984-85 season. The Lady Royals beat Bracken County 56-38 in the season opener, then, lost back-to-back games to Greenup County and Bourbon County.

Mason County reeled off four straight wins before losing to Rowan County by one point in Morehead.

The Lady Royals won the final 14 games of the regular season.

Mason County drew the St. Patrick Lady Saints in the first round of the district tournament. 1984-85 was the first season for girls' basketball at St. Patrick. Former Augusta and Murray State standout Marla Kelsch was the Lady Saints' coach. St. Patrick won five games and lost eight in the regular season.

The Lady Royals routed the Lady Saints 82-28 for their 20th win of the season.

Mason County beat Fleming County 58-53 in the championship game.

Bluford scored 22 points, and Michelle Swartz added 20 to lead the Lady Royals to a 71-54 victory over Deming in the first round of the 10th Region Tournament.

Mason County edged Paris 54-51 in the semifinals.

The Lady Royals beat Harrison County 70-45 in the championship game for their third straight region title. Lisa Doyle scored 29 points, Swartz 16, and Bluford 12.

Mason County played three-time state champion Laurel County in the first round of the state tournament. After trailing by five at the end of the first quarter, Mason County outscored Laurel County 14-4 in the second quarter to lead 19-14 at halftime. The Lady Royals were up 36-26 after three quarters. Laurel County rallied to tie it at 38-38 with 2:37 left. Mason County turned the ball over with 2:19 to go. The Lady Cardinals tried to hold the ball for the last shot, but Swartz came up with a steal with 19 seconds remaining. The Lady Royals took a timeout with 15 seconds left. When play resumed, Swartz received a pass, drove across the lane and was fouled as she took an off-balanced shot. Swartz missed the first throw, but made the second one to give Mason County a 39-38 lead. Laurel County's desperation shot at the buzzer hit the side of the rim. The Lady Royals had pulled off the upset despite scoring just three points in the fourth quarter.[752]

"That was a good game," says Hutchison, "[The Lady Cardinals] were a good team; they were probably the best team in the tournament.

It was Mason County's 20th consecutive win. Bluford scored a game-high 16 points.

The Lady Royals faced 13th Region champion Whitley County in the quarterfinals. Mason County led 14-12 at the end of the first quarter, but trailed 28-23 at halftime. The Lady Colonels were up 41-33 at the end of the third quarter and by 10 early in the fourth quarter. Mason County rallied to cut the deficit to three on three different occasions, the last time at 56-53 with 15 seconds left. The Lady Royals came up with a steal, but missed a shot. Whitley County got the rebound and was fouled. Connie Brock made one of two free throws to make the final score: Whitley County 57, Mason County 53.

"They outplayed us," says Hutchison. "We couldn't press them. See, our whole game was pressing, you know, taking the ball away from people, and we couldn't do it. They got it up the floor good."

Bluford led all scorers with 20 points and was named to the all-tournament team. Doyle, who fouled out with 4:14 to play, scored 14 points. Swartz added 10 points.[753]

Mason County ended the season with a 25-4 record.

The Lady Royals opened the 1985-86 season with a 72-31 win over Russell.

Mason County lost to Scott County 64-63 in the second game of the season despite a 25-point game from Doyle.

The Lady Royals won their next 12 games by an average of 31.6 points. Bluford had a 25-point game against Rowan County. Doyle fired in 26 points against St. Patrick.

The winning streak was snapped by a 60-57 road loss to Notre Dame.

The Lady Royals bounced back with wins over Clark County, Ripley, Ohio, and Lewis County. Doyle scored 26 points, and Bluford added 21 against Clark County. Bluford had 29 in the 93-30 victory over Ripley.

Mason County lost to Henry Clay 62-51, then closed out the regular season with five straight victories.

Under the three-team format, Mason County only had to play one game in the district tournament, and the Lady Royals routed St. Patrick 78-22.

The three-team format gave the Lady Saints, under first-year coach John Chamberlain, a second chance, and they took advantage of it by beating Fleming County 39-32.

In the first round of the 10th Region Tournament, Doyle scored a career-high 33 points to lead Mason County to a 67-49 win over Estill County. St. Patrick lost to Bracken County 49-42 to end its second season with an 11-16 record.

Doyle scored 28 points, Bluford 13 and Angie Garrett 12 in Mason County's 64-43 victory over Harrison County in the semifinals.

Four Lady Royals scored in double figures in a 64-40 win over Bracken County in the championship game. Bluford scored 17 points, Doyle 15, Shannon Litton 12 and Mindy Sharp 10.

Mason County used its full court pressure to beat Ashland 62-52 in the first round of the state tournament. Garrett led the Lady Royals in scoring with 19 points. Bluford added 16 and Doyle followed with 14.

Mason County defeated Cumberland 57-37 in the quarterfinals. Doyle scored 19 points, Bluford 11, and Sharp 10.

The Lady Royals played Franklin-Simpson in the quarterfinals. Franklin-Simpson led 18-11 at the end of the first quarter, 34-24 at halftime and 48-32 after three quarters. Mason County cut the deficit to 10 midway through the fourth quarter, but could get no closer. The final score was Franklin-Simpson 56, Mason County 45.[754]

"That was a lucky game by them," says Hutchison. "They hit shots, 30 feet, just throwing them up."

Doyle scored 22 points and was named to the all-tournament team. Sharp added 10. The Lady Royals ended the season with a 27-4 record. Mason County had a four-year record of 110-15.

The Lady Royals opened the 1986-87 season with five straight wins followed by five consecutive losses.

Mason County snapped the losing streak with a 59-35 win over St. Patrick.

The Lady Royals lost four of their next seven games and had a 9-9 record with seven games left in the regular season.

Mason County won five straight games before losing to Conner 56-53.

The Lady Royals closed out the regular season with a 54-51 win over Greenup County.

Mason County played the St. Patrick Lady Saints in the 39th District Tournament to a tight 59-58 in overtime. St. Patrick led 15-10 at the end of the first quarter, 32-23 at the half and 42-31 after three quarters. St. Patrick was up 47-34 in the fourth quarter. Mason County ended the fourth quarter on a 17-4 run to tie the game at 51-51 and force overtime. The Lady Royals had a one-point as the overtime period was winding down, but Stephanie Briggs hit a putback at the buzzer to give the Lady Saints a 59-58 win. Vanessa Walton led St. Patrick in scoring with 15 points, Briggs tossed 13, Debbie Martin and Tammy Whaley each had 10. Garrett scored a game-high 25 points for Mason County before fouling out in overtime. Litton scored 16 points and Sharp added 10.[755]

Mason County, like St. Patrick the previous season, took advantage of a second chance under the three-team format and beat Fleming County 48-37 to advance to the regional tournament. St. Patrick was the district champion, and Mason County was the runner-up.

St. Patrick lost to Bourbon County 51-40 in the first round of the 10th Region Tournament despite a 20-point game by Walton. The Lady Saints ended the season with a 13-10 record- their first winning season.

Mason County's first round opponent was Paris. The Lady Royals had an 11-point lead with 5:11 left in the game. Paris rallied to tie it at 48-48 with 1:04 to go. Mason County took a timeout to set up a play for the last shot. The play did not go as it was drawn up, but Litton hit a long shot at the buzzer to give the Lady Royals a 50-48 victory. Garrett had a game-high 18 points. Lariena Cropper tossed in 12 points and Litton added 10.

Garrett scored 18 points and Sharp added 10 to lead Mason County past Clark County 42-28 in the semifinals.

The Lady Royals defeated Bourbon County 59-33 in the championship game for their fifth straight 10th Region title. Litton scored 19 points, Garrett 17 and Sharp 10.

Mason County played 2nd Region champion Christian County in the opening round of the state tournament. Jakki Whaley suffered an ankle injury in the first quarter and sat out the rest of the game. Garrett hit an 18-footer to tie the score at 40-all with 56 seconds left. Rochelle Castle came up with a steal with 30 seconds to play. Mason County took timeouts with 22 seconds to go and with 11 seconds remaining to set up a final play. The Lady Royals did not get off a shot and the game went to overtime. Litton made a field goal in the opening minute of the extra period to give Mason County a 42-40 lead, but Christian County scored the final six points to win 46-42. The Lady Royals finished the season at 19-12.

Mason County had a 21-5 regular season record in 1987-88 and had double digit wins in the district tournament and the first two rounds of the regional tournament.

In the championship game, the Lady Royals trailed the Clark County Lady Cardinals 16-10 at the half and 27-24 after three quarters.

Litton hit a three-pointer to tie the game at 31-31 with 4:08 left. Another three-pointer by Litton gave Mason County a 36-34 lead at the 2:37 mark. Clark County tied it with a putback. Litton drained another three-pointer to give the Lady Royals a 39-36 lead with two minutes to play. Clark County hit a field goal to get to within a point. Both teams missed the front end of the one-and-one. Sharp hit two free throws to push Mason County's lead back out to three at 41-38 with 44 seconds to go. Clark County scored to make it 41-40 with 31 seconds left. Clark County freshman Maisha Thomas stole an inbounds, missed a shot, got her own rebound and was fouled with 18 seconds to play. Thomas hit both free throws to give the Lady Cardinals a 42-41 lead. Clark County forced a held ball and the possession arrow favored the Lady Cardinals. Clark County made one of two free throws with seven seconds left to make it 43-41. The Lady Royals missed a half court shot and a follow shot. Mason County's streak of five straight regional titles was snapped.

The Lady Royals' record was 25-6.

Mason County won the 1989 district tournament, but lost to Clark County 48-35 in the semifinals of the regional tournament to finish the season with a 12-15 record. It was the Lady Royals' first losing season since 1978-79.

Lex Turner coached both the St. Patrick boys' and girls' teams in the 1987-88 season. The Lady Saints were the district runners-up and lost to Clark County in the first round of the regional tournament to finish the season at 12-12.

Danny McKay coached the Lady Saints in 1988-89. St. Patrick lost to Fleming County in the semifinals of the district tournament and had a record of 12-10.

Helen Smoot stepped down as Maysville's coach after the 1978-79 season and former Maysville football coach Dean Cvitkovic took over for one season. Former Fee High School boys' basketball coach John Fields coached the Maysville girls for three seasons, followed by Ralph Dunlap for one season and Charles Coffey for one season.

Maysville did not have a girls' varsity team during the 1985-86 and 1986-87 seasons. Joe McKay coached the junior varsity in 1986-87 and was the varsity coach the last two years Maysville had a girls' team-1987-88 and 1988-89.

Chapter 37 End of an Era

Doug Hines guided the Maysville Bulldogs to a 23-10 record in the 1989-90 season. Highlights of the season included winning the 10th Region All "A" Classic and advancing to the statewide tournament for small schools. Maysville edged Mayfield 71-70 in the first round and outlasted Walton-Verona 69-68 in double overtime in the quarterfinals before losing to Owsley County 60-56 in the semifinals.

St. Patrick lost to Maysville in the 39th District Tournament, but had its first winning season since 1985-86 with a 15-9 record.

Bryan Tolliver, who had a 35-point game against Nicholas County in February, scored a game-high 31 points to lead Mason County to a 77-67 upset win over Maysville in the championship game of the district tournament. "For their talent, they dug as deep as any team I've ever had," says former Mason County coach Allen Feldhaus.

Maysville beat Paris in the first round of the 10th Region Tournament, but lost to Clark County in the semifinals to close out the year at 23-10.

Mason County lost to Bourbon County in the first round of the regional tournament to finish at 10-17.

Hines resigned as the coach at Maysville to become the coach at Union County. Hines had a two-year record of 38-24 with one district title and a 10th Region All "A" championship.

Assistant coach Steve Appelman was promoted to head coach for what turned out to be Maysville's final season.

The Maysville Board of Education voted to merge with the Mason County Schools. The merger took effect in the 1990-91 school year, but Maysville High School did not close until the end of that school year.

Appelman did not know the merger was going to happen when he accepted the head coaching position. He met with the players to discuss plans for the summer, then, a short time later, he and his wife were on the senior trip to Florida when they heard the announcement of the merger.

"You go from, you know, you're really happy about the opportunity of getting a job to coach, then it's for one year," says Appelman. "Then, what's going to happen after that one year?"

"End of an Era" was the theme for Maysville's final season.

The Bulldogs lost seven of their first 10 games. "We wanted to play man-to-man defense, and played some really good teams," says Appelman. The man-to-man defense was not popular with the fans. Appelman remembers people saying, "It's not working. Maysville teams can only play zone defense; they can only play 2-3 zone."

Appelman admits, "It was a rough start." He received other suggestions from the fans.

"People in this community are so knowledgeable about sports," says Appelman. "It's funny how you get notes sent to you. A lot of times they're anonymous, and they have all kinds of suggestions ... notes about who should be playing, and when to press. And then, you top that by people that stop by and give you suggestions. That's what's so unique about this community - is the knowledge of the sports fan."

The Bulldogs kept playing man-to-man defense and reeled off 11 straight victories. Maysville averaged 86.9 points per game during the winning streak including a 105-81 victory over North Gallia, Ohio.

Maysville breezed through the 10th Region All "A" Classic. The Bulldogs defeated Deming 80-36 in the quarterfinals, St. Patrick 80-56 in the semifinals and Paris 90-70 in the championship game.

"When you come up here to Paris and you play them on their home floor, I mean they have a super ball club, and you're able to win by 20, that's saying a lot for your team," said Appelman on the postgame radio show. "We heard a saying last night that a team met the challenge, and they beat it. Well that's what we did tonight - we met one heck of a challenge here in Paris; we not only met it, but we defeated it, and it feels good."[756]

The Bulldogs defeated Cumberland 70-55 in the first round of the All "A" Classic. Junior Guard Orlando Myrick set a single game All "A" Classic record with 12 assists.

The winning streak came to an end with a 70-62 loss to Kentucky Country Day in the quarterfinals.

After beating Nicholas County 88-76 in Carlisle, Maysville lost to Paris 90-87 at Paris in what turned out to be the final game between the longtime rivals.

In their last game in the Maysville gym, the Bulldogs defeated Newport 86-83.

After 16 straight years at the Mason County Fieldhouse, the 39th District Tournament was moved to Fleming County in 1991.

Fleming County rallied from a 13-point deficit to beat Mason County 86-71 in the first round. The Royals ended the season with a 13-10 record.

The upper bracket semifinal game pitted St. Patrick against Tollesboro. The Saints had opened the season with four straight losses. The losing streak was snapped by an 87-70 win over Fleming County. Jason Stahl fired in 43 points. St. Patrick ended the regular season with five consecutive losses. Tollesboro beat St. Patrick 77-57. The Saints' record was 8-17.

Maysville beat Fleming County 76-50 in the lower bracket semifinal game.

The championship game was a high scoring classic. Tollesboro junior Chris Harrison, a University of Kentucky signee, fired in 59 points to lead the Wildcats to a 110-107 overtime win over Maysville.

"We had the game won if we could have hit free throws right at the end," says Appelman.

The Bulldogs cruised to a 91-64 victory over Pendleton County in the first round of the 10th Region Tournament.

"Whenever we pressed them, they just fell apart," says Appelman.

Maysville defeated Clark County 72-63 in the semifinals.

"It was probably one of our better games that year," says Appelman.

The Bulldogs were one win away from advancing to the state tournament in their final season.

Standing in their way were the Harrison County Thorobreds coached by former Maysville coach Mike Reitz.

Maysville led by as many as 13 in the first quarter. Harrison County had an 83-75 lead with 2:42 left in the game. Freshman Timmy Myrick hit back-to-back three-pointers, and his cousin, Orlando Myrick, made a layup to tie the score at 83-83 with 1:53 to play. Kris Reitz, the coach's son, hit a three-pointer to put Harrison County back in front with 1:42 left. David Bennett and Galon Thomas hit back-to-back baskets to give Maysville the lead at 87-86 with 1:02 left. Harrison County guard Jerry Fogle hit one of two free throws to tie the game with 46 seconds left. Orlando Myrick made the first of two free throws with 28 seconds remaining. He missed the second, but Thomas tipped it in to give the Bulldogs a 90-87 lead. Reitz tied the game with a three-pointer with 20 seconds to go. Brad Allison blocked Thomas' layup, and Fogle drove to the other end of the court and hit a shot at the buzzer to give Harrison County a 92-90 victory.[757]

"It was a tough game to lose, but it was a great ballgame," says Appelman.

Maysville's tradition-rich basketball program came to a sudden end. The final team's record was 19-11.

Two nights after the region finals, the Mason County Board of Education accepted Coach Allen Feldhaus' resignation and promoted assistant coach Fred Hester to head coach.

In 16 seasons at Mason County, Feldhaus compiled a record of 325-136. His teams won nine district titles and four region championships.

The Ledger-Independent

Front row (L-R): Assistant Coach Joe McKay, Brandon Nelson, Orlando Myrick, Shawn Nelson, Lamont Johnson, Assistant Coach Dickie Butler. Middle row (L-R): Julius King, Chris Dearing, Timmy Myrick, Galon Thomas, Head Coach Steve Appelman. Back row (L-R): manager Chad Sauer, Marlon Thomas, Jeremiah Jackson, David Bennett, William Steward, manager Matt Kielman.

Laurnie Caproni, former *Ledger Independent* sports editor, says Feldhaus "was the great stabilizer of that whole basketball program. He really was. He did so many things that were so good."

Appleman and Maysville assistant coach Dickie Butler would join Mason County assistant coach Henry Boone on the Royals' coaching staff the next season.

Maysville High School's final athletic banquet took place on May 8, 1991 at Ramada Inn.

An Alumni Day was held on June 1, 1991 to bid farewell to Maysville High School. Several former players returned for an alumni game in the sweltering heat in the Maysville gym.

Chapter 38 Successful Merger

New Mason County head coach Fred Hester had spent 13 seasons as an assistant coach under former Royals coach Allen Feldhaus. Hester was standout player at Mason County in the 1960s. He was a member of the Royals' 1967 state championship golf team. Hester was a successful head coach at Ripley High School in Ohio before returning to his alma mater.

The first order of business for Hester and his assistant coaches was to bring the Mason County players and the former Maysville players together for the 1991-92 season – the first year for the merged schools. "We tried to do all the things we could do to make everyone feel welcome, to not leave anybody out," says Hester. "We ordered extra uniforms just to make sure that everybody who wanted to play just about got to play. We hardly had any cuts."

The merger gave Mason County quality depth, enabling the Royals to play a full-court pressing defense and a fast break offense similar to what Coach Rick Pitino was using at the University of Kentucky. Hester says he and his assistants thought, "why not play as hard as we can as long as we can, get kids to buy in that they will go out for a minute, get back in, that we'll commit to eight or nine or 10 (players)."

Orlando Myrick and Darin Poe were the captains. Nine Royals scored in an 85-47 season-opening win over the Tollesboro Wildcats. Orlando Myrick led the way with 22 points, and his cousin, Timmy Myrick, had 19. William "Snapper" Steward added 18.

In its home opener, Mason County jumped out to a 15-0 lead and routed St. Patrick 93-42. Poe scored a game-high 24 points.

The Royals outscored West Union, Ohio, 23-9 in the second quarter on their way to an 83-36 victory.

Orlando Myrick fired in 36 points to lead Mason County to a 90-68 victory over Bourbon County. Myrick scored 24 points in the first half, including 18 in the second quarter.

Five Royals scored in double figures in a 78-70 win over Lexington Tates Creek. Orlando Myrick scored 17 points, Poe 15, John Fryman 14, Timmy Myrick 12 and Julius King 11.

Mason County edged Nicholas County 83-80 in double overtime

in Carlisle despite a 50-point performance by Nicholas County senior guard Daniel Brown.

The six-game season-opening winning streak was snapped by an 84-75 loss to Louisville Ballard in the first round of the Ashland Invitational Tournament.

After beating Bracken County 71-49 at home, the Royals traveled to Covington and lost to Holy Cross 65-62.

Mason County defeated Tollesboro 124-72 in the first round of the Mason County Invitational Tournament. The 124-point game is a school record. Twelve Royals scored. Eight scored in double figures - Fryman with 19, Timmy Myrick 17, Steward 16, Orlando Myrick 13, Darin Poe and Jim Belcher 11 apiece, Shawn Myrick (Timmy's brother) and Eric Goodwin 10 each.

The Royals beat Bracken County 88-69 in the semifinals.

Mason County played Harrison County in the championship game. The Thorobreds scored the first 10 points of the game, but the Royals rallied for an 83-82 win. Harrison County guard Jerry Fogle had a game-high 41 points.

Mason County had another close call against the Paris Greyhounds in Paris, but pulled out a 78-75 win.

Victories over Pendleton County and Augusta gave the Royals their second six-game winning streak.

The streak ended with a 64-52 loss to the Rowan County Vikings.

The Royals bounced back with lopsided wins over Ripley, Ohio, and Estill County.

Scott County hit two free throws with no time on the clock to beat Mason County 75-74.

Mason County won the final seven games of the regular season. The only close game during that winning streak was an 82-78 victory over Harrison County in Cynthiana.

Mason County and St. Patrick met in the semifinals of the district tournament. The Saints had compiled a 14-12 regular season record and reached the century mark in two games – a 107-42 victory Augusta and a 100-67 win over Deming.

It was Mason County that lit up the scoreboard in the district game as the Royals beat the Saints 92-54. The Royals then breezed past Fleming County 90-58 in the championship game.

Timmy Myrick fired in 39 points to lead Mason County to an 88-69 win over the Paris Greyhounds in the first round of the regional tournament.

Mason County defeated Montgomery County 75-59 in the semifinals. Timmy Myrick scored a game-high 21 points.

It was Mason County vs. Nicholas County in the championship game. The Bluejackets, in the regional finals for the first time since

1957, were looking to avenge the double overtime regular season loss to Mason County.

The Mason County Fieldhouse was almost full 90 minutes before game time. It was standing room only at tip-off.

Orlando Myrick scored 27 points to lead the Royals to a 94-70 victory. Steward added 21, and Timmy Myrick had 15.

Hester says the Royals' depth was a key in holding Nicholas County guard Daniel Brown to 27 points. "We had two or three [players] that we constantly rotated on him from the get-go - made him play 32 minutes hard to get passes, to get open, to get looks. We didn't think we would stop him, but to have the depth of being able to, you know, guard him that way rather than just with one person, I thought made the whole difference."

Mason County was headed to the state tournament with a 12-game winning streak.

The 1992 state tournament was played at Freedom Hall in Louisville.

The Royals' first round opponent was Region Two champion University Heights Academy, a private school located in Hopkinsville.

Mason County made just two of 13 field goal attempts in the first quarter and trailed 19-4 at the quarter break. The Royals outscored the Blazers 15-6 in the second quarter to only trail by six at intermission. The third quarter was eerily similar to the first quarter - Mason County was just two of 14 from the field, and the Blazers outscored the Royals 18-5 to lead 43-24. Mason County outscored UHA 28-22 in the fourth quarter, but it wasn't enough as the Blazers won 65-52 and went on to win the state championship.

Mason County was 18 of 55 from the field for the game for 32.7 percent. Nine of the 18 field goals were in the fourth quarter. The Royals were five of 15 on three-point shots for 33.3 percent.

"We just didn't get the ball in the basket," Hester said in the post game press conference. "A lot of that was due to their defense. When we scouted them in their regional semifinals and finals, I thought they were as good a half court defensive team as I've seen all year."

Hester thought his team played well on the defensive end.

"Their flex offense, with their personnel is really hard to stop, and I thought except for two or three breakdowns where they got some easy ones, we did a good job even on that. It was just one of those nights that the ball just wouldn't drop."

Mason County ended the season with a 27-5 record.

"I told the kids they've had a great year under a lot of adversity," Hester said. "A lot of people didn't think they could come together that quickly. They've been a great group of kids, and I really appreciate the opportunity to get to coach them."

Chapter 39 Mason County Keeps Winning

Mason County opened the 1992-93 season with just two returning starters - Timmy Myrick, a six-foot-one junior and William "Snapper" Steward, a six-foot senior.

Steward suffered a broken foot in the Royals' opening game - an 81-57 road victory over the Ashland Tomcats.

The Royals defeated Tollesboro 90-63 in their home opener.

Sophomore guard Shawn Myrick scored 24 points to lead Mason County to a 102-78 victory over the St. Patrick Saints.

Back-to-back wins over West Union, Ohio, and Bourbon County ran the season-opening winning streak to five games.

The Royals were held to 28 points under their average in a 63-60 loss to Lexington Tates Creek.

Mason County won its next 10 games. The streak included an 80-67 victory over the No. 1 team in the state, Lexington Catholic, in the semifinals of the Bluegrass Festival Tournament at Lexington Catholic. Shawn Myrick scored a game-high 29 points. "That was a big win," says Hester. The next night, the Royals beat Montgomery County 71-56 to win the tournament.

Mason County defeated Montgomery County again in the championship game of the Mason County Invitational Tournament.

Alvin Sims and Cory Dumphord combined for 63 points for Paris, but it wasn't enough as Shawn Myrick scored 26 points to lead the Royals to an 86-82 victory the Greyhounds.

Shawn Myrick fired in 29 points in an 81-64 victory over Pendleton County.

The winning streak was broken by a 74-69 road loss to the Rowan County Vikings.

Mason County won the final 11 games of the season by an average margin of 28.9 points. Kyle Sherman, the Royals' six-foot-three sophomore center, had his first big scoring game with 27 points in an 82-63 victory over Covington Holy Cross.

The Royals entered the district tournament with a 26-2 record. Timmy Myrick poured in 29 points in an 89-56 rout of Tollesboro in the semifinals.

Fleming County and St. Patrick met in the other semifinal. St.

Patrick had compiled a 12-10 record in the regular season. Kelly Greenwell scored 45 points in the Saints' 103-61 victory over Deming in the next to last game of the regular season. Fleming County edged St. Patrick 76-74 despite a 30-point game by Greenwell.

Shawn Myrick scored 24 as Mason County breezed past Fleming County 84-51 in the championship game.

Mason County drew Clark County in the first round of the regional tournament. The Cardinals played tough for three quarters, but the Royals pulled away for a 78-56 victory. Steward had a game-high 21 points.

The Royals beat Harrison County 73-64 in the semifinals despite a 32-point game by Jerry Fogle.

A blizzard on Saturday forced the postponement of the championship game between Mason County and Montgomery County. It was rescheduled on Monday night. Five Mason County players scored in double figures in an 84-61 win. Sherman scored 19 points, Julius King 18, Shawn Myrick 16, Timmy Myrick 15 and Steward 12.

Mason County played Pleasure Ridge Park in the opening game of the state tournament at Rupp Arena. Both teams played an up tempo style sparked by full court pressure defense. PRP, led by Western Kentucky University signee Danyell Macklin, was No. 5 in Dave Cantrell's ratings of the state tournament teams; Mason County was No. 6.[758]

PRP's press was too much for Mason County, and the Panthers beat the Royals 73-52. "Here locally and here regionally, we had great success pressing," says Hester, "but, you know, we just weren't as fast as those kids." The loss snapped the Royals' 16-game winning streak. Mason County had a 31-3 record.

Chapter 40 Royals Three-Peat

Mason County won the State AAU Tournament in the summer of 1993, and was No. 3 in the state in *The Courier-Journal's* poll of coaches heading into the 1993-94 season.

The Royals had four returning starters- brothers Timmy Myrick and Shawn Myrick, Kyle Sherman and Anthony "Kotchie" Thomas. Phil Doyle was the new member of the starting lineup.

In the season opener, Mason County outscored Ashland 59-34 in the second half for a 103-72 victory. Shawn Myrick scored 25 points.

The Royals rallied to beat Fairfield, Ohio 63-61 in a game at the Shoemaker Center in Cincinnati.

Shawn Myrick had another 25-point game in a 102-67 win over West Union, Ohio.

Thirteen Royals scored in a 100-54 victory over Bourbon County.

Mason County's tougher schedule included the first trip to the King of the Bluegrass Tournament at Fairdale High School just outside of Louisville. The Royals defeated Breckinridge County 83-64, Lexington Catholic 89-67 and Louisville Doss 72-66 to advance to the championship game against the Fairdale Bulldogs. Shawn Myrick scored 28 points, but Fairdale edged the Royals 91-89 to snap Mason County's season-opening seven-game winning streak.

The next night, Thomas scored 24 points to lead the Royals to a 95-75 victory over Bracken County. It was Mason County's fifth game in six nights.

Snow delayed the start of the Ashland Invitational Tournament by one day. After Louisville Ballard and Lexington Bryan Station dropped out of the tournament, Mason County only had to play two games. Shawn Myrick scored 26 points in a 91-70 win over Russell. Timmy Myrick scored 21 points to lead the Royals to an 81-78 victory over Ashland in the championship game. Shawn Myrick, Timmy Myrick and Sherman were named to the all-tournament team.

Mason County was ranked No.1 in the first Associated Press poll of the season released on January 4. It was the first time a Mason County team had been No. 1 in the state.

The Royals ran their record to 13-1 with three victories in the Mason County Invitational Tournament. Shawn Myrick scored 30 points in an 86-73 victory over Harrison County in the title game.

After a 75-71 road win over the Paris Greyhounds, the Royals did not play another game for 11 days because of snowy weather.

Mason County lost to Covington Holy Cross 63-62 at the Shoemaker Center in Cincinnati.

With Shawn Myrick leading the way with 37 points, the Royals started another winning streak with a 103-79 victory over the Tollesboro Wildcats.

Shawn Myrick had a 30-point game as Mason County ran its winning streak to seven games by beating Fleming County 90-58.

The streak was broken by an 86-73 loss to Harlan in the S.T. Roach Classic at Paul Laurance Dunbar High School in Lexington.

The Royals closed out the regular season with four straight victories. Doyle scored 26 points against Bath County. Shawn Myrick had 28 points in a win over Newport Central Catholic.

Mason County outscored Tollesboro 104-96 in the semifinals of the 39th District Tournament. The Royals scored 52 points in each half. Doyle made seven three-pointers and scored 24 points. Shawn Myrick tossed in 21 points. Brian Muchrison, a 6-3 junior, came off the bench to score 18 points, including 11 in the first quarter. Thomas added 16 points.

The Royals scored 61 points in the first half and defeated St. Patrick 113-74 in the championship game. Shawn Myrick had a team-high 27 points. Muchrison had another 18-point game. St. Patrick junior Aaron Rigdon had a game-high 32 points.

St. Patrick lost to Harrison County 89-50 in the first round of the 10th Region Tournament to end the season at 12-16.

Sherman scored 24 points to lead Mason County to a 109-81 win over Bourbon County in the first round. Twelve Royals scored.

Shawn Myrick scored 28 points in a 101-89 victory over Montgomery County in the semifinals.

Mason County, led by Sherman's 26 points, beat Clark County 75-67 in the championship game to become the first school to win three straight 10th Region titles since Maysville won four in a row from 1945 to 1948. It was the Royals' 61st consecutive victory against 10th Region teams.

"To me, the 61 straight in the region is just something that you can't hardly imagine in sports," said Hester on the post-game show. "Those kids come ready to play every night."

Mason County had another tough draw in the first round of the state tournament at Freedom Hall. The Royals' opponent, 7th Region champion Louisville Moore, was 28-3. The Mustangs' six-foot-eight senior center, Louis Richardson, averaged 32 points a game.

The Royals led 16-15 at the end of the first quarter. Moore had a

40-35 lead at halftime. Shawn Myrick scored nine of his team-high 22 points in the third quarter, and Mason County led 60-59 at the quarter break.

The Royals were up 77-74 with 1:15, but they missed the front end of the one-and-one four times in the final minute.

Richardson made a reverse layup to cut Mason County's lead to one with 27 seconds left. Moore junior guard Wesley Miller hit a three-pointer with 17 seconds left to give the Mustangs a 79-77 lead. Mason County missed a shot in the lane in the closing seconds. The Royals lost in the first round of the state tournament for the third straight year. Mason County was 2 of 8 from the free throw in the fourth quarter. "We'd been a real good free throw shooting team all year," says Hester. "And [the Mustangs] seemed to have their best quarter there at the end."

Hester says it was a winnable game. "Of the three [first round losses] there in a row, that was the most disappointing. We were as good as Moore."

Mason County ended the season with a 30-4 record.

Chapter 41 Saints Win First 10th Region All "A" Classic

Heading into the 1994-95 season, Mason County looked to be in good shape to make a run at a record-tying fourth straight 10th Region title. The graduation of Timmy Myrick was a huge loss, but four other starters were returning. The Royals also had a new player-senior guard Jay Fite - who decided to attend Mason County instead of going to Lewis County when Tollesboro High School closed following the 1993-94 school year.

The Royals opened the season with an 87-78 loss to Cincinnati Oak Hills at the Shoemaker Center in Cincinnati.

Shawn Myrick scored 35 points to lead Mason County to a 99-91 victory over St. Patrick in the home opener. Aaron Rigdon scored 26 points for the Saints.

After a 108-86 win over Bourbon County at the Fieldhouse, the Royals played their next five games on the road.

Myrick scored 30 points in an 87-85 loss to Louisville Male in the Panther Classic at Pleasure Ridge Park. The next game was a 93-83 loss to Ashland.

Myrick and Kyle Sherman scored 20 points apiece in a 111-72 victory over Bracken County.

Myrick fired in 26 points to lead Mason County to a 94-80 victory over Paul Laurence Dunbar in the first round of the Ashland Invitational Tournament. The Royals lost to Covington Holy Cross 71-47 in the semifinals.

Back home for the Mason County Invitational Tournament, the Royals routed Bracken County 93-57 in the first round and Pendleton County 102-75 in the semifinals. Mason County beat Harrison County 73-70 in the championship game.

Sherman scored 25 points in a 95-71 win over the Paris Greyhounds.

The four-game winning streak was snapped by a 95-84 loss to Pleasure Ridge Park in Mason County's first appearance in the Louisville Invitational Tournament. Junior guard Dominic Myrick (Shawn's cousin) had his first big scoring game with 23 points.

The Royals bounced back with an 80-77 victory over Covington Holy Cross avenging the earlier loss to the Indians.

Mason County scored the final 12 points of the game to upset top ranked Harlan 72-69 at the Fieldhouse.

Shawn Myrick and Anthony "Kotchie" Thomas each scored 21 points to the lead the Royals to 95-44 win over Estill County.

Mason County trailed by 45 points in the third quarter and was routed by Scott County 112-80 in Georgetown. The 112 points are the most ever allowed by Mason County.

The Royals started a five-game winning streak with a 103-64 victory Fleming County. The only close call during the streak was against Clark County. The Royals led by nine points in the third quarter and trailed by four in the fourth quarter before pulling out a 75-72 victory.

The Harrison County Thorobreds beat Mason County 92-85 at the Fieldhouse. The loss snapped the Royals' 72-game winning streak against 10th Region teams and their 56-game home court winning. The loss was the first to a 10th Region team since the merger with Maysville.

In the next game, Mason County lost to Newport Central Catholic 62-61. The Royals closed out the regular season with a 75-71 victory over Montgomery County.

Coach Lex Turner's St. Patrick Saints won seven of its first eight games including a 78-73 victory over Fleming County. Then, the Saints lost five of the next seven. In the 10th Region All "A" Classic at Paris, St. Patrick defeated Bracken County and Nicholas County to advance to the finals against the Paris Greyhounds.

The Saints had lost to the Greyhounds 79-74 in the first round of the Mason County Invitational Tournament.

St. Patrick avenged that loss with a 70-67 double overtime victory to earn its first trip to the All "A" Classic state tournament. "The kids really worked hard," says Turner. "Paris has always had the athletes. And our kids, I just thought, wanted it more, worked together more."

The Saints had balanced scoring in the championship game. Aaron Rigdon scored 17 points, Brian Tucker 16, Jacob Yunker 13 and Josh Owens 10.

St. Patrick had a huge crowd, including alumni who had moved away from Maysville, for the first round game in the All "A" Classic game at Eastern Kentucky University.

Bobby Gantley scored 26 points to lead St. Patrick to a 75-53 win over Louisville Holy Cross. Rigdon added 18 points.

The Saints lost to Lexington Catholic 102-62 in the quarterfinals.

St. Patrick went 3-3 in the final six games of the regular season including a 93-83 loss to Paris in the final game.

With the closing of Tollesboro High School, there were only three teams in the 39th District in 1995.

Mason County breezed past Fleming County 99-58 in the opening game of the district tournament.

Under the three-team format, Fleming County played St. Patrick which drew a bye. Patrick. Gantley scored 21 points to lead the Saints to a 70-62 win over the Panthers.

Mason County defeated St. Patrick 87-55 in the championship game. St. Patrick lost to Montgomery County 88-40 in the first round of the 10th Region Tournament to end the season with a 17-12 record.

Mason County, playing without Shawn Myrick, who was suspended from school for fighting, defeated Clark County 58-46 in the first round.

Shawn Myrick was back for the semifinal game against Harrison County. He scored 19 points, and Sherman had a career-high 28 points, including 14 in the first quarter, to lead the Royals to an 81-73 victory.

It was Mason County versus Montgomery County in the championship game. Mason County was trying to tie Maysville's record of four straight region championships. Montgomery County was shooting for its first region title. The game turned out to be one of the greatest 10th Region finals ever with two outstanding individual performances.

The Royals trailed 13-4 midway through the first quarter, but the score was tied at 13-13 at the end of the quarter. Montgomery County led 34-29 at halftime. Shawn Myrick was fouled on a three-point shot with one second left in the third quarter. He made all three free throws to give Mason County a 51-49 lead. The Royals led 72-69 with time winding down. Montgomery County's six-foot-eight senior forward Billy Fawns hit a three-pointer to tie the game with eight seconds left. Mason County could not get off a shot, and the two teams were headed to overtime. Fawns had scored 17 points in the fourth quarter.

Myrick hit both ends of the one-and-one to give Mason County an 82-79 lead with 26 seconds left in overtime. Fawns tied the game with another three-pointer with four seconds to go. The Indians came up with a steal to force a second overtime.

Montgomery County junior Chris Congleton hit a three-pointer to put Montgomery County up 85-82. Shawn Myrick hit a shot in the lane to make it 85-84 with 3:21 left. The Indians pulled away with a 10-1 run and won, 99-92.[759]

Hester says that is one game he has probably thought about more than any just because every year in the NCAA tournament, the question comes up – do you foul with a three-point lead or let it play out? Fawns scored a 10th Region finals record 47 points and grabbed 17 rebounds. Shawn Myrick scored a career-high 44 points. "It was a classic game," says Hester.

Mason County's final record was 21-9. Shawn Myrick is fourth on the Royals' all-time scoring list with 2,049 points. He played two seasons at the junior college level and two seasons at the University of Cincinnati.

Chapter 42 Another Historic Win for St. Patrick

Mason County graduated eight seniors from the 1994-95 team, and three other players transferred to Fleming County. The three returning players had only scored a total of 53 points in varsity action the previous year.

The group of inexperienced players came together under the direction of Coach Fred Hester and won 16 games in the regular season and captured the school's fifth consecutive district championship. The Royals lost to Montgomery County 74-67 in the first round of the regional tournament to end the season with an 18-11 record. Hester says that team played hard, sacrificed, over achieved and was "just a fun group."

The St. Patrick Saints lost to Fleming County in the semifinals of the district tournament to finish at 16-11.

After the 1995-96 season, Hester had concerns about balancing his coaching and athletic director's jobs as well as missing his daughter's activities. He expressed his concerns to Superintendent Joe Dan Gold who told Hester to "think about it and decide something later."

Hester says everything was pretty easy going during the summer, and he planned to continue coaching. But then with the 1996-97 season approaching, he says he felt he wasn't doing all he should as an athletic director for a lot of the other sports, and "I didn't feel like I was wanting in preseason to do as much." Then, when the son of one his friends transferred to Fleming County, Hester resigned as coach on the day of the season opener. "That was just enough to tell me that was a good time [to step down as coach]," says Hester.

Hester had a record of 127-32 in five seasons as the Royals' head coach. His teams won five district titles and three regional championships.

Assistant coach Steve Appelman was named the interim coach.

"I felt very good as an athletic director about the staff we had," says Hester. Assistant coaches Henry Boone and Dickie Butler were still there, and former Mason County player Chris O'Hearn had just joined the staff.

Appelman remembers meeting the players and telling them, "We're going to on, and we're going to play." He says it was "a tough situation" because the head coach has set the tone and had the practices.

"There was something that was just different that whole year. It was hard to put your finger on," says Appelman. "If Fred had certain plays he uses all the time, and he has a certain system. And if you have a different system, it was just hard to change. So we just decided to keep his system in place and do what we had done the last few years." Mason County opened the season with three straight victories, including a 63-52 win over St. Patrick.

The two teams met again in the championship game of the Mason County Invitational Tournament. Mason County had won five straight games. St. Patrick, under veteran coach Lex Turner, and with five senior starters, had a three-game winning streak.

The Saints led by as many as 13 points in the third quarter. The Royals twice closed the gap to three. The last time was at 56-53 with 42 seconds left in the game. But St. Patrick ended the game on a 5-1 run to beat Mason County for the first time. The final score was 61-54. "It was fantastic," says Turner.

The Royals had won the first 56 games in the series which began in 1961 during Mason County's first season. St. Patrick's six-foot-six foot center, Drew Beckett, had a double-double with 14 points and 12 rebounds. Robert Klee scored 14 points. Josh Owens and Michael Walton added 13 apiece.

Turner remembers celebrating right after the game and getting ready to head to the locker room when he heard the public address announcement about the trophy presentation. "I forgot it was the MCIT finals," says Turner. "And I'm sitting there thinking, 'My gosh, we get a trophy to boot.' ... the game was bigger than the tournament for sure."

St. Patrick made it two straight wins over Mason County with a 57-53 victory in the semifinals of the district tournament. Beckett had a game-high 19 points. Owens added 17 points. Mason County ended the season with an 18-10 record. It was the first time since 1991 that the Royals did not advance to the regional tournament.

St. Patrick defeated Fleming County 69-65 in the championship game for its first district championship. Owens scored 27 points, and Beckett added 24. It was the Saints' 20th win of the season.

Beckett scored 29 points as St. Patrick ran its winning streak to nine games with a 70-62 victory over Montgomery County in the first round of the 10th Region Tournament.

St. Patrick's season came to an end with a 54-42 loss to Harrison County in the semifinals. Owens scored 15 points, and Beckett had 14. The Saints record was 21-8.

Former Rowan County High School and Morehead State

University standout Kelly Wells was hired as the Mason County coach in the summer of 1997. Wells had guided Marion County to the 1997 state tournament.

"Mason County has been one of those storied traditions forever," Well says. "And I think the legacy and the history of the Fieldhouse always brings to mind great basketball and just the regional tournaments and the traditions and the players and the Coach Allen Feldhauses of the world and the Fred Hesters of the world, and the Ronnie Lyonses, just the tradition has always been something that all coaches and players dream about.

"I actually played in the Fieldhouse as an eighth grader, and I think that's where my first recollection of the program kinda got into my mind, and as there was an opportunity there. It was something I wanted to see if I could pursue."

Wells was Mason County's third coach in three years and he says there were a lot of challenges.

"Any time you take over a program, each situation is unique," says Wells. "Coaches take over for different reasons. This transition probably wasn't an ideal transition, and maybe I was too young to really to be too scared of it or too concerned with it, and I've become great friends with all people involved. But I think there was a little bit of a challenge coming through - player expectations and those kind of things were probably a little different. The program had always been successful so I wasn't going to make an impact in that way."

Mason County opened the 1997-98 season with two consecutive wins, but lost its next three including a 66-61 loss to St. Patrick. It was the Saints' third straight win over the Royals.

Mason County avenged the loss by beating St. Patrick 65-56 in the semifinals of the district tournament. The Saints ended the season with a 15-11 record.

Mason County lost to Fleming County 60-45 in the championship game of the district tournament.

The Royals defeated Bourbon County 64-58 in the first round of the regional tournament, but lost to Bishop Brossart 73-68 in the semifinals to end their first season under Wells at 16-13.

Mason County won the Mountain School Boy Classic at Belfry and the Mason County Invitational Tournament in the 1998-99 season and had a 16-9 record in the regular season. In one of the victories, Larry Myrick scored 41 points, and the Royals came from behind to beat Paris 72-66.

Across town, the St. Patrick Saints lost five of their first seven games and eight of their first 12.

The Saints won back-to-back games before heading into the 10th Region All "A" Classic.

St. Patrick defeated Deming 78-45 in the quarterfinals. Four Saints scored in double figures. Jordan Owens had a game-high 23 points, Cody Conway 14, Simon Welte 12 and Michael Glass 10.

In the semifinals, the Saints trailed Bracken County by eight points at the end of the third quarter and by five with 1:30 left, but ended the game on a 10-1 run to win 60-56. St. Patrick hit 17 of 20 free throws in the fourth quarter.[760] Once again, the Saints had balanced scoring. Cody Conway had 14 points, Davey Downs 12, Willie Conway 11 and Owens 10.

St. Patrick trailed Paris by five points with 2:28 remaining in the championship game. Downs made a field goal and two free throws to cut the deficit to one. After Paris missed three free throws, Glass was fouled. He made the first free throw to tie the game at 53-53. Glass missed the second shot and Paris got the rebound, but was tied up by St. Patrick. The Saints got the ball on the alternating possession, but couldn't score. The Greyhounds had the ball with 16 seconds left. St. Patrick forced a loose ball and time ran out. In the overtime period, Paris took a 55-53 lead. St. Patrick tied the game on a Cody Conway basket. After each team committed a turnover, Paris decided to hold the ball with two minutes left, but turned it over. Downs made two free throws to give the Saints the lead at 57-55 with 1:10 to go. Paris tied it again. Willie Conway hit a jump shot with 36 seconds left to give St. Patrick a 59-57 lead. Owens came up with a steal and was fouled. He hit both free throws to make it 61-57 with 26 seconds to play. Paris missed three three-pointers in the closing seconds.[761] St. Patrick was headed back to the All "A" Classic. Owens scored 16 points, Willie Conway 13, Downs 12 and Glass 10.

St. Patrick had 18 steals and Owens had a double-double with 31 points and 10 rebounds in a 64-57 victory over Hancock County in the first round of the All "A" Classic at Eastern Kentucky University. Cody Conway added 16 points.[762]

The Saints trailed St. Mary 42-39 with 1:42 left in the quarterfinal game. Cody Conway hit a three-pointer to tie the game. Owens hit two free throws to give the St. Patrick a 44-42 lead with 1:10 to play. St. Mary hit one of two free throws to get to within one. The Vikings made a field goal to regain the lead with 20 seconds left. Cody Conway made two free throws to give the Saints a 46-45 lead. Owens stole the ball and was fouled with 3.8 seconds left. He missed the free throw. St. Mary grabbed the rebound, but could not get off a shot. Owens led St. Patrick in scoring with 11 points. Downs added 10. It was the 300th career win for St. Patrick Coach Lex Turner.[763]

The Saints played the University Heights Academy Blazers in the semifinals. UHA had won the All "A" Classic four times and was the 1992 state champion. The Blazers led 16-13 at the end of the first quarter. St. Patrick was up 27-22 at the half. UHA led 36-34 at the end of the third quarter and 44-37 with 4:30 left in the game. Downs hit a three-pointer, Glass made two free throws and Owens hit a three-pointer to give the Saints a 45-44 lead.

UHA scored on a layup to regain the lead. Owens was fouled with 38 seconds to go. He made one of two free throws to tie the game 40-40.

UHA guard Wayne Watts drove the lane and made a shot just ahead of the buzzer to give the Blazers a 48-46 win.

Owens scored a game-high 17 points and was named to the all-tournament team. Glass added 11 points. UHA defeated Gallatin County in the championship game.[764]

St. Patrick won six straight games before losing to Paris 55-51 in the final game of the regular season.

Mason County defeated St. Patrick 62-47 in the semifinals of the district tournament. The Saints ended the season with a 17-11 record.

Mason County lost to Fleming County 72-69 in overtime in the district championship game. The Royals beat Bracken County 71-55 in the first round of the regional tournament, but lost to Harrison County 66-56 in the semifinals to end the season with an 18-11 record.

Chapter 43 Girls Coaching Changes

The Mason County Lady Royals had a 6-20 record in the 1989-90 season-their first losing season since 1978-79.

The Lady Royals won the 1991 39th District Tournament, but finished the season with an 8-21 record.

After the Maysville-Mason County merger, the Maysville Gymnasium became the home of the Lady Royals. The inside of the gym was painted blue and white. A few years later the playing floor was named "Earle D. Jones Court" in honor of the legendary coach of the Maysville Bulldogs

Mason County had winning records and won the district championship in each of Coach Bob Hutchison's final six seasons. The Lady Royals' records those seasons were 18-10, 21-6, 19-7, 18-9, 18-8 and 20-6. During that stretch, Mason County lost in the first round of the regional tournament every year but one. That was in 1995 when the Lady Royals beat Deming 62-30 in the first round, but lost to Harrison County 65-37 in the semifinals.

Hutchison retired after the 1996-97 season. In 22 seasons as the head coach at Mason County, Hutchison had a 405-201 record. His teams won 19 district championships and six region titles.

Leon Willett was Hutchison's long time assistant coach. Willet duties included scouting the Lady Royals' opponents. "He brought back everything they did," says Hutchison. "And he coached the 'B' team, and he calmed me down. That's unbelievable, but he'd get me calmed down."

Hutchison says he loved every minute of coaching, and he missed it after he retired.

"I wouldn't even go to a ball game, says Hutchison. "I go to a ball game now, and I wish I was back coaching."

Assistant Coach Jeff McEldowney was promoted to head coach. McEldowney's first team, the 1997-98 squad, won the first 10 games of the season. The Lady Royals closed out the regular season with six straight victories, won their eighth straight district title and routed Nicholas County 64-27 in the first round of the regional tournament. But Mason County's season came to end with a 68-60 loss to Bishop Brossart in the semifinals. The Lady Royals' record was 22-6.

Mason County closed out the 1990s with a 22-10 mark in the 1998-99 season. The Lady Royals won the district tournament, but lost to Bishop Brossart once again in the region semifinals.

The St. Patrick Lady Saints had four different head coaches in the 1990s. Victor McKay succeeded his brother, Danny, as the head coach for the 1989-90 season and stayed three seasons.

Ron Reule was the coach for three seasons. The Lady Saints' 16-12 record in 1993-94 snapped a string of four straight losing seasons.

A 50-47 loss to Pendleton County in overtime in the first round of the regional tournament dropped St. Patrick's record in the 1994-95 season to 13-14.

Jeannie Whitehead took over as the coach for the 1995-96 season and guided the Lady Saints to a 12-12 record. Whitehead stepped down after the 1996-97 season.

Former basketball official Jerry Ormes was hired as the Lady Saints' coach.

Margaret Klee, a 5-8 senior guard, scored 41 points to lead St. Patrick to a 74-48 season-opening win over Bracken County.

Klee scored a career-high 44 points in a 65-64 loss to Campbell County in the Lady Royal Invitational.

The Lady Saints ended the regular season with seven straight wins.

Klee fired in 32 points to lead St. Patrick to a 68-46 win over Augusta in the first round of the 39th District Tournament.

The Lady Saints lost to Mason County 50-39 in the semifinals to end the season with a 17-10 record.

Klee is the Lady Saints' all-time leading scorer with 2,012 career points.

St. Patrick had a 17-9 record in the 1998-99 season.

The Lady Saints won 20 regular season games in 1999-2000. Joanna Bess fired in 33 points to lead St. Patrick to a 92-41 rout of Pendleton County in the Lady Royal Invitational.

The Lady Saints defeated Fleming County 54-36 in the first round of the 39th District Tournament.

St. Patrick cruised past Deming 60-31 in the semifinals.

Bess scored 27 points in a 44-39 victory over Mason County in the championship game.

Bess had 26 points to lead St. Patrick to a 34-32 victory over Bourbon County in the first round of the 10th Region Tournament. It was the Lady Saints' first regional tournament win.

St. Patrick lost to Estill County 43-37 in the semifinals to end the season at 24-9.

Mason County edged Clark County 60-58 in the first round of the regional tournament but lost to Harrison County 66-37 in the semifinals to close out the season with a 20-10 record.

McEldowney stepped down after the season. He had a three-year record of 64-26. McEldowney guided the Lady Royals to two district championships.

Paula Buser, a standout player on Mason County's first team, was hired as the Lady Royals' coach. Buser was the head coach at Fleming County for three seasons.

In her first season Buser guided the Lady Royals to 18 regular season wins. Mason County defeated St. Patrick 47-35 in the semifinals. The Lady Saints closed out the 2000-01 season at 19-9. Mason County lost to Fleming County 61-49 in the championship game. A 38-36 loss to Harrison County in the first round of the 10th Region Tournament gave the Lady Royals a record of 20-10.

St. Patrick and Mason County drew each other in the first round of the 2002 district tournament. The Lady Saints had won the regular season game 54-35. Mary Klee scored 23 points to lead St. Patrick to a 60-43 victory in the district tournament game. Mason County ended the year with an 8-20 record. It was the Lady Royals' first losing season since 1990-91.

The Lady Saints beat Augusta 70-48 in the semifinals and Fleming County 44-41 in the championship game for their second district title in three seasons.

St. Patrick edged Paris 48-46 in the first round of the 10th Region Tournament, but lost to Bishop Brossart 51-46 in the semifinals to end the season at 15-16.

The Lady Saints had their second straight losing season in 2002-03. The season ended with a 59-48 loss to Mason County in the first round of the district tournament.

The Lady Royals routed Deming 93-34 in the semifinals, then, rallied from a 20-point deficit to beat Fleming County 58-52 in overtime in the championship game. Seventh grader De'Sarae Chambers led the Lady Royals in scoring with 21 points.

Mason County lost to Harrison County 48-43 in the first round of the 10th Region Tournament. The Lady Royals finished with a 12-16 record for their second consecutive losing season.

The Lady Royals would rack up many points and numerous victories in the coming seasons as they looked to win a region title for the first time since 1987.

Chapter 44 2000 to 2001

The St. Patrick Saints opened the 1999-2000 season with six straight wins including a 75-57 victory over Mason County, but lost four of their next five games.

The Saints routed Deming 101-29 and headed to the 10th Region All "A" Classic with an 8-4 record.

St. Patrick had four double digit wins in the tournament to advance to the All "A" Classic for the third time. The Saints lost to Paducah St. Mary 53-49 in the first round.

St. Patrick beat Deming 75-55 in the semifinals of the 39th District Tournament.

Jordan Owens scored a career-high 39 points to lead the Saints to an 88-76 victory over the Mason County Royals in the championship game.

The Saints routed Estill County 89-57 in the first round of the 10th Region Tournament, but lost to Bishop Brossart 61-60 in the semifinals to end the season at 20-9.

Mason County and Bishop Brossart met in the championship game. The Royals had bounced back from the loss to St. Patrick in the district finals with wins over Clark County (55-52) and Campbell County (69-61).

The Royals suffered another heart breaking loss in the regional finals when Justin Seiter hit a shot at the buzzer to give Bishop Brossart a 52-50 victory. The Royals closed out the year with a 17-14 mark.

Freshman Chris Lofton led Mason County in scoring in the 2000-2001 season. Lofton, a sharp-shooting guard, scored 13 points in the second game of the season, and had a season-high 31 points in a victory over Lewis County.

Mason County beat St. Patrick 57-47 in the championship game of the district tournament.

St. Patrick lost to Montgomery County in the first round of the regional tournament to end the season with a 9-18 record.

Mason County beat Clark County 83-62 in the first round and Bishop Brossart 74-60 in the semifinals.

The Royals were in the region finals for the second straight year. Mason County had an eight-point lead over Campbell County at halftime. But the Royals only scored six points in the third quarter and lost 72-59 to finish the season with a 25-7 record.

The losses in the region finals in back-to-back years were tough for Coach Kelly Wells.

"Those were character builders for me as a coach," says Wells, "and philosophy builders for me as a coach too. You don't come off what you do and believe in because you don't win a game. And that was a challenge for me. I spent many nights at my computer and my desk, you know, pulling my hair out thinking of what we could have done differently. And you learn from those things and try to build from those. It ended up being probably the best things that happened in my career and kept me very humble and very hungry to continue to succeed."

Lofton set the Mason County freshman scoring records for a single game (31) and a season (407). Lofton would set many more records and take the Royals to new heights in the next three seasons.

Chapter 45 Lofton Leads Royals to State

For the first time since Kelly Wells had become the coach at Mason County, the Royals had a big post player when six-foot-five senior G.G. Lofton made the roster for the 2001-2002 season. The Royals finally had an inside presence to compliment their outside scoring threat.

Mason County had a 33-7 lead at halftime and beat St. Patrick 69-50 in the season opener.

After a 66-48 road loss to the Bourbon County Colonels, the Royals reeled off six straight victories, including a 74-70 win over Bourbon County in the Fifth-Third Bank Classic at Lexington Catholic.

Mason County lost back-to-back games to Westminster Academy and Highlands in the Fifth-Third Bank Classic.

The Royals had easy victories over Harrison County, Bishop Brossart and Montgomery County to win the Mason County Invitational Tournament. Robert Myrick made a school-record nine three-pointers and scored a career-high 39 points in the championship game.

An 85-59 win over the Paris Greyhounds ran Mason County's record to 11-3.

After consecutive losses to Scott County and Lexington Catholic, the Royals won the final 11 games of the regular season. The only close call during the winning streak was a 67-66 victory over Clark County.

The Royals averaged 85 points a game during the streak. Sophomore guard Chris Lofton scored 33 points in a 111-63 rout of Bracken County.

Mason County routed Augusta 93-53 in the semifinals of the 39th District Tournament.

Chris Lofton scored 19 points, G.G. Lofton 18 and Myrick 16 in a 68-58 victory over St. Patrick in the championship game. John Demoya had a game-high 21 points for the Saints.

St. Patrick lost to Montgomery County 66-42 in the first round of the 10th Region Tournament to finish the season with a 16-12 record.

G.G. Lofton scored a career-high 23 points to lead Mason County past Bishop Brossart 89-77 in the first round of the regional tournament.

The Royals played Bourbon County in the semifinals. Mason County led by 12 points, then, trailed by five before pulling out a 79-76 win. Chris Lofton led the Royals in scoring with 21 points.

Mason County jumped out to a 9-0 lead over Montgomery County in the championship game. The Royals led by 12 in the third quarter. The Indians rallied and took a four-point lead early in the fourth quarter. Mason County came back to win 63-59. Chris Lofton scored a game-high 31 points. It was the Royals' first 10th Region title since 1994.

Mason County hit a state tournament record 13 three-pointers in a 93-66 rout of Louisville Butler in the first round of the state tournament. Myrick hit seven three-pointers and scored 23 points. Chris Lofton made six three pointers and had a game-high 29 points.

The Royals only hit three three-pointers, and Myrick and Chris Lofton were held to six points apiece in a 64-51 loss to Paducah Tilghman in the quarterfinals. Tee Commodore led the Royals in scoring with 11 points. Nathan Myrick added 10. Mason County ended the season with a 28-6 record. Robert Myrick and Chris Lofton were named to the all-tournament team.

Chapter 46 Mason County Wins State Championship

Tragedy struck the Mason County basketball program in the spring of 2002. Assistant coach Pat Moore was seriously injured in an automobile accident in April. He was recovering at home in May when he became ill and died at Meadowview Regional Medical Center. Moore was a star on Maysville's 1988 10th Region champion team. Another star on that team, Mike Case, was killed in an automobile accident in 1990.

Moore's funeral was held in the Mason County Fieldhouse.

Mason County's 2002-03 season opener was pushed back in anticipation of a long run in the playoffs by the football team.

Three starters on the basketball team were also stars on the football field - Chris Lofton was a wide receiver and defensive end, Dustin Grutza was the quarterback, and Nathan Myrick was the team's top running back. One of the top substitutes on the basketball team, Derek Gilbert, also played football.

The football team lost to Russell 11-8 in the region championship game on November 22.

The Royals opened the basketball season on December 10. Jarrod Litzinger and Wes Jones were the other two starters. Gilbert, Andrew Tibbs and Seth Vice were the main subs. Lofton scored 20 points to lead Mason County to an 84-51 victory over the St. Patrick Saints in the season opener. Myrick, the only senior in the starting lineup, led the way with 21 points in an 88-43 win over the Bourbon County Colonels.

Mason County headed to Louisville for the King of the Bluegrass Tournament. The Royals' first round opponent, Louisville Eastern, was led by future NBA all-star Rajon Rondo. Lofton was the star of the game with 31 points. Rondo scored 20. There were 10 ties and 14 lead changes. Mason County outscored Eastern 29-13 in the fourth quarter and won 95-80.

With University of Louisville coach Rick Pitino looking on, Lofton hit seven three-pointers and scored 42 points to lead the Royals past North Hardin 95-81.

Mason County outscored Miami Senior 24-15 in the fourth quarter for a 74-65 victory in the quarterfinals. Lofton scored 21 points.

The Royals' season-opening five-game winning streak was broken with a 75-71 overtime loss to Apollo in the championship. Jones led Mason County in scoring with 23 points. He was 10-of-13 from the field.

The day after Christmas, Mason County defeated University Heights Academy 76-55 in the first round of the Fifth Third Bank Kentucky Holiday Classic at Lexington Catholic. Lofton hit five three-pointers and scored a game-high 20 points. Grutza tossed in 19.

In the quarterfinals against Highlands, Mason County blew a 17-point lead and trailed by four. But the Royals rallied. An old fashion three-point play by Lofton with seven seconds left gave Mason County a 48-47 victory. Lofton drained six three-pointers and had a game-high 30 points.

Grutza scored 18 points to lead Mason County to a 73-53 win over Louisville Trinity in the semifinals.

The Royals shot 62 percent from the field and defeated top ranked Lexington Catholic 93-89 in the championship game.

Lofton had 22 points, eight rebounds and five assists, and was named the Most Valuable Player.

Myrick also scored 22 points. Jones followed with 18, and Grutza added 12.

After eight straight road games, Mason County returned home on January 3 and beat Ashland 66-47.

Myrick scored 24 points, and Jones 20 in an 89-52 road victory over Fleming County. The Royals led 30-3 at the end of the first quarter.

Next up was the Mason County Invitational Tournament. Lofton was 9-of-12 from the field and scored 23 points, and Litzinger was 7-of-10 from the field and followed with 18 points in an 82-57 win over Campbell County in the first round.

In the semifinal game against Montgomery County, the Royals led 39-15 at halftime and won 63-40.

Lofton made six three-pointers and scored 28 points to lead Mason County to a 69-52 victory over Bishop Brossart in the championship game.

As the Royals headed to the locker room at halftime with a seven-point lead over the Paris Greyhounds at Paris, several of the Greyhounds' fans chanted "over rated." Mason County outscored Paris 56-23 in the second half for a 106-66 win. Grutza had 23 points and 13 rebounds. Lofton scored 21 points, Litzinger 20 and Jones 15.

Mason County traveled to Georgetown and beat Scott County 90-81. It was the Royals' first win over the Cardinals since 1994. All five starters scored in double figures- Grutza with 21, Lofton 20, Jones 17, Myrick 12 and Litzinger 14.

The Royals were ranked No. 1 in the Associated Press when they headed to Campbell County to play the Camels on January 21. Lofton scored 21 points to lead Mason County to an 88-63 victory.

The Fieldhouse was packed for the rematch with Lexington Catholic. The Knights won 76-75 despite a 25-point game by Lofton. The loss snapped the Royals' 12-game winning streak.

Mason County started another winning streak by beating Montgomery County 68-35. The Royals led 22-2 at the end of the first quarter and 42-10 at halftime.

Jones fired in 27 points in a 107-63 rout of Lewis County. The Royals scored 66 points in the first half.

Mason County shot 52 percent from the field in a 70-63 win over Rowan County.

Lofton was 7-of-9 from the field, including 5-of-6 on three pointers, and made both of his free throws for a 21-point game in a 67-35 victory over Russell in the Kentucky Prep Classic.

The next two games were close calls against 10th Region opponents. The Royals pulled out a 58-54 win over Bishop Brossart, despite shooting just 35.8 percent from the field. Mason County edged Clark County 68-66 in Winchester.

The Royals led 16-2 at the end of the first quarter on their way to a 76-46 victory over Harrison County.

Mason County closed out the regular season with an 89-67 win over Pendleton County. Lofton had a double-double with 24 points and 11 rebounds.

Mason County was back at No. 1 in the final Associated Press poll of the season.

Lofton and Grutza scored 23 points apiece to lead the Royals past St. Patrick 80-56 in the first round of the 39th District Tournament. St. Patrick closed out the season with a 10-12 record.

Mason County routed Deming 95-39 in the semifinals. The Royals were up 28-6 at the end of the first quarter and 54-22 at halftime.

Lofton and Myrick both scored 23 points in a 90-66 victory over Fleming County in the championship game.

Grutza scored 22 points to lead the Royals to an 85-53 win over Montgomery County in the first round of the 10th Region Tournament.

Bourbon County stayed with Mason County for a half in the semifinals, but the Royals outscored the Colonels 53-27 in the second half for a 91-58 victory. Jones led the Royals in scoring with 21 points.

Lofton scored 30 points to lead Mason County to a 78-51 win over the Clark County in the championship game. After leading by just five points at halftime, the Royals outscored the Cardinals 50-27 in the second half.

Several of the state's best teams including Lexington Catholic were upset in the regional tournament. Mason County was No. 1

in Dave Cantrall's Sweet Sixteen ratings.[765] The Royals' first round opponent, Ninth Region Champion St. Henry, won the Touchstone Energy All 'A" Classic in February. The Crusaders, making their first appearance in the state tournament, had a 30-4 record and a 19-game winning streak.

St. Henry had a 28-14 lead at halftime. The Royals outscored the Crusaders 25-14 in the third quarter. Mason County was leading 59-57 when Myrick came up with a steal and called time out with two seconds to play. After the timeout, the Royals ran out the clock for their 15 consecutive victory. Mason County scored 18 points off St. Henry's 23 turnovers. Lofton and Jones scored 17 points apiece.

Mason County played Eighth Region champion Oldham County in the quarterfinals. The Royals made their first eight shots and had a 20-6 lead with 3:11 to play in the first quarter. Mason County made its first five shots of the second quarter and used a 13-0 run to lead 35-14 with 5:05 remaining in the half. The Colonels switched from a man-to-man defense to a 2-3 zone and closed the gap to 37-26 by the end of the half.

Oldham County cut the Royals' lead to 39-36 with 4:16 to go in the third quarter. Lofton answered with a three-pointer. Myrick came up with a steal and made a layup. Jones scored on a putback, and Lofton hit another three-pointer to push the lead out to 11. Lofton made two free throws, Myrick had a putback, and Lofton added a basket to complete a 14-4 run. The Royals were up 53-40 heading into the fourth quarter. Oldham County could get no closer than nine. The final score: Mason County 63, Oldham County 50. Lofton ended up with 19 points. Jones had 14. Grutza and Litzinger added 12 apiece.

The Royals advanced to the semifinals to play a very athletic Hopkinsville team. The Tigers, the Second Region champions, had won 27 straight games.

There were seven ties in the first quarter. Hopkinsville was up 18-17 at the end of the first quarter and 31-30 at halftime. There were two ties and five lead changes in the third quarter. The Tigers lead 49-47 at the end of the third quarter. After Hopkinsville scored the first two points of the fourth quarter, Mason County scored nine straight points to lead 56-51. The Royals continued to pull away and won 75-63. Lofton scored a game-high 30 points and had six rebounds. Jones scored 19 points, and Grutza added 12.

Louisville Ballard defeated Lexington Henry Clay 84-77 in the other semifinal. Ballard was a three-time state champion. The Bruins, like the Royals, were not very big, but they used their quickness to press and play an up tempo style.

Lofton took his game to another level in the championship game. He made his first five shots including three three-pointers, and the

The Ledger-Indepedent

The Royals finally won their first state championship in 2003, returning the title to Mason County for the first time since Maysville's 1947 win.

Royals led 21-16 at the end of the first quarter.

Lofton hit three more three-pointers in the second quarter and Mason County went to the locker room at halftime with a 42-28 lead.

The Royals led by as many as 20 points in the third quarter. Lofton hit his seventh and eighth three-pointers of the game in the third quarter, and Mason County was up 62-48 heading into the fourth quarter.

The Bruins closed the gap to 68-58 with 4:47 left, but the Royals answered with an 11-2 run to push their lead back out to 19. The run included Lofton's ninth three-pointer which tied the record for three-pointers in a state tournament game set by Clay County guard Richie Farmer in the 1998 championship game. Fans wanted Lofton to break the record, but he did not attempt another three-pointer before leaving the game with 1:04 to go. Mason County scored the final seven points of the game for an 86-65 victory.

"I couldn't be happier for my guys," said Wells during the post game celebration. "They have earned everything that they have got. I'm proud as I could be of my fellows."

Wells said Lofton's shooting performance made his job pretty easy, "Get out of his way; let him shoot in the basket. He's a fine player, but it was a great team effort."

It was Mason County's first state championship and the first state title for a 10th Region team since Maysville won it in 1947.

"We're glad to bring it back to Maysville [and] Mason County where it belongs," said Wells.

Lofton finished with 39 points. He was 11-of-17 from the field including 9-of-12 on three-pointers and was 8-of-8 on free throws.

"I was just feeling it, and my teammates gave the ball to me, and I just shot and it went in," said Lofton.

Mason County hit 14 three-pointers in the game breaking the record of 13 the Royals set in 2002 in a first round win over Louisville Butler. Lofton broke the record for most three-pointers in a state tournament with 17.

Dustin Grutza with 11 points was the only other Royal in double figures in the championship game. Tibbs scored nine points. Myrick had eight points and six assists. Vice hit two three-pointers and scored eight points. Jones had seven points and Gilbert added 4.

Lofton was named the Most Valuable Player. He was joined on the all-tournament team by Grutza and Jones.

Mason County fans partied in a ballroom at the Lexington Center.

Sheriff, police and fire department vehicles escorted the team bus from the county line to the Fieldhouse for a celebration Sunday afternoon.

The team went to Frankfort on Monday. The House and Senate passed resolutions honoring the state champions. A parade was held in downtown Maysville eight days after the championship game. The Maysville Lions Club held a dinner for the Royals at the Maysville Country Club in May. The players, coaches and support staff received their state championship rings in June.

Other members of the team not previously mentioned were Robert White, Chris Schumacher, Casey Pfeffer, Tyler Murray, John Rice, Zach Harrison, Jonathan Dunn and Chris Hopper.

The community continued to celebrate the state championship while also thinking about the next season when four starters would return.

Chapter 47 State Runner-up Finish for Royals

The Mason County football team moved up to Class AAA for the 2003 season. Quarterback Dustin Grutza, who rushed for a school-record six touchdowns in the region finals, and wide receiver Chris Lofton led the Royals to a 12-2 record.

The Royals lost to 15-time state champion Highlands 21-14 in the state semifinals. Eight days later, Grutza, Lofton and the rest of the basketball team, ranked No. 1 in the Herald-Leader's pre-season coaches' poll, opened the season in the Marshall County Hoopfest. The defending state champions outscored Dudley High School of Greensboro, NC, 105-93. All five starters scored in double figures. Jarrod Litzinger led the way with 25 points. Grutza and Wes Jones had 22 apiece, Andrew Tibbs 17, and Lofton 16.

Mason County routed St. Patrick 84-31 in its home opener. Lofton had a double-double with 21 points and 13 rebounds.

Lofton fired in 26 points and Jones added 21 to lead the Royals past Cardinal Ritter of St. Louis 84-59 in the Kentucky Bank Classic at Bourbon County.

The Royals were out rebounded 33-19 and did not make a three-pointer, but they shot 54 percent from the field to beat Ashland 60-47.

Mason County hosted the River City Classic the week leading up to Christmas. Jones scored 29 points to lead the Royals to a 78-60 victory over Paul Laurance Dunbar in the first round.

Lofton scored 50 points and had 10 rebounds in a 94-71 win over Louisville Doss in the morning semifinal. Lofton was 20-of-30 from the field including 6-of-11 on three-pointers. He made 4-of-5 free throws and hit a half-court shot at the end of the third quarter.

"It was about that time for me to have a game like this," said Lofton. "I haven't been playing well all season, my defense has been suspect, and I just felt like it was time to start playing."

The championship game was played that night. Lofton scored 37 points, and Grutza added 28 as the Royals routed Clark County 110-63. Lofton was 13-of-18 from the field including 5-of-9 on three-pointers. He was 6-of-6 from the free throw line. Grutza was 10-of-13 from the field including 7-of-9 on three-pointers. Mason County shot 63 percent from the field.

After a brief Christmas break, the Royals opened play in the Fifth Third Bank Kentucky Holiday Classic at Lexington Catholic with a 72-41 win over Louisville Manual. Litzinger hit 10-of-14 shots and scored 25 points.

Grutza scored 20 points, and Lofton scored his 2,000th career point in an 88-55 rout of Daviess County in the quarterfinals.

The Royals outscored Louisville DeSales 25-12 in the fourth quarter for a 77-58 victory. Lofton scored 25 points. Litzinger followed with 17. Tibbs had a double-double with 16 points and 11 rebounds.

The championship game between Mason County and Lexington Catholic turned out to be an instant classic. The gym was filled to capacity, and many fans were turned away.

The Knights led 21-11 at the end of the first quarter. The Royals were up 35-31 at halftime. Lexington Catholic had a 56-46 lead after three quarters. Litzinger hit a three-pointer to close the gap to 71-70 with 10 seconds to go. Lexington Catholic hit two free throws with 4.6 seconds left.

After a Lexington Catholic timeout, Lofton received the inbounds pass, drove into front court and hit a 30-footer at the buzzer to send the game to overtime.

The Royals outscored the Knights 11-8 in the extra period for an 84-81 win. Lofton scored 32 points. Grutza had a double-double with 26 points and 13 rebounds. Litzinger added 15 points.

Mason County was 11-0 and had won 29 consecutive games dating back to the previous January.

The Royals traveled to Indianapolis on January 2 to play North Central in the Circle City Classic at Hinkle Fieldhouse on the campus of Butler University. Lofton hit six three-pointers and scored 29 points, but the Royals lost 92-75.

The next night, Mason County hosted Fleming County. It was the Royals' sixth game in eight days. Lofton scored 25 points, and Jones had 20 in a 74-53 victory.

Mason County shot 59 percent from the field in an 88-48 rout of Bracken County in the first round of the Mason County Invitational Tournament.

Jones scored 24 points, and Lofton had 22 points and nine rebounds in a 78-52 victory over Campbell County in the semifinals.

Lofton scored 26 points, Jones 25, and Litzinger 23 in a 92-79 win over Pendleton County.

The Royals ran their record to 16-1 with a 99-63 rout of Paris. Lofton scored 25 points, and Litzinger added 22.

The next day, Shelby Starns, the infant daughter of assistant coach Mark Starns, died of sudden infant death syndrome. The basketball team, the schools, and the community mourned with the Starns family. Mason County's game on the following Friday was postponed. Selby's funeral was held in Lexington that Saturday. Six days later, the Royals returned to action with heavy hearts.

The rematch with Lexington Catholic was moved to Memorial Coliseum on the campus of the University of Kentucky to accommodate the large crowd. The game was televised by Lexington station WKYT.

Mason County led 38-28 at halftime, but the Knights outscored the Royals 32-18 in the third quarter to lead by 14 heading into the fourth quarter. Mason County closed to within three in the closing minutes, but Lexington Catholic held on for an 82-75 victory. Lofton scored a game-high 25 points.

The Royals bounced back with an 87-46 win over Montgomery County. Lofton scored 27 points, and Litzinger added 21.

Litzinger scored a career-high 33 points and had 10 rebounds and Lofton added 29 points in a 106-80 victory over Scott County.

The Royals had a 51-19 lead over Rowan County and won 89-48. Mason County was 30-of-47 from the field for 63.8 percent. Lofton made five three-pointers and scored a game-high 24 points.

Jones scored 22 points to lead Mason County past Bishop Brossart 62-51.

Lofton hit five three-pointers and scored 42 points in an 84-72 win over Clark County.

Mason County had to rally to beat Lexington Lafayette. The Royals outscored the Generals 27-13 in the fourth quarter for an 87-79 road win. Jones had 26 points and nine rebounds. Lofton and Grutza scored 20 points apiece. Litzinger had a double-double with 16 points and 10 rebounds.

Litzinger was diagnosed with mononucleosis and missed the next three games. Casey Pfeffer took Litzinger's place in the starting lineup.

Lofton scored 30 points on 20 field goals and 10 free throws, grabbed 11 rebounds and had seven assists to lead the Royals past Harrison County 84-62. Jones added 21 points.

The next night, Lofton scored 41 points and had 10 assists as Mason County defeated Louisville Iroquois 104-79 in the Adolph Rupp Classic at Lexington Catholic. Jones scored 26 points. Eighth grader Darius Miller saw his first varsity action and scored three points.

Few people knew that Wells was dealing with a serious health problem until a feature story on the Royals in the February 25 edition of *USA Today* revealed that he needed a kidney transplant.[766]

Lofton made eight three-pointers and scored a career-high 54 points to lead the Royals to a 99-83 victory over the Pendleton County Wildcats on Senior Night. Lofton was 20-of-32 from the field including 8-of-15 on three-pointers. He was six-of-six from the free throw line.

He also had 10 rebounds. Lofton hit five consecutive three-pointers in the fourth quarter. Grutza added 20 points. The Royals made 12 three-pointers.

In the first game of the 39th District Tournament, Fleming County topped St. Patrick 71-44. The Saints' record was 4-21.

Mason County drew a first round bye and played Fleming County in the semifinals. Lofton made seven three-pointers and had another double-double with 42 points and 12 rebounds to lead the Royals to a 77-56 win. Lofton was 16-of-25 from the field including seven-of-11 from behind the arc. He was three-of-three on free throws. Grutza scored 15 points. Litzinger returned to action and scored 7 points.

The Royals led 58-20 at halftime on their way to an 85-39 rout of Deming in the championship game. Lofton played less than half the game and had a game-high 18 points.

Despite having the flu, Lofton scored 35 points and had 11 rebounds as Mason County beat Clark County 83-72 in the first round of the 10th Region Tournament. Lofton hit seven three-pointers and had five assists.

A feature on the Royals appeared on *NBC Nightly News with Tom Brokaw* on the night of the semifinals.

Lofton scored 27 points and became the Royals' all-time leading scorer in Mason County's 94-74 win over Pendleton County. Litzinger had 21 points and eight rebounds.

Mason County was a heavy favorite in the championship game against the Bourbon County Colonels. Bourbon County led 12-8 in the first quarter, but the Royals scored 16 straight points, led by 20 at halftime and won 101-70. Litzinger scored 11 straight points in the second quarter and finished with a game-high 28. Grutza had 20, Jones 19, and Lofton 17.

It was the Royals' third straight region title and their 53rd consecutive win against 10th Region teams. Mason County ran its home court winning streak to 25 games going back to the previous season.

The 101 points and 31-point margin of victory are 10th Region Tournament championship game records.

The community was stunned by the news that Jones was dismissed from the team two days before the state tournament for violating the team's code of conduct.

Mason County was looking to become the first back-to-back state champion since 1990-91. The task would be much more difficult without Jones.

Pfeffer replaced Jones in the starting lineup. The Royals played 12th Region champion Wayne County in the opening game. Mason County jumped out to a 12-0 lead and won 71-57. Lofton had a double-

double with 34 points and 10 rebounds. Litzinger added 22 points and eight rebounds.

"I thought tonight was a gutty performance by our kids," said Wells. "They just continue to amaze me, and they're very resilient; they overcome a lot of obstacles."

Mason County's quarterfinal opponent, Louisville Trinity, a football powerhouse, was in the state tournament for the first time. The Shamrocks defeated University Heights Academy 75-57 in the first round.

Trinity slowed the tempo against Mason County and led 18-11 in the second quarter. The Royals ended the half on an 8-1 run to tie the game at 19-19. The Shamrocks were up 33-32 after three quarters and 44-38 with 41 seconds left in the game. Pfeffer drained a three-pointer with 34 seconds to go. Then, Pfeffer forced a Trinity turnover. The Shamrocks committed a couple of common fouls. After the second foul, Lofton inbounded the ball to Litzinger with nine seconds to play. Litzinger passed the ball back to Lofton who drove off a pick and hit a game-tying three-pointer with 2.8 seconds left. After a timeout, Trinity missed a shot from behind the time line as the buzzer sounded.

Grutza fouled out with 3:31 left in overtime. The Royals led 48-45 with 3:09 to go, but the Shamrocks scored five straight points to take a two-point lead. Litzinger drove along the left baseline and hit a short shot to tie the game at 50-50. Trinity played for the last shot, but missed an open layup with one second left.

With the score tied at 52-52 with 41 seconds left in the second overtime, Trinity took a timeout. The Shamrocks again played for the last shot, but didn't get off a shot.

In the third overtime, Lofton hit two free throws, Litzinger had a field goal, and Chris Schumacher made one of two free throws to give the Royals a 57-52 lead with 2:19 left. Trinity would get no closer than four. A runout dunk by in Lofton in the closing seconds made the final score Mason County 66, Trinity 59.

"The kids have a heart of a champion, and I gotta give it up to them," said Wells. "They amaze me most nights, and again tonight, they did that as well."

Lofton, who finished with 29 points and 11 rebounds, was asked about his game-tying three-pointer.

"Coach just designed the play, and I found an opening," said Lofton at the post game press conference. "I was a little off balance, if I missed it, it would have probably been a bad shot. But it went in."

Litzinger had 17 points and eight rebounds. There were seven ties and 12 lead changes in the game.

Mason County played Scott County in the semifinals. The Royals led by as many 13 in the third quarter. The Cardinals went on a 21-10 run to close to within 70-68 with 28 seconds left in the game.

Grutza hit two free throws to make it 72-68 with 23 seconds remaining.

Scott County guard Tyler Hicks, the son of Cardinals' coach Billy Hicks, made a layup, came up with a steal and hit another layup to tie the game.

Litzinger missed a three-pointer and the two teams headed to overtime.

Scott County scored the first four points of the extra period, but Mason County bounced back with a 12-2 run to win 84-78.

Mason County made 27 of 33 free throws in the game including six of six in the overtime period.

Grutza led the Royals in scoring with 24 points. Lofton had 23 points and 11 rebounds. Litzinger and Tibbs added 14 points apiece.

Mason County advanced to the championship game to play 4th Region champion Warren Central. Mason County was trying to become just the sixth school to win back-to-back championships.

The second largest crowd in state tournament history - 20,252 - turned out for the game.

Warren Central led 25-14 at the end of the first quarter and 39-27 at halftime. The Dragons were up 48-31 with 2:57 left in the third quarter. Mason County cut the deficit to 10 at 52-42 at the end of the third quarter.

The Royals kept chipping away at Warren Central's lead in the fourth quarter. Lofton made a three-pointer to close the gap to 57-51 with 5:20 remaining. Warren Central made one of two free throws for a seven point lead. Miller, the 8th grader, drained a three-pointer to cut it to 58-54 with 4:01 to play.

Lonnell Dewalt, a six-foot-six senior forward, had back-to-back monstrous dunks on offensive follows for Warren Central. The second dunk was a one-handed slam that gave the Dragons a 62-54 lead with 2:08 to go. Lofton made two free throws with 1:23 left. Warren Central scored the final four points for a 66-56 win.

"I didn't think we had our 'A' game tonight," said Wells. "I thought Warren Central was on top of their game. I don't think they could have played any better. But I'm thrilled with my kids' effort. They never quit; we kept fighting to the end. We just got outplayed today."

Wells said he told the players he loved each one of them as he took them to the sideline after the game.

"They've had a ton of character. We haven't played well this whole tournament, but we've scratched, and we've clawed to get in the finals here. I couldn't be any more proud of a group of kids that will go down in history as one of the best high school teams ever."

Margie Appelman

The Royals were 23 of 67 from the field for 34.3 percent. Warren Central shot 55.6 percent from the field on 26 of 45.

Lofton scored a game-high 26 points, and Litzinger added 16. Warren Central senior forward Brock Whitney hit six three-pointers and scored 24 points. He was named the Most Valuable Player of the tournament.

Lofton, Grutza and Litzinger were named to the all-tournament team.

The loss snapped Mason County's 17-game winning streak. The Royals ended the season with a 33-3 record.

The members of the 2003-2004 team were: Zach Harrison, Chris Lofton, Chase Crawford, Chris Schumacher, Drew Stahl, Andrew Tibbs, Casey Pfeffer, Darius Miller, Brad Pawsat, Jarrod Litzinger, Mario Turner, Dustin Grutza, Chris Hopper, Micah Turner, Chris Stapleton, Eric Stitt and Barron Conley.

A rally for the Royals was held at the Fieldhouse on Sunday afternoon.

Wells received the *Herald-Leader* Coach of the Year award for the second straight season.

Lofton, the Royals' all-time leading scorer with 2,763 points, was named to the Associated Press, *The Courier-Journal* and *Herald-Leader* all-state teams. He was named the Kentucky Gatorade Player of the Year.

In a ceremony at the state capitol on April 16, Lofton became the first Mason County player to be named Mr. Basketball. Five days later, Wells had a kidney transplant. His wife, Shawne, was the donor.

The annual Kentucky-Indiana All-Star series was played in June. Wells coached the Kentucky All-Stars. Litzinger joined Lofton on the team. Lofton, who had signed to play at the University of Tennessee, scored 41 points to lead Kentucky to an 89-81 win in Owensboro. In the rematch in Indianapolis, Lofton scored 13 points before he left the game with a badly sprained ankle late in the first half. Indiana won 93-90.

After being snubbed by the University of Kentucky and the University of Louisville, Lofton had a phenomenal career at Tennessee. He scored 2,131 points and made a Southeastern Conference record 431 three-pointers. Lofton was the 2007 SEC Player of the Year and was named to UT's 20-man All-Century Team. He has played professionally in Turkey, Spain, Russia and in the NBA Development League.

Chapter 48 New Coaches for Royals and Saints

Two weeks after the start of the 2004-05 school year, Mason County coach Kelly Wells announced he had accepted the positions of assistant Athletic Director and assistant coach at Hawaii-Pacific University in Honolulu, Hawaii.

J.D. Barnett, the head coach and Athletic Director at Hawaii-Pacific, was the coach at the University of Tulsa when Wells played there.

"We talk to our kids all the time about chasing your dreams, and one of my dreams is to be a head Division I basketball coach in the near future," said Wells. "It's just a step we have to take in the process. We love it at Mason County; we're going to miss tremendously the people here and the school and the program. But it's a decision based solely on our career and nothing else."

In seven seasons at Mason County, Wells had a 172-56 record. He guided the Royals to five district championships, three region titles, a state championship and a state runner-up finish. The Royals' record in Wells' final three seasons was 96-11.

"It's hard to put into words the amount of pride we have in what we've established here, the friendships we've established here, and the players that have come through our program," said Wells. "We really feel the program is in awesome shape for many years to come. They'll have a chance again next year to be very good."

Former Mason County standout player Chris O'Hearn was named the new coach at Mason County on September 10. O'Hearn had been an assistant coach for Steve Appelman for one season and for Wells for four seasons. He moved into administration in the 2001-2002 school year and was the principal at the Mason County Middle School when Wells left for Hawaii.

"From way back when I first started coaching back in 1992, you know, I always had an eye on this job of coming home to Mason County," said O'Hearn at the press conference. "I know what a special place it is. I know what great facilities we have. I know what great kids we have. I know what great support we have from our community."

O'Hearn said he knew there was always going to be pressure when you were involved with the Mason County basketball program.

"Expectations are always high. I realize that. I'm ready to face that challenge, and I think our kids will be too."

Wes Jones, who was dismissed from the team prior to the 2004 state tournament, was allowed to play his senior season. He led the Royals in scoring with an average of 19.1 points per game.

Mason County's 64-game winning streak against 10th Region teams was snapped by a 64-61 loss to the Bourbon County Colonels.

Mason County breezed through the district tournament with lopsided wins over Deming, St. Patrick and Fleming County. The Royals' first season under O'Hearn came to end with a 60-54 loss to Harrison County in the first round of the 10th Region Tournament. Mason County's record was 22-9.

St. Patrick also had a new coach for the 2004-05 season. Scott High School freshman coach Tim Sullivan succeeded Lex Turner who retired after 28 seasons as the Saints' coach. Turner had a record of 365-375. He guided the Saints to their first win over Maysville in 1982, their first win in the regional tournament in 1982 and their first win over Mason County in 1997 (and four other wins over the Royals). Turner's St. Patrick teams won district titles in 1997 and 2000, and 10th Region All "A" Classic championships in 1995, 1999 and 2000. "I had a lot of great kids," says Turner.

Laurnie Caproni, former *Ledger Independent* sports editor, has high praise for the job Turner did at the small school.

"I don't think anybody ever did any better with what he had period," says Caproni. "Over all of those years, how could you have done better than he did? No one would have survived that. And about every 10 years if you look at the history of St. Patrick, and maybe 12, they'll cycle around and have a good team for a couple of years, then, they'll go under the long dark night."

Turner also coached the St. Patrick girls' team in the 1987-88 season.

Sullivan played basketball at Holmes High School and Brescia College.

The Saints had a record of 7-19 under Sullivan. The Saints lost to Mason County 69-28 in the district tournament. Sullivan stepped down as the St. Patrick coach after one season to become an assistant coach at Mason County.

Jason Hinson, a former assistant coach at Deming, was hired as the new coach at St. Patrick for the 2005-06 season.

Chapter 49 Back to State for Mason County

The Mason County Royals opened the 2005-06 season with seven consecutive victories including a 59-52 win over 10th Region rival Clark County in the semifinals of the Hoopin It Up Classic in London. The winning streak was snapped the next night by a 68-63 loss to defending state champion South Laurel in the championship game. The Royals led by five after three quarters, but were outscored 24-14 in the fourth quarter. Mikah Turner, Mason County's only senior, scored a career-high 25 points and grabbed 10 rebounds.

After going 2-2 in the Fifth Third Bank Classic at Lexington Catholic, the Royals returned home for the Mason County Invitational Tournament.

Mason County beat Bracken County 49-28 in the first round and Montgomery County 47-29 in the semifinals. The Royals lost to defending 10th Region champion Pendleton County 82-79 in double overtime in the championship game. There were eight ties and 16 lead changes in the game. Mason County missed potential game-winning shots at the end of regulation and at the end of the first overtime.

Scott County led 44-19 at halftime and 61-31 after three quarters in a 77-50 rout of the Royals.

Tyreese Scott, a five-foot-seven junior guard, hit five three-pointers and scored a career-high 33 points to lead Mason County an 80-69 overtime victory over Campbell County. Scott scored nine points in the overtime period.

The Royals lost to Lexington Catholic 73-53, beat Montgomery County 63-48 and lost to South Laurel 58-41 in the rematch at the Fieldhouse.

Mason County bounced back by with double digit wins over Fleming County, Rowan County and Bishop Brossart. Darius Miller scored 26 points in the 74-55 win over Rowan County.

The winning streak was broken by a 71-62 home loss to Clark County.

The Royals won the final three games of the regular season. Miller had another 26-point game in an 81-43 rout over Bracken County. Turner had a double-double with 20 points and 14 rebounds in a 54-43 victory over Harrison County. Mason County upset Pendleton

County 62-58. Miller scored 18 points, Russ Middleton had 14 and Turner celebrated Senior Night with another double-double-10 points and 11 rebounds.

The Royals jumped out to a 20-0 lead and beat Bracken County 65-42 in the semifinals of the district tournament. Miller scored a game-high 19 points. Turner had his third straight double-double with 11 points and 10 rebounds.

Augusta upset St. Patrick 68-63 in the other semifinal. The Saints ended the season with a 14-15 record.

Mason County was a huge favorite over Augusta in the championship game. The Royals led 20-11 at the end of the first quarter, but Augusta outscored Mason County 22-14 in the second quarter to cut the Royals' lead to one. Augusta guard Josh White led the comeback with eight second quarter points. Miller guarded White in the second half and held him to two points. The Royals ended the game on a 30-3 run and won 72-42. It was Mason County's 1,000th win. Miller had 18 points and nine rebounds. Turner had another double-double with 13 points and 13 rebounds. Scott added 14 points.

Mason County drew Deming in the first round of the 10th Region Tournament. The Black Devils came into the game with a 9-16 record but gave the Royals a game. It was tied 26-26 at halftime. Mason County outscored Deming 20-12 in the third quarter and 19-12 in the fourth quarter for a 65-50 victory. Turner and Miller both had a double-double. Turner had 19 points and 10 rebounds. Miller scored 16 points and grabbed 11 rebounds. Middleton added 16 points.

Miller scored 18 points to lead the Royals to a 50-45 win over Bishop Brossart in the semifinals. Turner scored 13 points and was one rebound away from recording his sixth straight double-double.

Clark County upset Pendleton County 72-68 in the other semifinal.

Mason County rallied from a seven-point deficit to beat Clark County 62-59 in the championship game. Miller scored 22 points, Middleton 18, and Scott 10. It was Mason County's fourth region title in five years.

Mason County played Warren Central in the opening round of the state tournament. Mason County coach Chris O'Hearn was concerned about the Dragons' state tournament experience. Warren Central was the state champion in 2004 and the state runner-up in 2005. Miller was the only Mason County player who had played in the state tournament, and that was as an 8th grader in 2004.

Warren Central led 16-14 at the end of the first quarter and 24-16 with 5:58 left in the second quarter. The Dragons were up 32-29 late in the second quarter. Tony Browning hit a three-pointer to tie the game. Turner came up with a steal and scored on a putback to give the Royals a 34-32 lead at halftime.

Mason County, playing without Middleton who left the game with a hamstring injury in the second quarter, led 46-45 at the end of the third quarter. There were three ties and four lead changes in the fourth quarter.

Mason County took a 59-57 lead when Scott drove past the defense and made a layup with 1:31 left. Warren Central tied it with 1:14 to go.

Browning hit the first of two free throws with 24 seconds left to give the Royals a 60-59 lead.

Brad Pawsat hit two free throws to push the lead to 62-59 with 14.6 seconds left.

Warren Central missed two three-pointers in the closing seconds, and Mason County won its ninth straight game.

"We talk to our kids about hanging their hats on the defensive end, and we were able to get stops there in the end when we needed them," said O'Hearn. "And we got stops in the second half which kept them from getting in their press, and I thought that was a huge key for us."

Turner had 17 points and 12 rebounds. Miller and Scott scored 14 points apiece. Browning tossed in 13. The Royals outrebounded the Dragons 36-20.

Middleton was unable to play in the quarterfinal game against Apollo. The Eagles led 23-16 at halftime. Mason County closed to within three in the third quarter, but did not score from 4:50 in the third quarter to 5:40 in the fourth quarter. Apollo scored the last seven points of the third quarter to lead 36-26. The Royals scored the first five points of the fourth quarter to cut the deficit in half. But the Eagles answered with an 8-0 run to lead 44-31 with 1:30 left. Apollo won, 48-36.

Turner scored 17 points. He was the only Mason County player in double figures. Turner was named to the all-tournament team. The Royals finished the season at 25-9.

Chapter 50 Miller Time & Another State Title

With four starters returning from a state quarterfinalist team, the Mason County Royals were in the Top 10 in the 2006-07 preseason rankings.

The Royals opened the season with 10 straight victories. The streak was snapped by a 64-59 loss to Lexington Catholic in the semifinals of the Fifth Third Bank Classic at Lexington Catholic.

The Royals had three easy wins in the Mason County Invitational Tournament.

After a 73-68 road loss to Scott County, Mason County closed out the regular season with 11 consecutive wins including a 62-54 victory over Clark County in Winchester.

The Royals routed Bracken County 94-54 in the semifinals of the 39th District Tournament. Augusta defeated St. Patrick 56-50 in the other semifinal. The Saints ended the season with a 12-14 record.

Mason County beat Augusta 90-36 in the championship game.

The Royals led 27-9 at the end of the first quarter and defeated Montgomery County 71-54 in the first round of the 10th Region Tournament.

Mason County played Bishop Brossart in the semifinals. The Royals had a 16-point lead with 7:38 left in the game, but the Mustangs closed to within four in the final minute. Tony Browning threw down a two-handed dunk to extend the lead to six points. Then, the Royals' press forced a turnover, and Darius Miller made a shot to make it 62-54. Mason County won, 63-57. It was the Royals' 15 straight win, their 20th consecutive home court victory, and their 24th straight win against 10th Region opponents.

Mason County put those streaks on the line against Clark County in the championship game.

There were 12 ties and 11 lead changes in the game. Clark County led 16-15 at the end of the first quarter. Mason County was up 26-25 at halftime and 41-40 after three quarters. The Cardinals had a seven-point lead with just over a minute to play. Mason County closed to within 62-59 and had a chance to the tie the game, but missed a three-pointer. Clark County hit one of two free throws with 13 seconds left and upset Mason County 63-59. Miller had 33 points and 10 rebounds.

Preston Knowles scored 33 points for Clark County.

Mason County closed the season with a 28-3 record.

Danny Boyd, the longtime statistician for the Royals, died suddenly in May 2007. Boyd was the official statistician for the 39th District and 10th Region tournaments. He was a substitute teacher at Mason County High School. Boyd ran the scoreboard at the Lady Royals' softball games, and he had been hired as the boys' golf coach for the 2007 season. The community mourned his death.

There was a lot of excitement leading up to the 2007-08 season. The Royals' schedule included a trip to Hawaii, Darius Miller had signed a national letter of intent with the University of Kentucky, and Mason County was ranked No.1 in the *Lexington Herald-Leader* pre-season ratings.

Mason County opened the season with back-to-back wins in the Mr. Basketball Classic at Tates Creek High School in Lexington. Miller scored 31 points, and Russ Middleton added 22 in an 84-71 victory over Bryan Station. Miller had 34 points, eight rebounds and six assists, and Middleton tossed in 20 points in an 85-73 win over Tates Creek.

A moment of silence was observed in memory of Boyd prior to the Royals' home opener against Covington Catholic. Miller had a double-double with 24 points and 12 rebounds and Trevor Setty scored 21 points to lead Mason County to a 66-56 win.

The Royals routed Scott 80-40. Middleton scored 25 points, Setty 20 and Miller 10.

Mason County beat Christ Presbyterian Academy of Nashville, Tennessee, 68-54 in the Farm Bureau Classic in Pikeville. Middleton and Setty each scored 19 points. Miller and Ethan King added 12 points apiece.

The next day the Royals flew to Honolulu, HI for the Iolani Prep Classic.

Mason County's first opponent in the tournament was Leilehua. The Royals led by as many as 44 points in the third quarter on their way to a 76-41 victory. Four players scored in double figures-Middleton with 19 points, Miller 15, Setty 14 and King 12.

The competition was much stronger in the second round. The Mt. Vernon Knights of New York were ranked 15th in the *USA Today* Super 25. Mt. Vernon, led by University of West Virginia signee Kevin Jones, was a two-time defending state champion. Mason County made 13 of 16 free throws in the fourth quarter and upset the Knights 73-69. Miller scored 23 points, Middleton 19 and Setty 13. Jones scored a game-high 36 points for Mt. Vernon.

Next up was Rice of New York City, which was No. 10 in the *USA Today* Super 25. The Raiders' star player was point guard

Kemba Walker who would lead Connecticut to the 2011 NCAA Championship. The Royals had a seven-point lead with 7:35 left, but Rice ended the game on a 26-8 run to beat Mason County 59-48. The loss snapped the Royals' season-opening seven-game winning streak.

Mason County bounced back with a 55-41 victory over the host school, Iolani. Miller led the way with 22 points. Middleton scored 13 and Setty added 12.

The trip to Hawaii included some sightseeing. The Royals went snorkeling in Hanauma Bay, visited Pearl Harbor, attended a luau and climbed Diamond Head. The team flew home on Christmas Eve.

Two days after Christmas, the Royals returned to action in the Lexington Catholic Holiday Classic. Mason County used a 14-1 run in the third quarter to defeat Lexington Christian Academy 71-38. Four Royals scored in double figures – Miller with, Middleton 13, Setty 11 and Jackson Tolle 10 on 5-of-5 shooting.

Mason County jumped out to a 9-0 lead and beat June Buchanan 68-58 in the quarterfinals. Setty led the Royals with 20 points. Middleton scored 19. Miller had 14 points, nine rebounds and nine assists. King added 10 points.

The Royals outscored Covington Catholic 40-18 in the second half to win 60-42 in the semifinals. Miller had a game-high 20 points. Middleton scored 18 and Setty added 10.

Lexington Catholic rallied from a 13-point second quarter deficit and beat Mason County 79-69 in the championship game. Middleton scored 19 points. Miller had 17 points and 11 rebounds. Setty scored 15 points and King had 14 points and 11 rebounds. Those four players were named to the all-tournament team.

The Royals had leads of 11-0 and 23-2 en route to a 77-33 win over Pendleton County in the opening round of the Mason County Invitational Tournament.

Mason County scored the first 19 points of the game in a 71-36 victory over Bishop Brossart in the semifinals. Setty, Miller and King were a combined 18 of 20 from the field. Setty scored 17 points, Miller 14, and King 12.

Miller had a double-double with 18 points and 14 rebounds to lead the Royals to a 69-55 win over in Montgomery County in the championship game. Miller also blocked six shots.

The three-game winning streak was snapped by a 76-64 home loss to Scott County. Miller played just 16 minutes and 13 seconds because of foul trouble. He scored five points before fouling out with 6:08 left in the game. Middleton led the Royals in scoring with 20 points.

Mason County used a 18-0 run in the third quarter to beat Centennial of Roswell, Georgia. 81-57 in the Nissan Shootout at Lexington Catholic. Miller scored a game-high 28 points. Setty followed with 20. Middleton scored 13 and King added 11.

Miller scored 29 points and grabbed 10 rebounds in an 80-63 win over Campbell County. Miller also had seven assists and blocked four shots.

The rematch against Lexington Catholic was played at Memorial Coliseum on the campus of the University of Kentucky and was televised live. Mason County trailed 64-53 with 6:20 left, but went on a 19-5 run to take a three-point lead. Nathan Novesel made one of two free throws to cut the Royals' lead to 72-70 with 29 seconds to play. After Mason County committed a turnover, Taylor Stewart hit a three-pointer to give the Knights a 73-72 lead with 8.6 seconds left. Miller hit a last second shot in the lane to give Mason County a 74-73 victory. Setty had 25 points. Miller finished with 18 points. Middleton scored 14, and King added 11.

The Royals scored 37 points off turnovers and routed Fern Creek 91-70 in the Kentucky Prep Classic at Montgomery County. Setty had 21 points and nine rebounds. Middleton scored 19 points, and Miller tossed in 14.

Miller had a double-double with 28 points and 11 rebounds to lead Mason County to a 63-45 victory over Henry Clay.

The Royals shot 62 percent from the field in a 94-48 rout of Rowan County. Miller made 9 of 10 shots and scored a game-high 25 points. Setty scored 18 points. King added 15 points on 7-of-7 from the field and 1-of-1 from the free throw line.

Mason County rallied from a six-point deficit in the fourth quarter to beat the Madison Central Indians 56-49 in Richmond. The Royals only had one turnover in the second half and made 9-of-11 free throws in the fourth quarter. Miller had a double-double with 17 points and 10 rebounds. Middleton scored nine of his 16 points in the fourth quarter.

The Royals were outrebounded 47-29 including 25-6 on the offensive boards but beat Montgomery County 71-65. Setty scored 21 points. Middleton followed with 19 points. Miller recorded another double-double with 16 points and 10 rebounds.

Mason County used a 21-3 run to defeat the Clark County Cardinals 67-50. The big run turned a five-point deficit in the second quarter into a 13-point lead in the third quarter. The Royals ended the first half on a 15-1 run. Miller scored a game-high 26 points. Setty scored 16 and King added 15.

Miller scored 17 points in the first quarter as the Royals raced out to a 32-15 lead over the Harrison County Thorobreds in Cynthiana. Mason County was up 65-31 at halftime. A reverse dunk by Miller off an alley oop pass gave their Royals their biggest lead-43 points- in the third quarter. The final score: Mason County 96, Harrison County

68. Miller and Middleton scored 23 points apiece. Setty scored 16 and King had 10.

The Royals shot 62 percent from the field and beat Elliott County 90-61. Elliott County, the top scoring team in the state, was held 26 points under its season average. Miller had another double-double with 29 points and 15 rebounds. Middleton added 27 points, and Setty tossed in 15.

Mason County's 11-game winning streak was snapped by a 65-54 loss to Bryan Station on Senior Night. Miller scored the Royals' first 11 points and ended up with a game-high 28 points. Bryan Station senior guard Shelvin Mack had 24 points and 13 rebounds.

Mason County routed St. Patrick 94-53 in the semifinals of the 39th District Tournament. Miller scored his 2,000th career point in the second quarter and had a game-high 22 points. St. Patrick senior Chris Owens scored his 2,000th career point in the third-quarter and had a team-high 13 points. St. Patrick ended the season with a 19-10 record.

The Royals cruised to a 104-49 win over Augusta in the championship game. Miller scored a game-high 22 points despite playing less than nine minutes.

For the first time since 1969 the 10th Region Tournament was not held at the Mason County Fieldhouse. It was the 40th District's turn to select the site, and the schools in the district voted to have the tournament at the Montgomery County High School Arena.

Mason County routed Deming 101-54 in the first round. Miller scored 22 points on 10-of-13 from the field including 2-of-2 on three-point shots.

Mason County played Clark County in the semifinals. The game was tied at 15-15 early in the second quarter. The Royals ended the half on a 16-3 run and scored the first nine points of the third quarter. The final score: Mason County 68, Clark County 45. The Royals had balanced scoring. Setty scored 15 points, Miller 14, Middleton 12, and King 11.

The Royals faced the Montgomery County Indians in the championship game. The game was tied 14-14 at the end of the first quarter. Mason County opened the second quarter on an 11-0 and led 37-22 at halftime. The Royals were up 62-43 after three quarters and won 82-61.

Miller scored 18 points in the first half and finished with a double-double-28 points and 13 rebounds. Setty hit five three-pointers in the second half and finished with 22 points. It was Mason County's fifth region title in seven years.

Miller was named the 10th Region Player of the Year by the Kentucky Association of Basketball and the Gatorade Player of the Year in Kentucky.

Mason County's first round game in the state tournament was a rematch against Elliott County. Prior to the game, a moment of silence was observed in memory of longtime Maysville scorekeeper Arthur "Punk" Griffin, who died in January. Griffin attended the state tournament every year beginning in 1947 when Maysville won the state championship. A spot on press row in the end zone remained vacant in Griffin's honor.

The Royals led by nine in the second quarter and had a 35-30 lead at halftime. The Royals led 43-41 after three quarters. Elliot County had a 57-50 lead with 4:17 left and was up 59-53 with 3:14 to play.

Mason County went on a 9-0 run that started with a three-pointer by Setty. Middleton buried a trey and Setty hit another three-pointer give the Royals a 62-61 lead with 1:45 to go. Elliott County made two free throws to cut the deficit to one.

Mason County twice missed the front end of the one and one, but the Royals got the rebound both times. After the second miss, Setty scored on a putback to give Mason County a 64-61 lead. Miller made two free throws to clinch the 66-61 victory.

Setty hit five three-pointers and scored 19 points including 11 in the fourth quarter. Miller had another double-double with 17 points and 10 rebounds. Russ Middleton scored 15 points and King added 11.

The Royals bolted out to a 10-0 lead over Paducah Tilghman in the quarterfinals and never looked back. Mason County was up 24-6 at the end of the first quarter and 39-11 at halftime. The Royals led by as many as 39 in the third quarter and won 73-46.

"We just came out focused and loose and shot the ball well and really just totally dismantled a pretty good Paducah Tilghman team," says Mason County coach Chris O'Hearn.

Miller scored 17 points on his 18th birthday. Middleton and King scored 12 points apiece, and Setty added 11.

The Holmes Bulldogs upset Lexington Catholic 57-50 in the upper bracket semifinal

Mason County played Shelby County in the lower bracket semifinal. The Royals led 16-15 at the end of the first quarter and 22-19 at halftime. Mason County increased its lead to 38-30 by the end of the third quarter. The Rockets closed to within two twice in the fourth quarter. The second time was at 48-46 with 2:19 left.

Keith Downing hit two free throws, blocked a Holmes shot and made two more free throws to give the Royals a 52-46 lead with 1:56 to go.

The Rockets cut the deficit in half with a three-pointer, but Mason County answered with a 6-0 run to lead 58-49 with 37 seconds left. The Royals won, 60-50.

Miller had 19 points and 10 rebounds. King followed with 18 points, and Middleton added 14.

One hour before the championship game, the Kentucky High School Athletic Association told O'Hearn that Setty would not be able to play in the game because of an incident that happened in the final minute of the semifinal game. Setty had left the bench and stepped on the floor when King was fouled hard on a drive to the basket. The KHSAA said Setty had been ejected from the game making him ineligible for the championship game. O'Hearn says the referee told him Setty was being assessed with an indirect technical foul but was not disqualified. O'Hearn says he told the KHSAA, "You need to call this referee. You need to get a hold of him; I'm telling you this is what he told me, 'He is not ejected.'"

O'Hearn says he also told the KHSAA he had sent Setty to the scorer's table to re-enter the semifinal game, but he didn't get in because there was not a dead ball before time expired.

The Royals took the floor for pre-game warm-ups thinking Setty was not going to get to play. O'Hearn says Setty was "just devastated, as any kid would be."

Word of the situation had spread along press row and among many of the fans.

But a few minutes later the Royals received good news. The KHSAA was allowing Setty to play. Setty joined his teammates on the court and was in the starting lineup.

The Royals were going up against a very talented Holmes team that had a 34-2 record. Senior guard Arrez Henderson was the team's leading scorer, and he had been a lockdown defender during the state tournament. Elijah Pittman, a six-foot-five sophomore, had been a junior varsity player most of the season, but he had become a star during the state tournament. He scored 19 points in the Bulldogs' quarterfinal round win over Paintsville and 15 against Lexington Catholic in the semifinals. Former Mason County assistant coach Tim Sullivan was an assistant coach for Holmes.

Mason County missed its first five shots, but led 13-9 at the end of the first quarter. Holmes scored the first four points of the second quarter to take a one-point lead. The Royals closed the first half on an 8-3 run to lead 21-16.

Mason County scored the first eight points of the third quarter to lead 29-16. The Royals led by as many as 15 points in the third quarter and were up 41-27 at the end of the quarter.

Holmes closed to within six points on four different occasions. The last time was at 52-46 with 55 seconds left.

Downing made one of two free throws with 51 seconds left.

Ryan Hamm was fouled with 39 seconds to go. His first free

Jason Butler

The 2008 Royals, led by Mr. Basketball Darius Miller, won Mason County's second state championship in six seasons.

throw looked to be short, but the ball hung on the rim and fell into the basket. Hamm made the second free throw to push the lead back out to nine.

Setty hit two free throws with 26 seconds left to give the Royals an 11-point lead.

Holmes scored on a putback with 16 seconds left. The final score was Mason County 57, Holmes 46. Mason County was the state champion for the second time in six seasons.

Miller scored 19 of his game-high 24 points in the second half and was named the Most Valuable Player. Middleton scored 13 points, and Downing added a career-high 10 points.

Miller, Middleton, and King were named to the all-tournament team.

The Royals were welcomed home with a celebration at the Fieldhouse.

"Welcome to our dream," O'Hearn told the crowd. "This is our dream. 1947, I guess, Maysville High School brought a state championship back to this community. It took about 56 years for that to happen again [with] that great [Mason County] team in 2003. Thanks to these guys behind me, it only took five years this time."

The team went to Frankfort on the following Wednesday and was honored by the state House and Senate.

Miller is third on the Royals' all-time scoring list. He was named Mr. Basketball during a ceremony in the Fieldhouse in April. He was named Second Team All-America by EA Sports and Third Team All-America by *Parade Magazine*. Miller was named Player of the Year by *The Courier-Journal*.

O'Hearn coached Miller's team in the Adidas Derby Festival Basketball Classic in Louisville.

As Mr. Basketball, Miller wore the No. 1 jersey for the Kentucky All-Stars in the annual series with the Indiana All-Stars.

Miller was a member of Team USA that won a gold medal at the U-19 World Championship in New Zealand in the summer of 2009. Miller was named MVP of the 2011 Southeastern Conference Tournament. He played for Team USA at the World University Games in China in the summer of 2011. After being a starter his sophomore and junior seasons, Miller was the sixth man on the University of Kentucky's 2012 National Championship team. He had 1,248 career points at UK and played in a school record 152 games. Miller presented a University of Kentucky jersey to President Barack Obama during the Wildcats' visit to the White House. Miller was selected by the New Orleans Hornets in the second round of the 2012 NBA Draft.

Chapter 51 The Lady Royals' Big 3

Eighth grader De'Sarae Chambers led the Mason County Lady Royals in scoring in the 2003-04 season. Mason County won the district tournament but lost to Harrison County 59-56 in the semifinals of the 10th Region Tournament to finish the year at 18-13.

The next season freshmen Lacey Cline, Chambers and Kasey Litzinger were the top three scorers. Mason County won the district tournament again and had a 10-game winning streak heading into the 10th Region Tournament championship game against Montgomery County. The Lady Royals had edged the Lady Indians 81-80 in overtime at home in January.

The regional tournament was played at Campbell County. Mason County had a nine-point in the fourth quarter and was up by three in the closing seconds, but Montgomery County hit a three-pointer to tie the game. The Lady Indians beat the Lady Royals 71-69 in overtime.

The Lady Royals were district champions again in 2006 but their season came to an end with a 53-49 loss to Montgomery County in the semifinals of the regional tournament. Mason County's record was 25-8. Cline, Chambers and Litzinger were once again the top three scorers.

Mason County won the 2007 district title and had an 11-game winning streak heading into another showdown against Montgomery County in the championship game of the regional tournament.

The Lady Royals had defeated the Lady Indians 77-67 in the regular season game at the Mason County Fieldhouse.

The regional tournament was played in the new Montgomery County High School Arena. The Lady Indians beat the Lady Royals 66-63. Mason County closed out the season with a 22-10 record.

The 2007-08 season was the last chance for seniors Chambers, Cline and Litzinger and coach Buser to win a region title. Buser announced she was going to retire at the end of the season.

Cline scored her 2,000th career point in the fifth game of the season-a 75-58 victory over Fleming County.

Chambers scored her 2,500th career point in an 85-70 loss to Hoover High of North Canton, Ohio.

Chambers scored 33 points and grabbed 11 rebounds and became

Mason County's all-time leading scorer (girl or boy) in an 80-76 loss to Rowan County. She passed Chris Lofton who scored 2,763 points for the Royals.

The Lady Royals won the 39th District Tournament for the sixth straight year, and for the second consecutive year and the third time in four years faced Montgomery County in the championship game of the 10th Region Tournament.

The game was tied with 3:45 left, but the Lady Indians ended the game on a 10-2 run to beat the Lady Royals 66-58. It was Montgomery County's fourth straight region title. Mason County ended the season with a 24-8 record.

Chambers finished her career with 2,967 points. She played college basketball at the University of Dayton. Cline is second on the Lady Royals' all-time scoring list with 2,543 points. She signed with Thomas More College, but she suffered a career ending knee injury. Litzinger is sixth on the scoring list with 1,572 points. She played at Lindsey Wilson College

In eight seasons as the Lady Royals' coach, Buser had a 153-93 record. Her teams won six district championships.

Stephen Butcher, the head coach at Pike County Central for three seasons, succeeded Buser.

Senior Keller Menke averaged 17.4 points a game in the 2009-10 season and is fifth on the Lady Royals' all-time scoring list with 1,637 points.

St. Patrick Lady Saints coach Jerry Ormes was fired after the 2006-07 season. In his last four seasons, the Lady Saints had records of 14-11, 9-17, 14-13 and 8-19. In 10 seasons, Ormes had a 146-129 record and guided the Lady Saints to two district titles. Assistant coach Elaine Douglas was promoted to head coach.

The Lady Saints won the district title in 2009. The Lady Royals won it 2010.

Chapter 52 Royals Rally for Region Title

The Mason County Royals opened the 2008-09 season with a 54-51 double overtime loss to the Highlands Bluebirds at the Fieldhouse. The loss snapped a couple of winning streaks. The Royals had won 13 straight season openers and 20 consecutive home openers.

Mason County won four straight games before losing to Franklin County 48-47 in the Kentucky Bank Shootout at Bourbon County.

The Royals traveled to Florida for the Daytona Beach Sunshine Classic. Russ Middleton scored 30 points in a 63-59 win over Harrison High of Kennesaw, Georgia, in the first round.

Mason County jumped out to a 10-1 lead and beat United Faith Academy of Charlotte, North Carolina, in the semifinals. Middleton scored 26 points. Phil Barner had a double-double with 10 points and 11 rebounds.

The Royals outscored Winton Woods, Ohio, 9-3 in overtime to win the championship game 50-44. Middleton scored 20 points and was named Most Valuable Player of the Tournament. Barner, Keith Downing, and Neal Pawsat were named to the all-tournament team.

Three victories in the Mason County Invitational Tournament extended the Royals' winning streak to six games.

Mason County traveled to Georgetown to play the Scott County Cardinals. Middleton scored 17 points in the first quarter, and the Royals led 20-13. Pawsat took an elbow to the head in the second quarter and sat out the rest of the game. Mason County was up 64-62 and headed to the free throw line for a one-and-one with 53 seconds left. The game was delayed for several minutes after a woman became ill behind the Royals' bench. When play resumed, Middleton missed the free throw, and Scott County ended the game on a 9-0 to win 71-64. Middleton scored a career-high 31 points.

Five Royals scored in double figures in a 95-63 rout of Pendleton County in Falmouth. Middleton scored 20 points and passed his dad, Kelly, on the Royals' all-time scoring list. Downing scored a career-high 14 points and had eight steals, five rebounds, five assists and three blocks. Treg Setty scored 14 points. Jordan Gilbert followed with 12 and Justin Lang added 10.

Mason County and Lexington Catholic played another classic at the Fieldhouse. The Royals led by 11 early in the third quarter. The Knights rallied and led by five in the fourth quarter. Middleton hit a shot at the buzzer to tie the game. Lexington Catholic outscored Mason County 9-3 in overtime to win 64-61. Treg Setty had a double-double with 29 points and 17 rebounds. Middleton scored 16 points. Downing had 13 rebounds.

The Royals bounced back with wins over Madison Central, Henry Clay and Campbell County. Setty had another double-double with 25 points and 12 rebounds in the victory over Campbell County.

The next game was against Clark County in Winchester. Mason County led by 10 points early in the fourth quarter, but Clark County rallied and tied the game. Middleton hit two free throws to give the Royals a two-point lead with 4.5 seconds to play. A foul was called as Clark County guard Robbie Stenzel launched a desperation three-point shot. With no time left on the clock, Stenzel stepped to the line and sank all three foul shots to give the Cardinals a 56-55 win. The loss snapped Mason County's 19-game winning streak against 10th Region teams.

The Royals scored 43 points off Fleming County's 26 turnovers in an 89-47 rout of the Panthers.

After an 86-71 loss to Elliott County in a packed gym in Sandy Hook, the Royals closed out the regular season with four straight wins.

Mason County breezed past Augusta 94-31 in the semifinals of the 39th District Tournament. Setty had a double-double with 19 points and 12 rebounds.

The Royals led 44-18 at halftime and routed St. Patrick 93-41 in the championship game.

All four first round games in the 10th Region Tournament were played on Saturday, March 7 at the Bank of Kentucky Center on the campus of Northern Kentucky University.

St. Patrick drew Clark County. After trailing 30-12 in the second quarter, the Saints went on a 22-10 run to close to within six at the end of the third quarter. Clark County opened the fourth quarter with an 11-4 to lead 51-38 with four minutes left. The Saints cut the deficit to nine but could get no closer. The final score was Clark County 58, St. Patrick 47. Stephen Mason had a double-double with 18 points and 10 rebounds for the Saints who ended the season with a 12-16-1 record. The tie was against Augusta late in the regular season. The score was tied at 58-58 when the power went off at the Augusta gym.

Mason County played Bishop Brossart in the final first round game of the regional tournament. The Royals scored the first nine points. The Mustangs hit two free throws. Then, Mason County scored 24 straight points for a 33-2 lead. Bishop Brossart did not make its first field goal until the 1:59 mark of the second quarter. Mason County won, 58-35.

The Royals scored 31 points off Montgomery County's 16 turnovers in a 75-45 victory in the semifinals.

It was Mason County versus Clark County in the championship game. Clark County used a 15-0 run to lead 18-6 early in the second quarter.

Mason County cut the deficit to nine at the end of the half. Stenzel opened the third quarter with a three-pointer to give the Cardinals a 27-15 lead. Mason County answered with an 8-0 run to get to within four. Clark County was up 35-34 at the end of the third quarter. Jordan Gilbert hit a three-pointer to give the Royals a 41-39 lead with 3:03 left. It was Mason County's first lead since the first quarter. The Royals outscored the Cardinals 10-4 the rest of the way for a 51-43 victory.

Mason County played 15th Region champion Shelby Valley in the first round of the state tournament.

The Royals led by eight in the second quarter and were up 24-18 at halftime. The Wildcats opened the third quarter on a 10-1 run and led 33-31 at the end of the quarter.

Shelby Valley led 37-31 with 5:58 left. Mason County tied the game at 39-39 with 3:51 to play, but did not score again until only 31 seconds remained. Shelby Valley won, 51-44. Mason County shot 27.7 percent from the field. Nine of the Royals' 13 field goals were three-pointers. Middleton made seven three-pointers and scored a game-high 24 points. He had all 12 of Mason County's first quarter points. "[Middleton] shot the lights out," says O'Hearn. "But we really struggled to score anywhere else." The Royals ended the season with a 24-7 record.

Chapter 53 A Region Three-Peat & a State Semifinal Finish

St. Patrick Saints coach Jason Hinson resigned in May 2009 to become the associate head coach at Augusta. He said it was a tough emotional day, "probably one of the hardest days of my life."

Hinson had been notified earlier in the spring that his teaching position at St. Patrick was being eliminated due to budget cuts.

Hinson coached four seasons at St. Patrick. His record was 57-55-1. Assistant coach Andy Arn was promoted to head coach.

Mason County was not at full strength when the 2009-10 season got underway. Neal Pawsat, the quarterback on Mason County's football team, suffered a knee injury in the final game of the regular season. Another football star, Josh Harris, suffered a severely sprained ankle on his first day of basketball practice.

The Royals opened the season with three straight wins. The streak was broken by a two-point loss to Highlands.

Mason County won three out of four games and took third place in the Citizens National Holiday Classic in Bowling Green.

The Royals jumped out to a 15-0 lead and withstood a rally by Christian County for a 53-50 win in the opening round of the Ashland Invitational Tournament.

Mason County made 19-of 21 free throws including 11-of-12 in fourth quarter to beat 10th Region rival Bishop Brossart 49-41 in the semifinals.

The Royals played Ashland in the championship game. Mason County led by as many as 19 points in the second quarter and 18 in the third quarter. Mason County had serious foul trouble in the third quarter. The Tomcats went on an 18-0 run and outscored the Royals 28-9 in the third quarter. The foul trouble was a blessing in disguise. Rheuben Bluford, a six-foot-five senior who had only scored four points in the first 10 games, came off the bench to score 13 points. Mason County outscored Ashland 24-11 in the fourth quarter and won, 64-53. The Royals made 11-of-12 free throws in the fourth quarter. Jordan Gilbert, Bradley Lang, Tyler Black and Treg Setty were named to the all-tournament team.

Mason County lost to defending state champion Holmes 53-47. Black suffered a knee injury and missed the next 11 games.

Setty had a double-double with 24 points and 17 rebounds, but the Royals blew a seven-point lead in the fourth quarter and lost to Campbell County 59-53. It was the Camels' first win over the Royals since the championship game of the 2001 10th Region Tournament.

Mason County won back-to-back games against Pendleton County and Madison Central. Setty had a game-high 18 points and Bluford had a double-double with 15 points and 12 rebounds in the victory over Madison Central.

The Royals shot just 37.8 percent from the field and lost to LaSalle 50-38 in the National Prep Classic in Wellston, Ohio.

In the rematch with Ashland, Mason County rallied from a 13-point second quarter deficit to beat the Tomcats 58-54. Justin Lang and Bradley Lang scored 13 points apiece. Setty had a double-double with 10 points and 11 rebounds.

Pawsat saw his first action of the season when the Royals hosted Henry Clay. Bluford had a double-double with 20 points and 13 rebounds, and Setty scored 19 points to lead Mason County to a 49-30 win.

The Royals lost to Lafayette 64-59. Setty had a game-high 21 points and grabbed nine rebounds. Bluford had another double-double with 16 points and 10 rebounds.

Mason County closed out the regular season with wins over Fleming County, Montgomery County, Harrison County, Covington Catholic and Bryan Station. The Royals had a 22-0 run against Montgomery County. With Black returning to action in the Bryan Station game, the Royals were at full strength for the first time. Gilbert led Mason County in scoring with 14 points. Bluford had a double-double with 10 points and 13 rebounds. He also blocked seven shots.

The Royals scored 17 straight points in the first quarter and defeated St. Patrick 84-55 in the semifinals of the 39th District Tournament. Gilbert had a game-high 21 points. The Saints ended the season with a 10-14 record.

Mason County shot 71.4 percent in the first half, including 8-of-10 in the second quarter and beat Bracken County 67-45 in the championship game. Five Royals scored in double figures. Gilbert had 13 points. Ryne King scored 12. Bluford had 11 points and 13 rebounds. Setty scored 11, and Justin Lang added 10.

The 10th Region Tournament returned to the Fieldhouse. After trailing by three points in the third quarter, the Royals ended the game on an 18-8 run to beat the Bishop Brossart Mustangs 51-46 in the first round. Setty scored 16 points, and Gilbert added 12.

Mason County jumped out to a 14-0 lead and defeated the Pendleton County Wildcats 65-52 in the semifinals. Bradley Lang was 6-of-7 from the field and scored a career-high 16 points. Gilbert also scored 16 points. Justin Lang added 10 points. Bluford had 12 rebounds.

Mason County and Clark County met in the championship game for the second straight year and the third time in four seasons.

Clark County was one of the top teams in the state with a 26-6 record. The Cardinals all junior starting lineup was big with six-foot-four Robbie Stenzel and six-foot-six Jaylen Daniel in the backcourt, and a front line of six-foot-five Corey Rogers, six-foot-eight Vinny Zollo and six-foot-seven Travis Purvis.

Mason County and Clark County had not met in the regular season. They were scheduled to play Feb. 5 at the Fieldhouse, but Clark County decided not to make the trip because the forecast called for a big snow. Stenzel happened to be sidelined with an ankle injury at the time. It rained that night, but the snow didn't fall until overnight.

Both teams were at full strength for the region championship game.

Clark County led 16-9 at the end of the first quarter, 30-29 at the half and 46-40 at the end of the third quarter.

The Cardinals were up 55-49 when the Royals began to rally. Setty hit a three-pointer to tie the game. Justin Lang made a run out layup to give Mason County a 57-55 lead. Rodgers hit a shot to tie the game. The Royals regained the lead when Gilbert made the front of the end of the 1-and-1. Gilbert missed the bonus free throw, but Justin Lang hit both ends of the 1-and-1 to put the Royals up 60-57 with 33 seconds left. Pawsat made 1-of-2 free throws to make it a two possession game at 61-57 with 18 seconds left. Zollo hit a three-pointer to cut Mason County's lead to one with 9.9 seconds to play. Justin Lang went back to the line for the double bonus with 8.8 seconds left. He missed the first free throw, but hit the second to make it 62-60. That turned out to be the final score as Clark County turned the ball over and time ran out. The Royals had pulled off the upset. Mason County was the 10th Region champion for the third straight year and the seventh time in nine seasons.

Gilbert and Justin Lang scored 16 points apiece. "Jordan and Justin both made play after play," says O'Hearn, "not only making shots in the second half, but some defensive plays that they made." He says those two were "just tough as nails." Setty added 10 points. Bluford had 11 rebounds.

"That was a great, great high school basketball game, one of my all-time favorites," says O'Hearn. "I would rank it right up there with the state championship."

Mason County played 5th Region champion North Hardin in the first round of the state tournament. The Royals led by 12 in the first quarter and were up 17-7 at the end of the first quarter, 25-22 at the half and 41-35 after three quarters. The Trojans rallied and took a 49-47 lead with 1:41 left. Gilbert made a layup to tie the game with 1:32 to go. North Hardin coach Ron Bevars said the Trojans were playing for the last shot, but took a shot early and missed. Mason County got the rebound, but a turnover gave the ball back to the Trojans with 11 seconds to play. North Hardin was called for a walk with eight seconds left. Gilbert missed a layup with four seconds to go. North Hardin missed a three-pointer at the buzzer.

A three-point play by Bluford gave the Royals a 56-54 lead with 1:37 left in overtime. North Hardin tied the game with 1:28 left. Mason County then spread the floor looking for the last shot. Gilbert drove to his right and banked in a running layup with four seconds to play to put Mason County up 58-56. The Trojans' desperation shot at the buzzer was an air ball. The Royals won their 11th straight game.

Gilbert and Bradley Lang scored 12 points apiece. Justin Lang added 10 points. Bluford had nine points and 14 rebounds.

The Butler Bears were Mason County's opponent in the quarterfinal round. The Royals trailed by nine in the second quarter and were down 24-19 at the half. Mason County shot just 28 percent from the field in the first half. "We struggled to score; we struggled to get in the press," says O'Hearn. Whatever O'Hearn said to his team at halftime worked. The Royals went to their run and jump press and outscored the Bears 21-10 in the third quarter to lead 40-34. O'Hearn says the Royals "played with a lot of emotion and energy, and really just blitzed them the second half." Mason County won 58-47. Black came off the bench to score 18 points. Gilbert and Pawsat scored 10 points apiece.

"That was a big win; I mean that puts you into playing on Saturday morning, playing on the last day of the season," says O'Hearn.

Mason County faced Shelby Valley in the semifinals. The Wildcats led 22-11 at the end of the first quarter and by as many as 14 in the second quarter. The Royals cut the deficit to seven, but Shelby Valley point guard Elisha Justice hit two free throws to give the Wildcats a 39-30 lead at the half. Mason County closed to within 41-36, but Justice hit a three-pointer and Shelby Valley began to pull away. Justice hit a three-pointer with four seconds left in the third quarter to give the Wildcats a 55-41 lead. Back-to-back baskets by Gilbert and Bluford in the opening minute of the fourth quarter cut the deficit to 10, but the Royals would get no closer. The final score was Shelby Valley 71, Mason County 51.

The Royals' game plan was to make Justice shoot from the perimeter and not let him get to the rim or create plays for his teammates. But Justice hit five of six shots from three-point range. "We thought that was his weakest part of his game, and he burned us," says O'Hearn.

Justice scored a game-high 31 points. Gilbert led Mason County in scoring with 15 points. Justin Lang added 10 points. Gilbert and Bluford were named to the all-tournament team.

Mason County ended the season with a 25-7 record. "It was a great finish, a great run, a great group of seniors that led us," says O'Hearn.

Shelby Valley beat Ballard 73-61 in the state championship game.

From the 2001-2002 season through the 2009-2010 season, Mason County had a 254-50 record (83.6%) with nine district titles, seven regional championships, two state championships, a state runner-up and a state semifinalist finish.

The Mason County Royals' streak of three straight 10th Region titles came to an end with a semifinal loss in the 2011 regional tournament. Earlier in the season, Mason County's official timer and team bus driver, Mike "Murph" Murphy, died at the age of 53. Murphy was also Mason County's head baseball coach. The Royals hosted the inaugural U.S. Bank Mike Murphy Classic during the 2011-12 basketball season. The Royals won their 12th consecutive district title in 2012, but lost to Clark County in the championship game of the 10th Region Tournament.

The St. Patrick Lady Saints won their first 10th Region All "A" Classic championship in 2011.

Endnotes & References

1. History of Basketball. Available: http://www.history-of-basketball.com/history.htm. Accessed April 26, 2011
2. Public Ledger. (Maysville, KY)
3. Public Ledger. June 29, 1895. "Ge Whiz."
4. Public Ledger. August 10, 1895. "Who Says Maysville Can't Play Ball? For the Second Time the Cincinnati Reds Go Down in Deserved Defeat."
5. Public Ledger. Feb. 3, 1897. Y.M.C.A Paragraphs.
6. Evening Bulletin. (Maysville, KY) April 5, 1987. Basket Ball.
7. Public Ledger. April 27, 1897. Y.M.C.A. Matters.
8. Public Ledger. March 26, 1897. Y.M.C.A Matters.
9. Evening Bulletin. March 26, 1897.
10. Public Ledger. April 5, 1897. Y.M.C.A. Matters.
11. Public Ledger. April 26, 1897. Y.M.C.A. Matters.
12. Public Ledger. December 17, 1898.
13. Public Ledger. Feb. 27, 1899.
14. Evening Bulletin. March 22, 1899.
15. Evening Bulletin. March 25, 1899.
16. Evening Bulletin. March 27, 1899.
17. Ibid.
18. Evening Bulletin. December 9, 1899.
19. Public Ledger. January 13, 1900.
20. Evening Bulletin. February 7, 1900. Basket Ball.
21. Public Ledger. February 14, 1901.
22. Public Ledger. February 27, 1901. "A Brief Outline of the Game As It Is Played at the Y.M.C.A."
23. Evening Bulletin. March 8, 1901. "The Heavyweights Won the Basket Ball Game Last Night At Y.M.C.A. Gym, Attracted a Big Crowd."
24. Evening Bulletin. June 13, 1901. Y.M.C.A. Statistics.
25. Evening Bulletin June 3, 1901. Basket Ball Thursday. "Cincinnati Y.M.C.A. to Meet Local Club."
26. Evening Bulletin. June 6, 1901. "Basket Ball Game Postponed."
27. Evening Bulletin. December 17,1901. "Y.M.C.A Basket Ball Games to Played This Evening."
28. Evening Bulletin. February 15, 1902. "Hard Fought Game: Covington Y.M.C.A. Basket Ball Team Defeated the Maysvilles, But They Were Given a Lively Fight."
29. Ibid.
30. Evening Bulletin. February 14, 1902. "An Exciting Game: You Should See the Basket Ball Contest at the Convent Hall To-Night."
31. Evening Bulletin. March 8, 1902. Basket Ball. "Glendale Won Last Night, But It Was a Fine Game-Score 36 to 33-Big Game This Afternoon."
32. Ibid.
33. Evening Bulletin. March 10, 1902. "Took Both Games: Glendale Again Defeated the Maysville Y.M.C.A. Basket Ball Team."
34. Public Ledger. April 12, 1904.
35. Public Ledger. April 23, 1904.

36. Public Ledger. January 18, 1905. "Basket Ball Tonight: Good Game at the Y.M.C.A., Trimmed With German Lunch."
37. Public Ledger. March 20, 1906.
38. Public Ledger. October 15, 1907. "Maysville Athletics Lining Up for Strenuous Campaign; High School Boys Organize."
39. Public Ledger. February 8, 1910. "Basket Ball Game Scheduled in Near Future by High School Girls."
40. Public Ledger. June 16, 1909. "First Commencement and Dedication of Maysville's New High School Building Occurs Tomorrow."
41. Public Ledger. November 2, 1909. "High School Girls' Basket Ball."
42. Public Ledger. February 21, 1910. "Mayslick vs. Maysville Basketball Game at High School Next Saturday Afternoon."
43. Public Ledger. November 15, 1909. "Maysville Girls Lose Basket Ball Game to Paris in Exciting Score of 25-9."
44. Ibid.
45. Public Ledger. Decmber 21, 1909. Basket Ball: "Maysville Girls Victorious in Game at Ashland Saturday."
46. Public Ledger. March 14, 1910. "Maysville 19, Ashland 3: Handsome Iron City Team Outclassed by Maysville High School Girls."
47. Public Ledger. February 23, 1910. "Lexington 38, Maysville 3."
48. Public Ledger. March 1, 1910. Basket Ball. "Maysville Wins from Mayslick; Other Games on the Schedule."
49. Public Ledger. February 28, 1910.
50. Public Ledger. March 8, 1910. Basket Ball. "Maysville Loses at Richmond and Winchester But Receives Warmest Hospitality."
51. Public Ledger. March 29, 1910. "The Girls' Defy."
52. Ibid.
53. Public Ledger. April 18, 1910. "Last Game of Basket Ball Next Tuesday Evening."
54. Public Ledger. February 18, 1910. Basket Ball. "Lewisburg and Mayslick Teams Play at Latter Place Tomorrow."
55. Public Ledger. October 13, 1910. "Athletic Association Organized by Minerva High School Athletic Association With Membership of 54 Will Contest Other County Schools."
56. Public Ledger. November 25, 1910.
57. Public Ledger. January 19, 1911.
58. Public Ledger. December 8, 1910.
59. Public Ledger. January 20, 1911.
60. Public Ledger. March 9, 1911.
61. Ibid.
62. Public Ledger. February 17, 1912. "Maysville Wins."
63. The Bourbon News. January 30, 1912.
64. Public Ledger. March 2, 1912. "Basketball."
65. Public Ledger. April 18, 1912. "M.H.S. Basket."
66. Ibid.
67. Public Ledger. November 29, 1912.
68. The Daily Bulletin. January 2, 1913. Basket Ball. "Maysville High School Team Defeats 'Lion Tamers' By Score of Eighteen to Ten."

69. Public Ledger. September 15, 1915. "High School Athletics to Start Soon."
70. The Daily Bulletin. January 31, 1913. Baskte Ball. "High School Girls' Teams Play Interesting Games While Boys Have Battle Royal."
71. The Bourbon News. February 18, 1913. "Paris Defeats Maysville Girls."
72. Public Ledger. February 19, 1914. "Girls Basket Ball Here Tomorrow Night Between Paris and Maysville High School Teams."
73. Public Ledger. February 7, 1914. "Basket Ball Tonight: Maysville High School Team Will Meet the Fast Portsmouth Boys at the High School Auditorium."
74. Public Ledger. February 7, 1914. "23 to 13 Portsmouth's Measure Taken by the Maysville High School Boys Last Night."
75. Public Ledger. November 7, 1914. "M.H.S. Lost at Germantown."
76. The Bourbon News (Paris, KY). December 22, 1914. "Paris Defeats Maysville."
77. Public Ledger. January 8, 1915. "Intercollegiate Basketball Season."
78. Public Ledger. January 9, 1915. "Maysville Takes Doubleheader."
79. Public Ledger. January 25, 1915. "Walloped: Ashland High School Team Defeats M.H.S. Team Saturday Night by the Score of 37 to 12."
80. Public Ledger. September 15, 1915. "High School Athletics to Start Soon."
81. Public Ledger. February 1, 1915. "Defeated at Augusta."
82. Public Ledger. February 20, 1915. "Maysville Lost at Portsmouth."
83. Public Ledger. February 13, 1915. "Dashing Game of Basketball Played at High School Auditorium Last Night Between Maysville and Newport Girls; Game Resulted in a 17 to 17 Tie."
84. Public Ledger. February 12, 1915. "Girls' Basketball."
85. Public Ledger. March 15, 1915. "Defeated at Newport."
86. Public Ledger. September 30, 1915. "Crowded Are the Rooms of the Mayslick School as Never Before."
87. Public Ledger. November 8, 1915. Basketball Notes. "Mayslick to Play Here Friday Evening."
88. Ibid.
89. Advocate, the MHS Yearbook. On file at the Kentucky Gateway Museum Center, Maysville, Kentucky.
90. Public Ledger. September 15, 1915. "High School Athletics to Start Soon."
91. Public Ledger. November 4, 1915. "Basketball Season to Open Friday."
92. Public Ledger. November 10, 1915. Basket Ball Notes. "M.H.S. Announces Official Basketball Schedule."
93. Public Ledger. November 18, 1915. Basketball Notes.
94. Public Ledger. January 5, 1916. Basket Ball Notes.
95. Public Ledger. November 8, 1915. Basket Ball Notes. "Mayslick to Play Here Friday Evening."
96. Public Ledger. November 13, 1915. Basket Ball Notes. "Maysville Takes Double Bill From Mayslick; Large Crowd Present."
97. Public Ledger. November 20, 1915. Basket Ball Notes. "M.H.S. Takes Scrappy Game From Brooksville; Good Sized Crowd Attends Game."
98. Public Ledger. November 12, 1915. Basket Ball Notes. "Mayslick vs. Maysville Tonight."
99. Public Ledger. November 18, 1915. Basket Ball Notes.
100. Public Ledger. November 23, 1915. Basket Ball Notes.

101. Public Ledger. November 27, 1915. "M.H.S. Trims Dayton Bunch: Maysville High School Basketball Team Takes Fast Game From Dayton; Captain Hampton Plays Stellar Game."
102. Public Ledger. December 4, 1915. "Maysville Wins Close Game From Germantown; Picked Girls' Teams Play Interesting Game."
103. Public Ledger. December 11, 1915. "Take Doubleheader: M.H.S. Trims Carlisle Twice; Delightful Times Given Players by Nicholas Citizens."
104. Advocate School Annual. On file at the Kentucky Gateway Museum Center, Maysville, Kentucky.
105. Public Ledger. January 10, 1916. "Maysville Won."
106. Public Ledger. January 13, 1916. "Leave on Trip Today."
107. Public Ledger. January 5, 1916. Basket Ball Notes.
108. Advocate School Annual. On file at the Kentucky Gateway Museum Center, Maysville, Kentucky.
109. Public Ledger. February 1, 1916. "Will Play Paris."
110. Public Ledger. February 5, 1916. "42 to 8: Pride of Bourbon Goes Down in Defeat Before Maysville High School Quintet."
111. Advocate School Annual. On file at the Kentucky Gateway Museum Center, Maysville, Kentucky.
112. Public Ledger. March 3, 1916. "Boys' Basketball Team of Maysville High School Hold Banquet; Speechless Delivered and Good Time Generally Had."
113. Advocate MHS Annual. On file at the Kentucky Gateway Museum Center, Maysville, Kentucky.
114. Public Ledger. December 11, 1915. "Take Doubleheader: M.H.S. Trims Carlisle Twice; Delightful Times Given Players By Nicholas Citizens."
115. Advocate MHS Annual. On file at the Kentucky Gateway Museum Center, Maysville, Kentucky.
116. Ibid.
117. The Calx MHS School Annual. On file at the Kentucky Gateway Museum Center, Maysville, Kentucky.
118. Public Ledger. January 6, 1917. "54 to 1, 55 to 6."
119. Public Ledger. January 22, 1917. "Girls Win; Boys Lose."
120. Public Ledger. January 27, 1917. "Maysville Girls Defeated."
121. The Daily Bulletin. January, 27, 1917. "Record."
122. Ibid.
123. Public Ledger. February 5, 1917. "By Narrow Margin."
124. Public Ledger. February 10, 1917. "Win Game."
125. Public Ledger. February 17, 1917. "Girls Lose at Paris."
126. The Calx, MHS Annual. On file at Kentucky Gateway Museum Center, Maysville, Kentucky.
127. Daily Public Ledger. November 4, 1916. "Will Begin Basketball."
128. Public Ledger. November 25, 1916. "Two Victories Mark the Opening of the Basketball Season of the Maysville High School; Germantown Boys Easily Defeated."
129. Public Ledger. November 29, 1916. "Manchester Team Will Try Their Skill at Defeating the Maysville Basketball Team Tonight in the High School Auditorium."
130. Public Ledger. December 1, 1916. "Manchester Licked in a Fast Game of

Basketball on the Floor of the High School Auditorium Wednesday Night."
131. Public Ledger. December 16, 1916. "Maysville Loses to Lexington in One of the Best Played Games Ever Seen on the Local Floor, Score 32-22."
132. The Calx, MHS Annual. On file at the Kentucky Gateway Museum Center, Maysville, Kentucky.
133. Public Ledger. December 30, 1916. "Alumni Victorious."
134. Public Ledger. January 6, 1917. "54 to 1; 55 to 6."
135. Public Ledger. January 19, 1917. "Paris Tonight."
136. Public Ledger. January 20, 1917. "Paris Defeated."
137. Public Ledger. February 5, 1917. "By Narrow Margin."
138. The Calx, MHS Annual. on file at the Kentucky Gateway Museum Center, Maysville, Kentucky.
139. Ibid.
140. Public Ledger. October 29, 1917.
141. The Calx, MHS Annual. On file at the Kentucky Gateway Museum Center, Maysville, Kentucky.
142. Ibid.
143. Public Ledger. February 25, 1918. "Maysville Goes Down in Defeat."
144. The Calx, MHS Annual. On file at the Kentucky Gateway Museum Center, Maysville, Kentucky.
145. Public Ledger. March 4, 1918.
146. The Calx, MHS Annual. On file at the Kentucky Gateway Museum Center, Maysville, Kentucky.
147. Ibid.
148. Public Ledger. February 9, 1918. "Maysville Wins Both Games."
149. Public Ledger. February 25, 1918. "Maysville Goes Down in Defeat."
150. Public Ledger. March 16, 1918. "Two Exciting Games."
151. The Calx, MHS Annual. On file at the Kentucky Gateway Museum Center, Maysville, Kentucky.
152. Public Ledger. October 7, 1918. "Schools, Churches And Theaters Closed."
153. Public Ledger. February 16, 1919. "Only 9 Schools in Mason to Finish Season."
154. Public Ledger. February 22, 1919. "Eighty Deaths in Mason County Due to 'Flu' Disease."
155. The Calx, MHS annual. On file at Kentucky Gateway Museum Center, Maysville, Kentucky.
156. Public Ledger. December 26, 1918. "Alumni Defeats the High School Squad."
157. Ibid.
158. Public Ledger. January 25, 1919. "Maysville High Takes One Sided Game From Bracken Boys Yesterday."
159. The Calx, MHS annual. On file at the Kentucky Gateway Museum Center, Maysville, Kentucky.
160. Public Ledger. February 1, 1919. "Maysville High Wins From Ashland Five."
161. Public Ledger. March 8, 1919. "Maysville Loses."
162. The Calx, MHS annual. On file at the Kentucky Gateway Museum Center, Maysville, Kentucky.
163. Ibid.

164. Ibid.
165. Public Ledger. October 27, 1919. "Minerva Clinches County Basketball Championship."
166. The Calx, 1920 MHS annual. On file at the Kentucky Gateway Museum Center, Maysville, Kentucky.
167. KHSAA Boys' State Basketball Tournament Records.
168. The Calx, 1920 MHS annual. On file at the Kentucky Gateway Museum Center, Maysville, Kentucky.
169. Ibid.
170. The Ledger Independent, Maysville, KY. March 23, 1972. "About Those 'Tough Sardis Girls ...'"
171. Team Photo.
172. The Ledger Independent. March 4, 1980. "The '22 Sardis Girls Were Something Else," by Evelyn Kwaczala.
173. Ibid.
174. The Calx, 1922 MHS annual. On file at the Kentucky Gateway Museum Center, Maysville, Kentucky.
175. Ibid.
176. The Calx, 1923 MHS annual. On file at the Kentucky Gateway Museum Center, Maysville, Kentucky.
177. Ibid.
178. Ibid.
179. The Calx, 1924 MHS annual. On file at the Kentucky Gateway Museum Center, Maysville, Kentucky.
180. The Daily Independent, Maysville, KY. March 15, 1924. "Suffers Broken Collar Bone in Ashland Game."
181. The Calx, 1924 MHS annual. On file at the Kentucky Gateway Museum Center, Maysville, Kentucky.
182. Ibid.
183. The Daily Independent. December 28, 1923. "Doubleheader Here Tonight."
184. The Daily Independent. October 9, 1924. "Bulldogs Ready for Second Game."
185. The Daily Independent. February 11, 1924. "Minerva Wins From Maysville."
186. The Daily Independent. March 10, 1924. "Minerva Wants Play for $500."
187. Public Ledger. December 2, 1925. "Local Quintets to Open Season Here on Friday Night."
188. Daily Independent. December 4, 1925. "First Basketball Game of Season."
189. Public Ledger. December 2, 1925. "Local Quintets to Open Season Here on Friday Night."
190. Public Ledger. December 5, 1925. "M.H.S. Net Teams Open Season Here Friday Evening."
191. Public Ledger. December 12, 1925. "Portsmouth Over Maysville."
192. Public Ledger. January 9, 1926. "Local Fives Score Double Victory Over Augusta."
193. The Daily Independent. January 26, 1926.
194. Public Ledger. "M.H.S. Fives Lose Double-Header to Georgetown Fives."

195. The Daily Independent. February 1, 1926.
196. Ibid.
197. The Daily Independent. February 15, 1926.
198. Public Ledger. February 27, 1926. "M.H.S. Fives Drop Double-Header at Georgetown Friday."
199. Public Ledger. March 2, 1926. "Hooray! M.H.S. Fives Hand Flemingsburg Trimming."
200. Public Ledger. March 5, 1926. "M.H.S Fives Win First Games at Tournament."
201. Public Ledger. March 8, 1926. "M.H.S Girls Cop District Flag at Brooksville Meet."
202. Ibid.
203. Daily Independent. March 9, 1926. "Awards Many in State Net Tournament."
204. Daily Independent. March 12, 1926. "Girls Win First Game in State Tournament."
205. Public Ledger. March 11, 1926. "Maysville Girls Win First Game by 24 to 12 Score."
206. The Daily Independent. March 12, 1926. "Girls Win First Game in State Tournament."
207. Public Ledger. March 12, 1926. "M.H.S. Girls Trim Shepherdsville to Enter Semi-Finals."
208. Public Ledger. March 13, 1926. "Maysville Wins Tournament by 23 to 16 Score."
209. Public Ledger. March 15, 1926. "State Basketball Champions."
210. Ibid.
211. Ibid.
212. The Daily Independent. March 16, 1926. "All Maysville Honoring Girls for Victory."
213. Public Ledger. March 17, 1926. "Rotarians Give Banquet Honoring Basketball Team."
214. Public Ledger. March 19, 1926. "Commercial Club Honors Basketball Team."
215. Public Ledger. January 4, 1930. "Local Fives Open New Gym With Double Victory."
216. Ibid.
217. Public Ledger. March 4, 1927. "Net Tournament at Bracken County Well Under Way."
218. The Daily Independent. March 4, 1927. "Girls to Play Flemingsburg; Boys Draw Bye."
219. Public Ledger. March 5, 1927. "Maysville Boys Down Augusta in Rousing Victory."
220. Public Ledger. March 12, 1927. "Maysville Girls Are Eliminated by Ashland Five."
221. The Daily Independent. March 12, 1927. "Ashland Teams Win Honors in Sixth Region."
222. Public Ledger. March 12, 1927. "Maysville Girls Are Eliminated by Ashland Five."

223. The Daily Independent. March 12, 1927. Ashland Teams Win Honors in Sixth Region."
224. The Daily Independent. March 17, 1927. "Germantown And Minerva First to Play."
225. Public Ledger. March 17, 1927. "Ashland Coach Gets New Deal in State Meet."
226. Public Ledger. March 18, 1927. "Covington Made Favorite by Win Over Manual."
227. The Daily Independent. March 21, 1927. "M.M.I And West Louisville Cop Championships."
228. Public Ledger. March 21, 1927. "Minerva Outplays M.M.I. Cadets for Three Quarters."
229. 1927 Minerva team photo. District Tournament Basketball: A 50-Year History, 1923-1972. Compiled by the May's Lick 4-Hers, Page 4.
230. The Daily Independent. March 3, 1928. "Gold And White Beats Augusta by Large Score."
231. Public Ledger. March 5, 1928. "Maysville Girls, District Champs, Play Paintsville."
232. Public Ledger. March 10, 1928. "M.H.S. Girls Go Down to Defeat Before Ashland."
233. The Daily Independent. March, 1928. "Ashland Teams Are Champs of Eighth Region."
234. Ibid
235. The Daily Independent. March 17, 1928. "Minerva Loses Running Guard for Tournament."
236. The Daily Independent. March 16, 1928. "Minerva Wins First Game in State Tourney."
237. Public Ledger. March 16, 1928. "Two Cases of Scarlet Fever at Minerva."
238. Ibid.
239. The Daily Independent. March 7, 1930. "Large Crowds Attend First Day of Tourney."
240. The Daily Independent. March 8, 1930. "Maysville Teams Reach Semi-Finals."
241. The Daily Independent. March 10, 1930. "Maysville Girls and Boys Win Tournament."
242. The Daily Independent. March 15, 1930. "Maysville Five Victor Over Mt. Sterling."
243. Public Ledger. March 17, 1930. "Ashland Girls And Mt. Sterling Boys Cop Titles."
244. Ibid.
245. Public Ledger. March 20, 1930. "Mayslick Five Wins First Game at State Meet."
246. The Daily Independent. March 22, 1930. "Mayslick Goes in the B Finals of Net Tourney."
247. The Daily Independent. March 24, 1930. "Corinth And Hazard Takes State Title."
248. Public Ledger. March 22, 1930. "Mayslick Girls Lose in B Finals."
249. The Daily Independent. March 7, 1931. "Tournament Champions Decided

Today."
250. Team photo on page 57 of *The Towns of Mason County: Their Past in Pictures*. By Jean Calvert and John Klee.
251. The Daily Independent. March 9, 1931. "Maysville Wins Third Straight Championship."
252. Ibid.
253. The Daily Independent. March 12, 1931. "Regional Meet Opens Tonight at Morehead."
254. The Daily Independent. March 14, 1931. "Mayslick And Minerva Score Easy Triumphs."
255. The Daily Independent. March 16, 1931. "Mayslick Girls Win Class B Regional Title."
256. The Daily Bulletin. March 16, 1931. "Tomcats."
257. The Daily Bulletin. March 20, 1931. "Defeat."
258. The Daily Independent. September 28, 1925. "Meeting Called to Elect Coach."
259. The Daily Independent. October 2, 1925. "Football Season Opens Here Today."
260. The Daily Independent. October 3, 1925. "Maysville Wins Opening Game of 1925 Season."
261. Ibid.
262. The Daily Independent. September 4, 1926. "Preparations Complete for School."
263. The Daily Independent. August 23, 1927. "Hobart Walker Named Coach to Succeed Long."
264. The Daily Independent. June, 6, 1927. "Hobart Walker Resigns Post at Maysville High."
265. The Daily Independent. September 1, 1928. "City Schools Open Tuesday; New Teacher."
266. Public Ledger. March 14, 1930.
267. The Daily Independent. September 26, 1930. "Hovater's Squad Working Good at Blue Licks' Camp."
268. The Daily Bulletin. February 10, 1931. "Miss Jones."
269. The Daily Independent. February 11, 1931. "Lawrenceburg Sardis Lose to Maysville."
270. The Daily Bulletin. February 13, 1932. "Tomcats."
271. The Daily Independent. February 14, 1932. "Victory."
272. Public Ledger. August 20, 1931. "Successor to Hovater Named by School Board."
273. Lexington Herald. August 20, 1931. "Earl Jones Appointed Maysville High Coach." Public Ledger. August 20, 1931. "Successor to Hovater Named by School Board."
274. Public Ledger. August 20, 1931. "Successor to Hovater Named by School Board."
275. Lexington Herald. August 20, 1931 "Earl Jones Appointed Maysville High Coach."
276. Ibid.
277. Public Ledger. February 27, 1931. "Girls Win But Boys Are Sunk by

Kavanaugh."
278. Lexington Herald. August 20, 1931. "Earl Jones Appointed Maysville High Coach."
279. Public Ledger. August 20, 1931. "Successor to Hovater Named by School Board."
280. The Courier-Journal (Louisville, KY). August 23, 1931. "Earl Jones Signs To Coach At Maysville."
281. Public Ledger. September 26, 1931. "Bulldogs Scored 19 to 7 Win in Season Opener."
282. Public Ledger. December 2, 1931. "Practice Begun by Coach Jones for Net Season."
283. *Maysville High Girls' Basketball, 1924-1932*. By Debbie Day.
284. Public Ledger. March 5, 1932. "Both Maysville Fives in Tourney Finals Tonight."
285. The Daily Independent. March 7, 1932. "Washington And Maysville in First Place."
286. Ibid.
287. Ibid.
288. The Daily Independent. March 10, 1932. "Regional Net Tournament Opens Tonight."
289. Public Ledger. March 11, 1932. "Vanceburg Girls, Mayslick, North Middletown Win."
290. Public Ledger. March 12, 1932. "Maysville Girls Beat Vanceburg Play Washington."
291. The Daily Independent. March 14, 1932. "Washington Swamps Clintonville."
292. Ibid.
293. The Daily Bulletin. March 14, 1932.
294. THE Daily Independent. March 14, 1932. "Washington Swamps Clintonville."
295. The Daily Bulletin. March 14, 1932.
296. The Daily Independent. March 14, 1932. "Regional Won by Paris and Washington."
297. Ibid.
298. The Daily Independent. March 14, 1932. "Nine Class B Teams Win Way to State Meet."
299. The Daily Independent. March 18, 1932. "Clay City Takes First Title From Washington."
300. The Daily Bulletin. March 18, 1932.
301. Public Ledger. January 19, 1937. "River Still on Way Up; Crest Put at 58 Feet."
302. Public Ledger. February 4, 1937. "River Drops Under Flood Stage Here Thursday."
303. Public Ledger. January 25, 1937. "Crest Near, 75 or 76 Feet."
304. Public Ledger. January 26, 1937. "May Get One to Two Feet."
305. Public Ledger. January 28, 1937. "Flood Waters Receding."
306. Public Ledger. February 4, 1937. "River Drops Under Flood Stage Here Thursday."
307. Public Ledger. February 10, 1937. "River Continues to Rise, Has Come Up

Over 10 Feet."
308. Public Ledger. February 11, 1937. "Bulldogs Trounce Versailles, 32-17."
309. Public Ledger. March 19, 1937. "Bulldogs Hold St. X to 25 to 22 Score."
310. Public Ledger. November 9, 1937. Local Net Team to Open Season at Mayslick Dec. 1."
311. Public Ledger. March 15, 1938. "Coach Jones Drills Cagers for State Meet."
312. Public Ledger. March 4, 1938. "Bulldogs Upset Dope; Play Augusta Tonight."
313. Ibid.
314. Public Ledger. March 11, 1938. "Bulldogs Defeat Flemingsburg 33-27."
315. "Bulldogs Trample Greyhounds."
316. Public Ledger. March 14, 1938. "Bulldogs, Regional Champs, Draw Russell."
317. Public Ledger. March 18, 1938. "Maysville Highland (sic) Tonigh."t
318. Public Ledger. March 19, 1938. "Bulldogs in Finals, Tonight, Play Sharpe."
319. Public Ledger. March 19, 1938. "Bulldogs in Finals, Tonight; Play Sharpe."
320. Courier-Journal article by Earl Ruby. Reprinted in the Public Ledger, March 21, 1938, "Bulldogs Are Toast of All Maysville."
321. Lexington Herald game story by Neville Dunn. Reprinted in the Public Ledger, March 21, 1938, "Bulldogs Are Toast of All Maysville."
322. State Tournament records.
323. Public Ledger. March 21, 1938. "Bulldogs Are Toast of All Maysville."
324. Public Ledger. February 26, 1940. "Bulldogs Dealt Blow As Ritchie Found Ineligible."
325. Public Ledger. February 28, 1940. "Maysville High School Suspended From K.H.S.A.A."
326. Letter from Adolph Rupp in Jones' scrapbook at Kentucky Gateway Museum Center, Maysville, Kentucky.
327. The Daily Independent, Page 1. September 2, 1930. "Formal Opening of New Colored School Today."
328. Public Ledger. February 24, 1927. Page 4. Colored News.
329. Public Ledger. February 28, 1927. Page 1. Colored News.
330. Public Ledger. February 15, 1927. Page 3. Colored News.
331. Daily Independent. March 28, 1927. Page 6. "Washington Lost First Game 14-10."
332. Public Ledger. February 27, 1928. Page 4. "Colored High School Fives Get Even Break."
333. Public Ledger. March 6, 1929. Page 2.
334. The Daily Bulletin. March 19, 1931. Page 4. "Colored High School Represented at Lexington."
335. The Daily Independent. March 20, 1931. Page 5. "Maysville's Fee Team Are Victors."
336. The Daily Independent. March 21, 1931. Page 8. "Fee Basket Five Wins One, Loses One."
337. The Daily Independent. February 11, 1932. Page 7. Colored News.
338. The Daily Independent. March 14, 1932. Page 1. "Fee Team."
339. The Daily Bulletin. January 21, 1932. Page 3. "Fee Hi News."
340. The Daily Bulletin. January 28, 1932. Page 4. "Fee Hi Weekly News."
341. The Daily Independent. January 28, 1932. Page 7. Colored News.
342. The Daily Independent. February 18, 1932. Colored News.

343. The Daily Independent. February 25, 1932. Page 8. Colored News.
344. The Daily Independent. March 14, 1932. Page 2. "Maysville Team Second in State Negro High Meet."
345. Ibid.
346. The Daily Bulletin. March 14, 1932. Page 1. "Fee Team."
347. Public Ledger. December 17, 1932. Page 4. Colored News.
348. Public Ledger. December 20, 1932. Page 3. Colored News.
349. Daily Independent. January 9, 1933. Page 8. Colored News. "Fee Hi Girls And Boys Swamp Lexington Team."
350. Public Ledger. January 14, 1933. Page 4. Colored News.
351. Public Ledger. January 31, 1933. Page 4. Colored News.
352. Daily Independent. January 23, 1933. Page 8. Colored News.
353. Public Ledger. February 6, 1933. Page 4. Colored News.
354. Public Ledger. February 11, 1933. Page 4. Colored News.
355. Public Ledger. February 13, 1933. Colored News.
356. Public Ledger. February 21, 1933. Page 4. Colored News.
357. Public Ledger. February 27, 1933. Page 4. Colored News.
358. Public Ledger. March 4, 1933. Colored News. "Fee Hi Defeats Ala. State College, 34-32."
359. Public Ledger. March 8, 1933. Page 4. Colored News.
360. Public Ledger. March 14, 1933. Page 4. Colored News. "Fee Wildcats Second Best in State Tournament."
361. Ibid.
362. The Daily Independent. March 20, 1933. Page 3. "Fee Girls Win State Basketball Championship."
363. The Daily Independent. January 7, 1933. Page 8. Colored News. "Fee High Basketball."
364. The Daily Independent. January 9, 1933. Page 8. Colored News. "Fee Hi Girls And Boys Swamp Lexington Team."
365. Public Ledger. January 14, 1933. Page 4. Colored News.
366. Public Ledger. January 31, 1933. Page 4. Colored News.
367. Public Ledger. February 6, 1933. Page 4. Colored News. "Richmond Easy Prey for Fee Hi."
368. Public Ledger. March 18, 1933. Page 4. "Fee Girls Win State Basketball Crown."
369. Ibid.
370. The Daily Independent. March 20, 1933. Page 3. "Fee Girls Win State Basketball Championship."
371. Ibid.
372. Team Photo on file at the Kentucky Gateway Museum Center, Maysville, Kentucky. The Daily Independent. March 20, 1933. Page 3. "Fee Girls Win State Basketball Championship."
373. Public Ledger. March 22, 1934. Page 2. Colored News. "Fee High Girls Depart for State Tourney."
374. Public Ledger. March 24, 1934. "Fee Girls Cop State Title Second Time."
375. Ibid.
376. Ibid.
377. Interview with Stella Jackson Bennett, September 13, 2011.

378. Public Ledger. February 10, 1939. Page 4. "Fee High Cagers Cop District Title."
379. Public Ledger. February 25, 1939. Page 4. "Fee Upset by Richmond And Lincoln Ridge in Tourney."
380. Public Ledger. March 14, 1939. Page 4. "Fee Hi to Tuskegee."
381. Public Ledger. March 19, 1940. Page 4. "Fee Hi Team Off to Tuskegee."
382. Public Ledger. March 14, 1941. Page 3. "Fee Hi Wins, 26-18."
383. Public Ledger. March 13, 1941. Page 3. "Fee High to State Tournament."
384. Public Ledger. March 12, 1946. "Fee High Cagers Win Region Title."
385. Public Ledger. March 15, 1946. "Fee Wldcats Lose to Henderson, 33-21."
386. Public Ledger. March 16, 1946. Colored News. "Fee Wins Consolation Title in State Tourney."
387. Public Ledger. March 3, 1947. Page 2. Colored News. "Regional Tournament at Fee High School."
388. Public Ledger. February 22, 1947. Page 3. Colored News. "Tournament Plans Nearing Completion."
389. Public Ledger. March 7, 1947. "Fee Wildcats Win Opener in 2 Overtimes."
390. Public Ledger. March 8, 1947. "Fee Wins Thriller; In Finals Tonight."
391. Public Ledger. March 10, 1947. "Ashland Cops Eastern Mountain Cage Title."
392. Public Ledger. March 8, 1948. Colored News. "Fee High to Close Season."
393. Public Ledger. March 5, 1949. Basketball Games. "Fee High Wins Two; To Play in Semi-finals This Afternoon."
394. Public Ledger. March 7, 1949. "Fee High Cops Eastern District Meet by Downing Ashland, 51-44."
395. Public Ledger. March 11, 1949. Basketball. "Fee High Eliminated in Regional Tournament."
396. Public Ledger. September 14, 1942. Intramural Sports to Replace Football Here.
397. Coach Jones' letter, dated August 27, 1943, on file at Kentucky Gateway Museum Center, Maysville, Kentucky.
398. Public Ledger. March 16, 1945. "Bulldogs Lose to Male by Only 3 Points, 44-41."
399. Public Ledger. February 25, 1946. Basketball Games. "Bulldogs Close With Great Victory Over Male, 41-25."
400. Public Ledger. February 19, 1946. Basketball Games. "Get Revenge; Sink Bears 57-40."
401. Public Ledger. March 13, 1946. "Breck Favored; Bulldogs Are Third Choice, 6-1."
402. Public Ledger. March 15, 1946. "Bulldogs Win First Title; Play Ft. Knox Tonight."
403. University of Louisville Basketball Guide
404. Public Ledger. August 11, 1950. "Kenny Reeves Signs $4,500 Contract With Boston Celtics."
405. Kenny Reeves 10th Region Hall of Fame induction speech, March 26, 2007.
406. *St. Patrick Record Book*, compiled by Tony Sapp and Rick Swartz.
407. Public Ledger. December 24, 1937. "Mert Blanton Entrant in Boxing Tournament."

408. Public Ledger. March 11, 1946. "Banquet Pays Tribute to St. Patrick's Cagers And Coach."
409. Public Ledger. March 11, 1946. "Banquet Pays Tribute To St. Patrick's Cagers And Coach."
410. Public Ledger. October 31, 1945. "St. Patrick's Has 23-Game Schedule."
411. Public Ledger. January 14, 1945. "St. Pat Has Three Games Coming Up."
412. Public Ledger. February 21, 1946. "Basketball Irish Lose Final Game to Portsmouth Catholic."
413. Public Ledger. November 13, 1945. "Fighting Irish Take on Tigers Tonight."
414. *St. Patrick Record Book*, compiled by Tony Sapp and Rick Swartz.
415. Public Ledger. February 22, 1947. "Full House Expected For Title Here Sunday."
416. Public Ledger. March 9, 1948. "Local Teams to Be at Full Strength."
417. Public Ledger. March 10, 1948. "St. Patrick Loses But Bulldogs Win."
418. *St. Patrick Record Book*, compiled by Tony Sapp and Rick Swartz.
419. Public Ledger. November 20, 1946. "Basketball Bulldogs Unimpressive But Cop Opener, 30-17."
420. Public Ledger. November 23, 1946. Basketball Games. "Bulldogs Perk Up to Swamp Morgan, 73-26."
421. Public Ledger. November 28, 1947. Basketball Games. "Bulldogs Take Measure of Lewis County Lions, 59-23.
422. Public Ledger. January 24, 1947. Basketball Games. "Bracken County Polar Bears Defeat Bulldogs in Two Overtimes."
423. Public Ledger. January 29, 1947. Basketball Games. "Comets Pull Away in Fourth Quarter to Beat Bulldogs, 44-34."
424. Public Ledger. February 3, 1947. Basketball Games. "Inez Comes From Behind in Closing Minutes."
425. Public Ledger. February 8, 1947. Basketball Games. "Lafayette Downs Bulldogs in Well Played Game, 35-32."
426. Public Ledger. February 15, 1947. Basketball Games. "Bulldogs Trounced by Inez, 54-32, After Poor First Half.
427. Public Ledger. February 19, 1947. Basketball Games. "Bulldogs Take Measure of Polar Bears, 54-39."
428. Public Ledger. February 27, 1947. Basketball Games. "Bulldogs Barely Squeak Past Orangeburg, 26-24."
429. Public Ledger. March 1, 1947. Basketball Games. "Bulldogs Close Campaign With 56-48 Win Over Manual."
430. Public Ledger. March 7, 1947. "Bulldogs Versus Tigers in Finals of Meet Tonight."
431. Public Ledger. March 8, 1947. "Bulldogs Defeat Tigers, 34-24, for District Title."
432. Public Ledger. March 13, 1947. "Bulldogs Play Morgan Tonight at 8 O'clock."
433. Public Ledger. March 14, 1947. "Bulldogs Versus Polar Bears in Finals Tonight."
434. Public Ledger. March 15, 1947. "Bulldogs Down Bears, 34-31, for Regional Crown."
435. Public Ledger. March 18, 1947. "Bulldogs to Hit the Road Tomorrow."
436. Ibid.

437. The Courier-Journal. March 30, 1947. "Jones, Bulldogs Mentor, Chosen Coach of Year."
438. Public Ledger. March 21, 1947. "Bulldogs Upset Corbin, 39 to 30; Play Magnolia."
439. Public Ledger. March 22, 1947. "Bulldogs Upset Owensboro, 56-41."
440. Ibid.
441. Public Ledger. March 24, 1947. "Bulldogs Win Championship; Underdogs Play Great Ball to Mount Throne."
442. Ibid.
443. Ibid.
444. Public Ledger. March 24, 1947. "Triumphal Parade to Champion."
445. Ibid.
446. Ibid.
447. Public Ledger. March 25, 1947. "Trophies Shown at Merz Brothers."
448. Public Ledger. March 26, 1946. "Champions' Coach Says Victory Was Reward Sufficient."
449. Public Ledger. April 4, 1947. "Lions Give Billfolds to Champ And Coach."
450. Public Ledger. March 31, 1947. "Jones, Bulldog Mentor, Chosen Coach of Year."
451. Ibid.
452. Letter to Jones from Adolph Rupp in Jones' scrapbook at the Kentucky Gateway Museum Center, Maysville, Kentucky.
453. Letters from Southern Coach and Athlete in Jones' scrapbook at the Kentucky Gateway Museum Center, Maysville, Kentucky.
454. A letter from Canton Public Schools Superintendent N.R. Haworth in Jones' scrapbook at the Kentucky Gateway Museum Center, Maysville, Kentucky.
455. Public Ledger. February 2, 1948. Basketball Games. "Bulldogs Fall Before Inez As Three Players Foul Out."
456. Public Ledger. February 21, 1948. Basketball Games. "Bulldogs Turn Tables on Indians; Scalp 'Em 57-41."
457. Public Ledger. March 9, 1948. "Local Teams to Be at Full Strength."
458. Public Ledger. March 13, 1948. "Bulldogs Grab Title in Thrilling Finish, Nosing Out Paris, 48-44."
459. Ibid.
460. Ibid.
461. Public Ledger. March 17, 1948. "Brewers, Owensboro Favored in Ratings."
462. Public Ledger. March 19, 1948. "Bulldogs Play Owensboro at 8:30 Tonight."
463. Public Ledger. March 22, 1948. "Fatigue Main Factor in Title Loss by Bulldogs to Brewers Dribble Dope." By Bill Mathews.
464. Game story written by Bob Adair in the Herald-Leader, March 21, 1948, and reprinted in the Public Ledger, March 22, 1948.
465. Game story written by Johnny Carrico in The Courier-Journal and reprinted in the Public Ledger, March 22, 1948.
466. Ibid.
467. Ibid.
468. Public Ledger. March 22, 1948. "Welcome Tells Team How It Stands in Hearts of Fans Here."
469. Public Ledger. March 29, 1948. "Two Bulldogs Named; Tarry Coach of Year."

470. Public Ledger. March 26, 1948. "Jaycees' Ceremony for Bulldogs on Air."
471. Public Ledger. April 2, 1948. "Lions Entertain M.H.S. Basketeers And Coach."
472. Public Ledger. April 15, 1948. "Community Banquet Climaxes Feteing of Maysville Bulldogs."
473. Public Ledger. April 2, 1948. "Lions Entertain M.H.S. Basketeers And Coach."
474. Public Ledger. February 19, 1949. "Bulldogs Again Beat Clark Co., 49-45."
475. Public Ledger. February 19, 1949. "Maysville Needs Bigger Gym."
476. Public Ledger. March 9, 1949. "Bulldogs Lose Heart-Breaker; Paris Wins in Two Overtimes."
477. Public Ledger. March 10, 1949. "Cynthiana Win; 'Dogs 'Loss' Uppermost."
478. Public Ledger. March 10, 1950. "Ormes Not Expected to Play Tonight."
479. Public Ledger. March 11, 1950. "Bulldogs Play Paris in Finals Tonight; Jonesmen Hard Pressed to Down Augusta, 47-39."
480. Public Ledger. March 11, 1950. "Cage Fans Stampede at Sale of Tickets; Near Tragedy."
481. Public Ledger. March 13, 1950. "Fans Apply for Tourney Tickets."
482. Public Ledger. March 14, 1950. "Fans Get 32 More Ducats Than Promised."
483. Public Ledger. March 13, 1950. "Can Bulldogs Defeat Devils Again, Question"
484. Public Ledger. March 16, 1950. "Maysville Bulldogs Stage Final Quarter Spree to Rout Owensboro by 56-40."
485. Public Ledger. March 18, 1950. "Foe's Height, Chicken Dish Tell Tale of Bulldogs' Loss."
486. Ibid.
487. Ibid.
488. Big Blue History.net.
489. Public Ledger. March 3, 1955. "Jones a Respected Coach; Crum's Choice Is Popular."
490. Ibid.
491. Ibid.
492. Public Ledger. March 5, 1956. "Panthers Beat 'Dogs in 42-41 Thriller."
493. Public Ledger. March 12, 1956. "MHS Bulldogs, Region Champs, Meet Bell County in State Play Thursday; Tucker's 15-Foot Shot Is Lethal to Blue Jackets."
494. Public Ledger. March 16, 1956. "Bell Co. Boys Too Big for Bulldogs."
495. Public Ledger. February 15, 1956. "School Integration Here This Fall."
496. Public Ledger. January 14, 1950. Colored News. "Lincoln-Grant Defeats Fee Wildcats, 58-31."
497. Public Ledger. March 4, 1950. Colored News. "Fee 54, Somerset 43."
498. Public Ledger. March 6, 1950. Colored News. "Fee Third in District Play; Goes to Regional."
499. Public Ledger. March 10, 1950. Colored News. "Dunbar Too Much for Fee in Regional Game 49-31."
500. Public Ledger. February 23, 1951. Colored News. "Fee Drops Heartbreaker to Paris in Double Overtime by 60 to 58."
501. Public Ledger. February 22, 1952. Colored News. "Fee vs. Paris in Net Finals Tonight."

502. Public Ledger. February 23, 1952. Colored News. "Paris Upsets Fee to Take Tourney Title."
503. Colored News. "Fee Wildcats Lost Tourney Title in Overtime Contest."
504. Public Ledger. March 6, 1952. Colored News. "Fee Wildcats Dump Somerset Trojans, 75-47."
505. Public Ledger. March 8, 1952. Colored News "Fee Romps Over Dunbar to Earn Tickets to State Play."
506. Public Ledger. March 15, 1952. Colored News. " Fee Slips by Bowling Green in 51-48 Thriller at State."
507. Public Ledger. March 17, 1952. "History Repeats for Wildcats As Fee Is Runner Up to State Champs."
508. Public Ledger. March 2, 1953. Colored News. "Fee Wildcats Win District Game Against Cynthiana."
509. Public Ledger. March 9, 1953. Colored News. "Fee High Ranks Fifth Tournament."
510. Public Ledger. March 13, 1953. Colored News. "Fee Loses to Somerset, 75-68, in Sectional Meet."
511. Public Ledger. February 27, 1954. "Fee Victorious in District Tourney Title."
512. Public Ledger. March 1, 1954. Colored News. "Fee Loses to Paris in Tournament Finals."
513. Public Ledger. March 8, 1954. Colored News. "Fee, Losing Two of Three, to See No Further Action."
514. Public Ledger. February 28, 1955. Colored News. "Fee And Winchester Are in This Week's Regional Play at Paris."
515. Public Ledger. March 7, 1955. Colored News. "Fee Loses Two Games in Blue Grass Tourney."
516. Public Ledger. February 18, 1956. Colored News. "Fee Slips Past Ashland 58 to 57 in Year's Final."
517. Public Ledger. February 20, 1956. Colored News. "Fee to Meet Mt. Sterling in District Play Saturday."
518. Public Ledger. February 27, 1956. Colored News. "Fee's Netters Down Mt. Sterling And Winchester to Win."
519. Ibid.
520. Public Ledger. March 5, 1956. Colored News. "Fee Gets Third Place in Regional Tournament."
521. Public Ledger. March 10, 1956. Colored News. "Fee Sparkles Over Harlan to Win Berth in State Tourney."
522. Public Ledger. March 12, 1956. Colored News. "Fee Is Runnerup in Sectional; Meets Louisville Team."
523. Public Ledger. March 15, 1956. "Fee's Debut in 'State' to Be Friday Night."
524. Public Ledger. March 17, 1956. Colored News. "Fee Loses to Louisville Central in Tourney Play."
525. Public Ledger. March 20, 1956. Colored News. "Fee High Player Rates an All State Berth."
526. Public Ledger. March 20, 1956. Colored News. "Fee High School Athletes Are Honored at Annual Banquet."
527. Public Ledger. September 5, 1956. "City School Have 1,457 Registration Total Opening Day."

528. Public Ledger. October 11, 1956. "Bulldogs Have 28 Games Booked for '56-57 Basketball Season."
529. Public Ledger. November 1, 1956. "Coach Crum Reveals Lineup for Opener."
530. Public Ledger. November 3, 1956. Basketball Games. "Bulldogs Begin '56 Season With 83 to 29 Victory."
531. Public Ledger. November 15, 1956. "Bulldogs Open Home Season With 70 to 49 Victory.
532. Public Ledger. November 15, 1956. "'Dogs Away Friday; Meet Clark County."
533. Public Ledger. December 29, 1956. Basketball Games. "Last Second Points Hopping Pays Off for Ashland Over Bulldogs."
534. Public Ledger. December 31, 1956. Basketball Games. "Ashland Winner, MHS Third in Holiday Invitational Tournament."
535. Public Ledger. January 17, 1957. "Dogs' Away Friday; Play Here Saturday."
536. Public Ledger. January 21, 1957. Basketball Games. "MHS Needs Double Overtime to Tame Thoroughbreds 71-68."
537. Public Ledger. January 23, 1957. Basketball Games. "MHS Sets Scoring Record Against Breckinridge, 101-45."
538. Public Ledger. January 26, 1957. Basketball Games. "M.H.S. Bulldogs Romp Over Inez Indians, 74-57."
539. Public Ledger. February 2, 1957. Basketball Games. "MHS Beats Nicholas Co. 68-63 on Jackets' Court."
540. Public Ledger. January 30, 1957. Basketball Games. "Bulldogs Overcome Comets on Olive Hill Court."
541. Public Ledger. February 2, 1957. Basketball Games. "MHS Beats Nicholas Co. 68-63 on Jackets' Court."
542. Public Ledger. February 4, 1957. Basketball Games. "Bulldogs Sparkle As They Defeat Paintsville, 85 to 70."
543. Ibid.
544. Public Ledger. February 9, 1951. Basketball Games. "'Dogs Need Extra Time to Quell Clark Co., 62-60."
545. Public Ledger. February 14, 1957. "Litkenhous Rating Kept by Maysville."
546. Public Ledger. February 16, 1957. Basketball News. "'Dogs Halt Harrison Co. Home Win Streak, 56-45."
547. Public Ledger. February 23, 1957. Basketball News. "MHS Bulldogs Trounce Mt. Sterling, 62-31."
548. Public Ledger. February 23, 1957. Basketball Games. "Bulldogs End Season With 72-44 Win Over Boone Co."
549. Ibid.
550. Public Ledger. February 26, 1957. "In 103 to 53 Win, Bulldogs Hang Up Record."
551. Public Ledger. March 1, 1957. "Wildcats Make Valiant Fight Against 'Dogs."
552. Public Ledger. March 4, 1957. "MHS Takes District Tourney Title, 80-50."
553. Public Ledger. March 7, 1957. "Bulldogs, Scott County Win in Region Tourney."
554. Public Ledger. March 9, 1957. "Bulldogs One Win From State Tourney Berth."
555. Public Ledger. February 20, 1957. "In 39th District Meet, T'boro, Fleming

County Serious Threat To 'Dogs."
556. Public Ledger. March 11, 1957. "Blue Jackets Rout of 'Dogs Biggest Upset."
557. Inside Kentucky Sports. March 1974. "Maysville Has Many Memories of Sweet 16."
558. Public Ledger. February 19, 1958. "Henry O'Cull Sparks 102-46 Orangeburg Win."
559. Public Ledger. March 4, 1958. "Favorites Win Opener of District Tourney."
560. Public Ledger. June 6, 1958. "Bulldogs Return As State Titlists."
561. Public Ledger. December 6, 1958. All Sports. "'Top-Rated' Bulldogs Soar Over Harrison County for Easy Win, 70-68."
562. Public Ledger. December 20, 1958. All Sports. "After 10 Straight Wins, Bulldogs Meet Match in Louisville."
563. Public Ledger. December 24, 1958. All Sports. "Maysville Drops to 4th."
564. Public Ledger. January 22, 1958. All Sports. "Bulldogs Rated Tenth."
565. Public Ledger. March 14, 1959. "'Dogs Squeak Past Nicholas Co.; Win, 45-44, in Last 10 Seconds."
566. Public Ledger. March 16, 1959. "Bulldogs Rout Scott Co. for Regional Title."
567. Ibid.
568. Ibid.
569. Public Ledger. March 19, 1959. "Maysville Wins 78-67."
570. Public Ledger. March 20, 1959. "'Dogs Bite Dust; Tumbled 62-75."
571. Public Ledger. August 20, 1949. "Blanton Quits As Coach of St. Patrick High; Lustic Successor."
572. Public Ledger. January 30, 1950. "Stahl Believed to Have Established Scoring Record."
573. Public Ledger. March 27, 1950. "Cooke, Stahl, Ormes on All-State Teams."
574. Public Ledger. April 8, 1950. "'Fanny' Stahl Gets Scholarship."
575. Public Ledger. September 19, 1955. "Five Parochial School Boys Hurt in Crash."
576. Ibid.
577. Public Ledger. November 5, 1956. Basketball Games. "Paddies Open Their New Gym With Win Over St. Mary's."
578. Public Ledger. December 3, 1956. "Bishop Blesses St. Patrick Addition."
579. Ibid.
580. Public Ledger. October 21, 1959. "Schedule-Rich Bulldogs Prep for Nov. 10 Road Opener."
581. Ibid.
582. Ibid.
583. Public Ledger. February 13, 1960. "Louisville Manual Coming Here Friday."
584. Public Ledger. March 1, 1960. "Maysville Wins 1st Game of Tournament."
585. Public Ledger. March 2, 1960. "Paddies And Tigers Second Night Victors."
586. Ibid.
587. Public Ledger. March 2, 1960. "Coach Gets a 'Shower.'"
588. Public Ledger. March 4, 1960. "Paddies, Bulldogs Cop Semi-Finals."
589. Public Ledger. March 4, 1960. "No Saturday Bath."
590. Ibid.
591. Public Ledger. March 7, 1960. "Maysville Wallops St. Patrick 83-43."
592. Public Ledger. March 10, 1960. "Bulldogs Gun Down Paddies; Win 63-34."

593. Public Ledger. March 12, 1960. "Bulldogs, Wildcats in 10th Region Finals."
594. Public Ledger. March 14, 1960. "Bulldogs Blast Wildcats for Title in 10th."
595. Public Ledger. March 14, 1960. "Opponents Are New Champions of 16th Region."
596. Ibid.
597. Public Ledger. March 17, 1960. "Bulldogs Defeat Tomcats, 61 to 58, in Tourney Bow."
598. Public Ledger. March 19, 1960. "Lose Heartbreaker to Louisville Flaget, 59-56."
599. Public Ledger. April 4, 1960. All Sports. ""Chuck" Hall Selected on Herald-Leader Team."
600. Public Ledger. April 4, 1960. All Sports. ""Chuck" Hall Is Selected on CJ's Second All-State Team."
601. Public Ledger. March 5, 1943. "Cardinals Beat Vols to Win Tourney Title."
602. Public Ledger. June 6, 1960. "Central High School Basketball Team Will Be Royals."
603. Public Ledger. November 9, 1961. All Sports. "Mason County Royals Off to Victory in Opening Game With Owingsville."
604. Public Ledger. April 6, 1960. "Jesse Amburgey Named Coach at Deming High."
605. Public Ledger. January 7, 1961. All Sports. "Mason County Royals Edge Paddies 64-59."
606. Public Ledger. January 30, 1961. All Sports. "Maysville Defeats Royals Before Capacity Crowd Here."
607. Public Ledger. March 4, 1961. "All Finals Tickets Have Been Sold."
608. Public Ledger. March 6, 1961. "Royals Cage Kings."
609. Ibid.
610. Public Ledger. March 9, 1961. "Polar Bears Eliminate Royals 62-58 in Region.
611. Rusty Ryan's comments at 10th Region Hall of Fame Banquet.
612. Public Ledger. March 10, 1961. "Dogs Perform Perfectly to Down Scott County."
613. Public Ledger. March 11, 1961. "Maysville Will Meet Harrison Co. in Finals."
614. Public Ledger. March 13, 1961. "Harrison Co. Edges Maysville, 57-56, for Region 10 Title.
615. Public Ledger. March 10, 1962. "Harrison Co., Maysville Meet in 10th Region Final."
616. Public Ledger. March 12, 1962. "Harrison Co. Edges Maysville, 78-76, for 10th Region Title."
617. Public Ledger. March 8, 1963. "'Dogs Down Deming."
618. Public Ledger. February 5, 1963. "Bulldogs' Hall Improving, Sidelined by Hepatitis."
619. Public Ledger. March 9, 1963. "'Dogs Meet Bourbon for Title at 8 P.M."
620. Public Ledger. March 11, 1963. "All the Way, Maysville Chants! Dogs Down Colonels 59-49 to Take 10th Region Title."
621. Public Ledger. March 11, 1963. "City Hails Champions."
622. Public Ledger. March 14, 1963. "Battling Bulldogs Win Out With Heroic Closing Rally."

623. Public Ledger. August 24, 1963. "Pulaski Countian Named Coach at Mason Co. High."
624. Ibid.
625. LSUSports.net. October 29, 2009. "LSU Announces 'Foundation Era' All-Alex Box Team." Available: www.lsusports.net/ViewArticle.dbml?DB_OEM_ID=5200&ATCLID=1435239.
626. Public Ledger. December 18, 1962. "Verville Appears Low Bidder on School Job."
627. Ibid.
628. Public Ledger. December 21, 1962. "School Board Asks Rejection of All Construction Bids."
629. Public Ledger. January 23, 1963. "East End's Basic Bid Lower of 2 on School Construction."
630. Public Ledger. January 11, 1965. "Mason Co. School Patrons Have Their Finest Hour."
631. Ibid.
632. Public Ledger. January 16, 1965. "Royals Open New Gym With Victory; First Game Witnessed By 2,000-2,500."
633. Public Ledger. January 20, 1965. "Royals Down Bulldogs 70-58; 3,900 Look On."
634. Public Ledger. March 5, 1965. "Coach Adolph Rupp, UK Mentor, Scouts Bobby Hiles."
635. Public Ledger. September 25, 1965. "2,500 See Hawks Rip Royals 122-105."
636. Public Ledger. November 20, 1965. "Saints Sink Singing (sic) Springs 81-52; Stahl's 41 Points Top School Record."
637. Public Ledger. March 10, 1967. "Pendleton Nudges Royals 66-65 in Last Few Seconds."
638. Public Ledger. February 19, 1968. "Mason County Star Home After Surgery."
639. Ibid.
640. Public Ledger. February 27, 1968. "Royals Ease Past St. Patrick, 37-15; Meet Bulldogs Wednesday Night At 8."
641. Public Ledger. February 29, 1968. "Royals Subdue Battling Bulldogs 69-64 to Gain Spot in 39th District Final."
642. Public Ledger. March 11, 1968. "Clark County Wears Down Mason County in Final Frame to Take Title, 65-58."
643. Public Ledger/Daily Independent (Maysville, KY). December 4, 1968. "Blakefield Stars in Saints OT Win."
644. Public Ledger/Daily Independent. December 9, 1968. "Blakefield Is Hurt; Saints Lose 64-50."
645. The Ledger Independent (Maysville, KY). January 26, 1970. "'Dogs Come From Nine Down to Beat Royals 59-55."
646. The Ledger Independent. February 9, 1970.
647. The Ledger Independent. February 17, 1970. "Harlan Nips Mason 75-73 in OT; Lyons Sails in 45."
648. The Ledger Independent. February 21, 1970.
649. The Ledger Independent. March 9, 1970. "Royals Win Fifth Straight District

Title."
650. The Ledger Independent. March 12, 1970. "Royals Scratch From Behind to Rub Out Harrison County."
651. The Ledger Independent. April 6, 1970. "Lyons Gets 14 As 'Stars Win 87-81 in Dapper Dan. By Laurnie Caproni."
652. The Ledger Independent. June 22, 1970. "Indiana Wins; Lyons Gets 2.
653. The Ledger Independent. June 29, 1970. "Lyons Tosses in 22, But Kentucky Loses."
654. The Ledger Independent. March 8, 1971. "Maysville Wins District Tournament; Smith Rips Home 36 to Key Victory." By Laurnie Caproni.
655. The Ledger Independent. March 15, 1971. "Royals Lose in Region Finals."
656. The Ledger- Independent. December 9, 1971. "Louisville Central Leads AP Poll."
657. The Ledger Independent. December 23, 1971. "Central First; 'Dogs Fourth."
658. The Ledger Independent. December 30, 1971. "Maysville Continues to Rank High in Polls."
659. The Ledger Independent. January 10, 1971. "Royals Bump Catholic for Ninth Win in a Row."
660. The Ledger Independent. January 18, 1972. "Royals Rally to Whip 'Dogs, 77-67."
661. The Ledger Independent. January 31, 1972. "Walker, Smith in Gear As 'Dogs Devour Johnson."
662. The Ledger Independent. January 31, 1972. "Royals Notch 14th-in-a-Row in OT Win Over Newport Cath."
663. The Ledger Independent. Feb 9, 1972. "Royals Zip to 9th in AP Poll."
664. The Ledger Independent. February 14, 1972. "Mason County Streak Hits 21."
665. Ibid.
666. The Ledger Independent. February 9, 1972. "Walker Leads Maysville to Easy 81-63 Victory."
667. The Ledger Independent. March 6, 1972. "Bulldogs Overpower Royals for Title."
668. Ibid.
669. The Ledger Independent. March 10, 1972. "Mason, Pendleton Post 10th Region Victories."
670. The Ledger Independent. March 13, 1972. "The Semi-Finals." By Laurnie Caproni.
671. Ibid.
672. The Ledger Independent. March 13, 1972. "Maysville High Is Going to State!"
673. The Ledger- Independent. March 16, 1972. "'Dogs Zip From Behind to Whip Christian County."
674. The Ledger- Independent. March 20, 1972. "Big, Bad Central Wasn't So Big And Bad After All." By Laurnie Caproni.
675. The Ledger Independent. March 20, 1972. "'Dogs Bring Home 3rd Place Trophy."
676. Ibid.
677. The Ledger Independent. January 8, 1979. "Saints, 'Dogs, Royals Lose to

Northern Kentucky Catholics."
678. The Ledger Independent. January 15, 1973. "Fogeless 'Breds Nip 'Dogs; Purcell Knocks Off Mason."
679. The Ledger Independent.January 22, 1973. "'Dogs Nail Pendleton; Fleming Belts Bracken."
680. The Ledger Independent. January 24, 1973. "Polar Bears Roar by Royals; Bulldogs Chew up Rowan Co."
681. The Ledger Independent. January 29, 1973. "'Dogs Now 15-4 After Wins at Paintsville, Johnson Central."
682. The Ledger Independent. January 31, 1973. "'Dogs, Panthers Win; Royals Fall to Breck."
683. The Ledger Independent. February 5, 1973. "Bulldogs Clout Lexington Catholic; Trojans Slip Past Mason County."
684. The Ledger Independent. February 8, 1973. "High-Flying Maysville, Bracken Ground."
685. The Ledger Independent. February 12, 1973. "Royals Squeeze Past Estill; Saggin' Bulldogs Lose Again."
686. The Ledger Independent. February 13, 1973. "'Dogs Snap Mini-Skid With Win Over Bath."
687. The Ledger Independent. February 20, 1973. "'Dog's Clip Ashland; Royals Split."
688. The Ledger Independent. February 21, 1973. "'Dogs Clout Catholic."
689. The Ledger Independent. March 5, 1973. "'Dogs Whip Fleming for District Title."
690. The Ledger Independent. March 8, 1973. "Maysville Downs Clark, 77-68."
691. The Ledger Independent. March 12, 1973. "The Semi-Finals." By Laurnie Caproni.
692. The Ledger Independent. March 12, 1973. "'Dogs Zap Fleming to Win 10th."
693. The Ledger Independent. March 16, 1973. "Bulldogs Chop Down Lee, 76-65."
694. The Ledger Independent. March 19, 1973. "Bulldogs' Run for Glory Squashed by Unlikely Hickman County."
695. The Ledger Independent. May 15, 1973. Jim Mitchell Resigns Mason County Post."
696. The Ledger Independent. June 19, 1973. "Gary Jefferson Named Head Coach at MCHS."
697. Ibid.
698. The Ledger Independent. January 15, 1974. "Royals Race From Behind to Nip 'Dogs, 58-56."
699. The Ledger Independent. February 27, 1974. "Fleming County, Maysville Clash Tonight."
700. The Ledger Independent. February 15, 1974. "11 Games on Tap for Weekend."
701. The Ledger Independent. February 28, 1974. "Panthers Shade 'Dogs' to Gain Region Berth."
702. The Ledger Independent. March 4, 1974. "Fleming Wins First Title Since '56."

703. The Ledger Independent. March 7, 1974. "Mason Resists Bracken; Bourbon Wins." By Laurnie Caproni.
704. The Ledger Independent. July 3, 1974. "Elza Whalen New Principal at Maysville."
705. The Ledger Independent. July 9, 1974. "Lyle Dunbar Named MHS Basketball Coach."
706. Interview with Lyle Dunbar, March 2011.
707. The Ledger Independent. June 17, 1975. "Pikeville Scholarship Goes to Tim Purdon."
708. The Ledger Independent. March 7, 1975. "Fieldhouse Scene of Brawl After Wednesday Night Game."
709. The Ledger Independent. March 7, 1975. "Girls Will Play."
710. The Ledger Independent. March 10, 1974. "Fleming Girls Shock MHS 32-29 in District."
711. The Ledger Independent. April 7, 1975. "MHS Team Gets Suspended Until Jan. 1."
712. The Ledger Independent. May 6, 1975. "Mason County Looking for a New Coach.
713. The Ledger Independent. May 30, 1975. "Pete Gill New Mason Coach."
714. The Ledger Independent. July 21, 1975. "Mason Board Seeks Successor After Pete Gill's Resignation."
715. The Ledger Independent. July 22, 1975. "Hall Replaces Dunbar As Maysville High Coach."
716. Lyle Dunbar interview, March 2011.
717. The Ledger Independent. April 24, 1975. "School Board Votes 3-1 to Reinstate Hall As Fleming Coach."
718. The Ledger Independent. June 16, 1975. "Bob Hall Declines Job Offer."
719. The Ledger Independent. March 22, 1976. "Mason County's Girls Win 3rd Place Trophy."
720. The Ledger Independent. March 18, 1976. "Mason Girls Blitz Caldwell, 52-42."
721. The Ledger Independent. March 22, 1976. "Royals Work Miracle in Double-Overtime Victory."
722. The Ledger Independent. March 22, 1976. "Mason County's Girls Win 3rd Place Trophy."
723. The Ledger Independent. February 7, 1977. "'Dogs Destroy Bourbon County."
724. The Ledger Independent. February 4, 1977. "Mason County Schools Plan to Reopen February 9."
725. The Ledger Independent. March 6, 1978. "Bulldogs Edge Mason in OT Thriller." By Laurnie Caproni.
726. The Ledger Independent. March 23, 1978. "'Dogs Miracle Comeback Bid Falls Short by One."
727. The Ledger Independent. March 18, 1981. "City Proclamation."
728. The Ledger Independent. February 12, 1982. "Patient And Poised St. Patrick Roars From Behind to Pin 58-55 Shocker on Maysville." By Laurnie Caproni.
729. The Ledger Independent. March 8, 1982. "Royals Whip St. Pat to Win

District."
730. The Ledger Independent. March 11, 1982. "Mason and Clark Win; Showdown Is Friday."
731. The Ledger Independent. March 1982. "Mason Survives in Overtime Thriller; Paris Holds Off Pawsat, St. Patrick."
732. Ibid.
733. The Ledger Independent. March 15, 1982. "Mason County's Big Blue WINS AGAIN! Region 13 Next for 30-and-Zip Royals."
734. The Ledger Independent. March 26, 1982. "Royals Shoot Down Middlesboro." By Laurnie Caproni.
735. The Ledger Independent. March 27, 1982. "Royals Bow to Virgie; Record Is 31-1."
736. The Ledger Independent. November 20, 1982. "Frey And His Bulldogs Are Preparing to Play Very Hard."
737. The Ledger Independent. March 1, 1985. "Irish Rub Out Bulldogs, 46-44." By David Williams.
738. The Ledger Independent. March 8, 1985. "St. Pat Derails Engineers." By David Williams.
739. The Ledger Independent. March 11, 1985. "Royals Bound for State Tourneys. By David Williams.
740. The Kentucky Post (Covington, KY). March 21, 1985. "Winners Never Quit." By Terry Boehmker.
741. Lexington Herald-Leader. March 23, 1985. "Doss Boots Mason 64-63 in Overtime."
742. The Ledger Independent. March 13, 1986. "Mason, MMI Roll to First Round Wins."
743. The Ledger Independent. March 14, 1986. "'Dogs Hang on, Win by One." By Matt Stahl.
744. The Ledger Independent. March 28, 1987. "Ballard Wins on Goal at Buzzer." By Matt Stahl.
745. The Kentucky Post. April 6, 1987. "The Best in Basketball." By Dan Weber.
746. The Ledger Independent. March 7, 1988. "Running Score."
747. The Ledger Independent. March 10, 1988. "'Dogs Stay on Road to Louisville."
748. The Ledger Independent. March 14, 1988. "Dogs Superb in Pressure-Cooker Victory."
749. The Ledger Independent. March 18, 1988. "Last Seconds Tick From MHS Year." By Richard Skinner.
750. The Ledger Independent. August 18, 1988. Hines Named Coach at Maysville." By Richard Skinner.
751. The Ledger Independent. March 22, 1984. "Lady Royals Fall 42-40 in 'Sweet 16.'"
752. The Courier-Journal. March 14, 1985. "Mason Jars Laurel Co. on Swartz Free Throw." By Tony Moton.
753. The Ledger Independent. March 16, 1985. "Season Ends for Lady Royals As Furious Rally Falls Short Against Whitley County."
754. The Ledger Independent. March 30, 1986. "Well Done, Lady Royals." By Laurnie Caproni.

755. The Ledger Independent. March 3, 1987. "St. Pat Girls Shellshock Mason County."
756. WFTM postgame interview, conducted by Russ Curtis.
757. The Ledger-Independent. March 11, 1991. "Maysville Era Ends on Shot at Buzzer."
758. Lexington Herald-Leader. March 17, 1983. "Mason Co.-PRP an Early Match Built for Speed."
759. The Ledger Independent. March 13, 1995. "Royals Denied; Indians Win First Region Title." By Rick Greene.
760. The Ledger-Independent. January 23, 1999. "St. Patrick Rallies Late in Fourth Quarter to Defeat Polar Bears." By Chuck Truesdell.
761. The Ledger Independent. January 25, 1999. "St. Patrick Ready for Richmond." By James Mulcahy.
762. The Ledger Independent. January 29, 1999. "Irish Enter Elite Eight." By Chuck Truesdell.
763. The Ledger Independent. January 30, 1999. "Saints in Semis With 46-45."
764. The Ledger Independent. February 1, 1999. "St. Patrick Stunned at the Buzzer." By Chuck Truesdell.
765. Lexington Herald-Leader. March 19, 2003. "High School Boys' State Tournament Preview."
766. USA Today. February 25, 2004. "Kentucky High School Power Is Throwback."

Index

C

D

E

F

G

H

I

L

M

O

P

Q

R

S

T

U

V

W

X

Y

Z